Ross-Ade

Ross-Ade
Their Purdue Stories, Stadium, and Legacies

Robert C. Kriebel

Purdue University Press

Copyright © 2009 by Purdue University. All rights reserved.

Front cover photo courtesy of Purdue University Sports Information Archives.

The typeface used on the front cover for the title and subtitle is CentaurMT. The typeface Centaur was designed by Bruce Rogers, Purdue University class of 1890.

Library of Congress Cataloging-in-Publication Data
Kriebel, Robert C., 1932-
  Ross-Ade : their Purdue stories, stadium, and legacies / by Robert C. Kriebel.
    p. cm. -- (The founders series)
  ISBN 978-1-55753-522-1
  1. Ross, David, 1871-1943. 2. Ade, George, 1866-1944. 3. Purdue University--Benefactors--Biography. 4. Ross-Ade Stadium (West Lafayette, Ind.)--History. I. Title.
  LD4672.65.R67.K75 2009
  378.772'95--dc22
  [B]
                            2009006172

Contents

Acknowledgments ix
Introduction xi
PART I Ross-Ade: Their Stories
Like being in jail 3
Mechanic or farmer? 7
A good spectator 9
Much of the time lonely 15
In the Big Arena 19
A different breed of cat 43
Chicago, here he came 51
Meanwhile, down on the farm 65
"Fables" and more 73
Plays and more plays 91
Made for the movies 111
Peace and War 123
At war with Purdue 133
Together at last 141
Walter Scholer 149
Ross-Ade 163

PART II Ross-Ade: Their Stadium

A time for reflection	185
Out of the Joke Division	191
Events of great importance	197
Governor Leslie	209
Darkest memories	217
Maybe sports?	227
Fast growing seeds	233
Promising news, growing Depression	241
A time of change	249
Purdue Airport	257
Earhart at Purdue	265
The "Flying Laboratory"	277
Pride, sadness, mystery, hope	287
A new season of pride	299
Golf courses, parties, and war	305
The Hall of Music	311
Getting serious	319
Wartime!	327
"A multiplier of the power of men"	333
"Home is the Hoosier"	343
Hovde for Elliott	347
Gaining in value	353
The "Golden Girl" and "Purdue Pete"	355
"I am an American"	359

A hallowed centerpiece	365
The "PAT" era	371
Not your average Joe	377
Bermuda and "The Boilermaker"	381
An economic plus	385
And then some	389
References	393
Index	395

Acknowledgments

The author is indebted to the following persons for their helpful cooperation in the preparation of *Ross-Ade: Their Purdue Stories, Stadium, and Legacies:*

Byron L. Anderson, Purdue Alumni Association, West Lafayette

James F. Blakesley, West Lafayette, President, Purdue Class of 1950

Richard "Dick" Freeman, International Pacific, Corona del Mar, California, Purdue Distinguished Engineering Alumnus, 1973.

Amanda Grossman, Library Assistant, Purdue Archives and Special Collections

Kelly Hiller, Director of Creative Communication and Editor, *The Purdue Alumnus.*

Chris Horney, President, Sigma Chi Fraternity, Purdue University, West Lafayette

David Hovde, Associate Professor, Purdue University Libraries

Fern Martin, West Lafayette

Kathryn Matter, Purdue University Department of Bands

Joanne Mendes, Archives Assistant, Purdue Archives and Special Collections, Purdue University Libraries

Sammie L. Morris, Assistant Professor of Library Science and Head of Archives and Special Collections, Purdue University Libraries.

Cory Palm, Purdue University Sports Information Department.

Nicki (Reas) Meneley, Assistant Executive Director, Purdue Alumni Association.

Tom Schott, Assistant Athletic Director-Communications, Purdue University

C. Wesley Shook, President, The Area Plan Commission of Tippecanoe County, West Lafayette

James C. Shook, Senior Chairman of North Central Health Services Inc.'s Board of Directors, West Lafayette

Bernie Sergesketter, Winnetka, Illinois, Sigma Chi Fraternity

Philip R. Steele, Sigma Chi Fraternity

The late Robert W. Topping (1925-2009), retired Senior Editor, Purdue University Publications

Paula Alexander Woods, retired from the staff of the Lafayette-West Lafayette Convention and Visitors Bureau

Introduction

As the crow flies (they measure distance that-a-way in Indiana), the country towns of Brookston and Kentland lie thirty-six miles apart. Between them the crows out there flap over level fields of corn, oats, soybeans, wheat, and hay.

With Purdue University off to the south, Brookston and Kentland have formed a triangle for more than a century. As the crows fly, Purdue is fourteen miles from Brookston, thirty-seven miles southeast of Kentland.

In the space of fifty-eight years, a remarkable thing took place in that triangle. Two boys from farms near Brookston and Kentland attended Purdue. One turned dreamer and became a writer. The other mastered drawing and invented machines. After graduations six years apart, both men earned fames and fortunes.

Distant strangers as Purdue alumni, they met at last in 1922, in a county judge's office. That afternoon they got dust on their good leather shoes by hiking shallow hills and weeds on an old farm. They stood on a stretch of high ground and shared a vision that day, made a deal, shook hands, bought the farm, and on it started a football stadium still booming at Purdue.

The strangers were Dave Ross and George Ade. Because they met, the rest is history.

Robert C. Kriebel
Lafayette, Indiana
May 2009

Part I
Ross-Ade: Their Stories

Like being in jail

Teenage John Ade sailed over to the United States from a brewery job in Lewes, England, in the summer of 1840. His family spent a week in New York City, then tried Cincinnati. John took up schoolwork and drove a team for a contractor. He married Adaline Bush when he was twenty-three and she was eighteen. Adaline's mother was an Adair. Coincidentally, England's Ades were kin to Scotland's Adairs. When opportunity knocked in 1852, the newlywed Ades moved to rural Morocco in Jasper County of northwestern Indiana.

John Ade farmed and managed a country store in Morocco. In 1853, He became Morocco's first postmaster, too, under Whig-Republican Millard Fillmore's presidency. But when Franklin Pierce reached the White House, Democrat kingmakers fired Postmaster Ade for "offensive partisanship." A Republican he was, by God, and a Republican he would stay.

In 1859, Indiana government snipped off part of Jasper County and Morocco and with those acres formed Newton—Indiana's last county. The voters in Newton County elected their grocer friend John Ade to be Recorder. The Ades left Morocco for Kentland, four miles from the Illinois line. Kentland was where the new courthouse would go and where the Recorder's office would be. The Ades' little story-and-a-half frame house, the second one to go up in Kentland, faced the south side of the courthouse square. That house became the birthplace of George, the fifth of John and Adaline Ade's six children, on February 9, 1866.

John quit storekeeping to hammer out a living as a blacksmith and finally to put on a suit and be cashier of the new Discount and Deposit Bank in Kentland.

George grew up in a happy enough home in the town of six hundred. He had two brothers and three sisters. He would call his mother's goodness "unbounded," remembering her as being so rooted in "unruffled common sense and entire lack of theatrical emotionalism that I sometimes marveled at the fact that, from no merit of my own, I was privileged to have such a remarkable mother." (Kelly, *Ade*, 21)

Sons and daughters alike in those days carried out their chores and attended some dinky village or township school. George, although dismissed by some as a hopeless work-dodger and daydreamer, did at least show an early love for drama and literature. Writing, and doing so with a droll sense of humor, came to George naturally, early, and easily.

"When I was a small boy," he still recalled when he was fifty-two, "being on a farm the year round was a good deal like being in jail, except that the prisoners in jail were not required to work fourteen hours a day. The good old days were not so good, and the nights were worse." Describing the same general era and his boyhood job of lighting the household lamps, George wrote:

> I had to climb a ladder and struggle with slow-burning brimstone matches to touch off the charred wick and eventually flood a few square feet with modified gloom. The old-fashioned coal-oil lamp threw out a weak yellow glare. After you had one lighted you had to start another so you could tell where you had put the first one. (Kelly, *Ade*, 24)

As for the Indiana farmland spreading for miles around him, George would record:

> The explorer could start from anywhere out on the prairie and move in any direction and find a slough, and in the center of it an open pond of dead water. Then a border of swaying cattails, tall rushes, reedy blades sharp as razors, out to the upland, spangled

with the gorgeous blue and yellow flowers of the virgin plain. A million frogs sang together each evening and a billion mosquitoes came out to forage when the breeze died away. The old-fashioned flimsy mosquito netting would not keep out anything under the size of a barn swallow. (Kelly, *Ade*, 22)

In Ade's boyhood, Kentland boasted one watch repairman, a druggist, a blacksmith, Keefe's grocery, and four saloons—six-hundred-or-so people and, in all of Newton County, fewer than four thousand.

When George began going to school, *McGuffey Reader* introduced him to prose and poetry by noted authors who glorified honest work, truth, and other virtues. Already good at reading the words in *Youth's Companion, Harper's Young People,* and *Harper's Weekly*, the schoolboy George Ade found *McGuffey* almost too easy. Because he could be so thoroughly absorbed when reading, his family, friends, and schoolmates labeled him a dreamer early in his life. Mother once asked him to carry in an armload of kitchen firewood. He hauled it through the parlor and put it on the floor, slumped back into his chair and picked up his book. Until reminded by Mother, he thought he had left the wood in the kitchen. As a first-grader he learned a shortcut to school along a weedy railroad. However, before a predicted snow, Mother sensed that daydreaming George might walk home backward, against the shrieking wind, and would neither see nor hear a train. Right she was. George wrote about it in a school essay, "A Mother's Intuition." One of George's simplest morning chores was to turn the cow out of the barn to go to pasture, then lead it in at night. The day he forgot the morning part his father found the cow still in the barn at night and lamented, "I'm afraid, George, you're always going to be a dreamer."

George excelled in school, especially spelling. Sometimes George could beat even his teachers in spelling bees. If he had a boyhood problem at all, it was to find enough to read. Kentland had no public library, but John and Adaline put Dickens and other greats on the family bookshelves. That is how George came to know Mark Twain and how *Life on the Mississippi* stood as an all-time favorite.

Kentland acquaintances came to believe that, while it was fine to invite George to parties, it behooved them to hide their books and magazines or else he would pay attention to nothing else. George liked parties all right, even though he stayed at arm's-length from the girls.

One of George's earliest memories—"as far back as I can reach into the past"—was of sitting out on a fence the crisp, starry night of October 8, 1871. He was peering north-northwest at "a blur of illumination" in the sky. He was seeing the Great Chicago Fire burning roughly eighty miles away. With droll understatement, he would tell years later of watching Chicago "burning up in a highly successful manner." Had George gazed southeast earlier in that summer of '71, he might have seen another, quite different brilliance: David Edward Ross, coming into life, in Brookston, on August. 25.

Mechanic or farmer?

The Ross family story began taking shape in 1827 when baby David's grandfather, another David Ross, a settler from eastern Pennsylvania, reached Lafayette, Indiana. Lafayette was a promising town on the Wabash River. The settler Ross stayed only a day or two, then plodded on through level but open, swampy wilderness northwest to what is now Chicago and stayed for about two years. But he returned to Lafayette, took up farm work, clerked in a general store, saved his money, bought a little shop on the courthouse square, and conducted business on his own.

Married, he fathered a son, George Henderson Ross, in about 1839. The original Dave Ross had a brother-in-law named Billy Henderson, who rode off to hunt for California gold in 1849. But before he left, Billy arranged for Original Dave, as his agent, to buy him a thousand mushy acres in White County, to the north of Lafayette. As Billy envisioned it, draining that land might be a problem but if and when dry, that rich, moist, black soil could yield amazing corn crops.

As the years went by, young George Henderson Ross met and married Susanna Booth. They moved to Billy Henderson's thousand-acre wetland and farmed it for him from a two-story home about four miles west of the White County seat of Brookston. There, six weeks and two days before the Great Chicago Fire, George and Susannah Ross became parents of little David Edward Ross. The name honored the baby's grandparents, *David* Ross and *Edward* Booth.

In about 1878, young Dave Ross started in a public school in Brookston. Ten-mile passenger train trips to Lafayette, though seldom, provided him with a certain amount of fun. That was because sometimes Susannah would leave Dave at her sister's place on a farm, or in Lafayette with his uncles William Edward "Uncle Will" Ross or David Linn "Uncle Linn" Ross. Uncle Will is said to have taught the boy, "Needles and pins, needles and pins / When a man marries, his trouble begins."

Whether that alone influenced little Dave to choose the single life remains questionable, but there was no mystery about the boy's keen interest in machines. His parents once took him on a Wabash River excursion steamboat ride. He wandered off from their notice for a while, and in a panic, they feared he had fallen overboard. They found him not in the river but in the ship's smelly engine room, awed by all the hissing and clanking machines. Later at his Uncle Linn's wedding, Dave dropped down to the basement to work the movable parts of a furnace.

"I wonder," his dad said, "if he's going to become a mechanic instead of sticking to the farm" (Kelly, *Ross*, 17).

A good spectator

The cool weather months—September through April, the months containing the letter "R"—gave George Ade, during his errand-running years in Kentland, a good reason to visit Keefe's Grocery, because Keefe sometimes carried fresh oysters. For a quarter a boy could take home a cardboard bucket with a wire handle containing enough oysters for a family dinner. George liked ice cream, too, and rarely found enough.

Meanwhile, as a lanky teen, he was gaining respect for the spoken word. "The famous orators," he would remember, "were those who could cause jurors to weep. The popular preachers could make the most noise while picturing hellfire. A really successful funeral could be heard a mile away. Religious convictions were vivid and concrete. Satan devoted all his time to frying those who had failed to attend church" (Kelly, *Ade,* 34).

And yet George lost interest in church early in life. In this choice he joined his brother Joe, who avoided sermons when he could. However, his brother Bill became an ardent churchgoer. George did at least seem to have memorized every Methodist hymn he ever heard before he backslid. He appeared to make no great effort to learn hymns, but words and music sank so deeply into his memory that they were his for life. Stories of his amazing memory for people, places, events, and song lyrics also followed him.

Along this early path George also let the theater stir his curiosity. One of his first stacks of saved pennies is said to have gone for a book of popular songs by the team of Harrigan and Hart. George digested song hits from the American stage, especially minstrel shows.

He was a good spectator, too. Minor troupes from Indianapolis played McCullough's Hall in Kentland, including the Graham Earle Stock Company and the Harry Hotta Players. George wrangled his way into some McCullough's Hall events by passing out the manager's handbills. A few times John Ade took George to Chicago to see plays and musicals.

During these formative years, George also felt exposure to Republican politics. He wrote both seriously and amusingly about them: "It was a time when one of the chief lunacies was the belief that voters could best prove the fervor of their political convictions and the high character of their patriotism by walking mile after mile carrying torches and permitting kerosene to drip on their clothing" (Kelly, *Ade*, 38). In Newton County, "the first lessons learned were those of political hatred. We studied our [Thomas] Nast cartoons before we tackled the primer." George was brought up to believe that if Democrats won anything "the whole solar system would be disarranged" (ibid.).

Even as a young teen, through his father, George met political celebrities. One was Albert G. Porter, Indiana Governor and U.S. Minister to Italy. Another was Schuyler Colfax from South Bend. The U.S. Vice President at the time, Colfax once even visited the Ade home. In the autumn of 1876, George bounced across a prairie road seated in a carriage beside Benjamin Harrison. Harrison was running for Indiana Governor against Democrat James D. "Blue Jeans" Williams. Ade remembered only that Harrison wore gloves and said nothing for twenty-five miles.

As a young teen, George also took to puttering around the office of the *Gazette*, Kentland's Republican weekly paper. For the *Gazette* George carried out menial duties "mostly for the glory of the Republican cause." His main claim to fame was his brazen theft, from the nearby rival paper's office, of proof sheets that alerted Republicans to last-minute attacks coming from Democrats. The victimized editor, never able to find the culprit, wrote that the air of his sanctum must never again be contaminated by the "fumes emanating from the infamous skunk's filthy carcass."

The lessons continued for the growing boy: "I learned to smoke, by painful efforts, when I was a small boy, starting in on corn-silk and graduating up to the stub-tailed cheroots which came in small paper boxes and sold three for a nickel" (Tobin 13).

The law at that time required only two years of high school. During his two years, George felt trapped into honest farm work and hated it, yet found it rich in raw material for writing. "The distrust with which I regarded horses at that time has never been overcome," he wrote later. One task involved pulling cockle-burrs out of corn. "It was pretty hard to look over a field of cockle-burrs and find the corn," he wrote. "Sometimes the corn crop would fail and sometimes the oat crop would fail but the cockle-burr crop and the mustard crop never failed." John Ade would shake his head sadly. What was to become of a farm son who detested farming and had no talent for anything else?

In October 1881, the answer began to take shape. George's high school teacher assigned all the seniors to write themes. George procrastinated. In a last-minute effort, he chose his own subject and titled it "A Basket of Potatoes."

The teacher liked it. John Ade liked it. So did the editor of the *Gazette*. The result was George Ade's first published literary work at age fifteen. He spoke of it in an interview in 1902: "Did I ever write anything humorous as a kid? Yes. But I didn't know it. My sister found the piece called 'A Basket of Potatoes,' that I had written when I was fifteen. I then wrote a good deal for the Kentland paper, for nothing. That article told how, when you shake a basket of potatoes, the big ones come to the top. I have no doubt it set the younger members of the community to thinking. But I never meant it for humor." The essay concluded:

"And so it is everywhere, life is but a basket of potatoes. When the hard jolts come the big will rise and the small will fall. The true, the honest, and the brave will go to the top. The small-minded and ignorant must go to the bottom...Now is the time for you to say whether or not in the battle of life you will be a small or large potato. If you would be a large potato get education, be honest, observing and careful and you will be jolted to the top. If you would be a small potato, neglect these things and you will get to the bottom of your own accord. Break off your bad habits, keep away from rotten potatoes and you will get to the top. Be careless of these things and you will reach the bottom in due time. Everything rests with you. Prepare for the jolting." (Kelly, *Ade*, 45)

The mild attention George gained from the essay inspired no less than Mr. Hershman himself, the county superintendent of schools, to come out and see John Ade. George was the sort, Hershman said, who could gain much from a college education. George's older brothers, Will and Joe, had shrugged off college. John never saw George as college material, either. Too dreamy. Too lazy. But if George didn't go, what *could* he do? Not many local boys had tried college. College might cost two hundred fifty dollars a year, a thousand for the four-year course. What college should it be? Indiana University at Bloomington was one hundred and fifty miles away. What people were calling "a little agricultural college near Lafayette" was closer, at fifty miles. In September 1882, John applied for a scholarship through the Newton County Commissioners (all Republican). Politics didn't matter, though. No one else in the county even applied. George had the necessary "good moral character" for one.

However, Mother wished to be heard. She considered George too young, just past sixteen, to go so far from home. She pictured the temptations he might face as a farm boy on a campus across a river from Lafayette, a city of fifteen thousand. So George stayed in Kentland and took special courses in high school to prepare.

Even when the big day came in the fall of 1883, John Ade feared the worst. Only two other boys in Newton County were going off to college, and George alone was going to try Purdue.

Much of the time lonely

When Dave Ross was five years old, he learned a lesson about the value of education. A younger brother and sister took sick with diphtheria. An old doctor named Mendenhall came out to the farm. The father, George Ross, also sent for a younger doctor named Robert O'Ferrall who had opened an office in Brookston. "Diphtheria is a *germ* disease," said O'Ferrall. "The other children will catch it if you don't get them out of here."

"You and your *germs*!" Mendenhall snorted. "Diphtheria is a *constitutional* disease. You get it or you don't. They're as safe here as anywhere."

The parent Rosses heeded the young doctor, schooled in Europe and in the American East. There was no trouble getting their three oldest children to a safe place. The kids visited relatives in Lafayette. Those children lived. The two little sick children died. Dave never forgot that one doctor knew what he was talking about and the other did not.

At age six, Dave started in the public school in Brookston. People noticed he was shy and uneasy around older or stranger boys. However, he knew ways to amuse himself. He learned to imitate the low "meow" of a cat. Teacher and pupils never suspected the deadpan Ross boy.

They said Dave made friends with many boys yet returned from school alone. He never had a really close chum. Much of the time he was lonely. Sometimes his parents left him in Lafayette to visit his uncles Will and Linn Ross, their sister Eleanor, or Uncle Billy Henderson who was home from California. The four adults all seemed to enjoy being single so much that Dave may then and there have seen reasons to stay single, too.

In 1880, Dave's parents decided to move to Lafayette so that his mother, a sickly sort, would be nearer to her sisters. Soon Dave was deep into *McGuffey's Fourth Reader*, "The Wreck of the Hesperus" and "The Old Oaken Bucket." He got along well in the city school and made a normal amount of friends. He became interested in baseball and wished he had a baseball suit. One of his aunts offered to sew him one if she could find a pattern. Dave lay on a sheet of brown wrapping paper, drew his own outline in chalk, and then filled in the space for her pattern.

But nagging problems on the White County farm pulled George Ross and family back there to live again. From the farm, Dave walked two miles to his country school. Tiring of the muddy or dusty paths he had to tramp, Dave threatened once to quit school. He didn't, but the threat coupled with other factors persuaded the family to move from the farm back into Brookston.

The boy started high school there in September 1887. He impressed his teachers as "solid." He made average grades and lamented that he did not grow more. He wanted to be a big, tall man but remained short and, in the middle, a little wider than average.

Dave and his father sometimes rode farm horses a few miles east to the Tippecanoe River for fishing, boating, and swimming. But the day came when Dave decided that he wanted to go to college. To George Ross, that idea was nonsense; college was a waste of time and money. Dave should be getting into something practical. Four years studying agriculture seemed bad enough to George Ross, but Dave had in mind four years of *engineering*. Purdue University, across the river from Lafayette, had eight buildings and courses in mechanical and civil engineering, and was adding electrical engineering with the belief that there would be a future for electricity.

People around Lafayette were proud enough of Purdue University, but there were dark stories such as the case of Sheriff McCutcheon's son John. John had finished Purdue but had become an *artist*—good God!—working for a newspaper in Chicago. What good had four years of college been to him? Then there was the kid named Ade whose dad was the banker up in Kentland. With his new Bachelor of Science degree, Ade was only writing short items for six dollars a week for a little Lafayette paper. He could have done that without wasting money in college.

Late in August 1889, Dave Ross confronted his father about enrolling in Purdue. "You're needed on the farm," said George Ross. "If I were better educated," the boy responded, "I could be more help." George Ross replied, "Maybe later on. I don't think we can manage it now. In a year or so we'll see."

It was crunch time. Dave wrote to tell Uncle Will of his plight. Uncle Will divined the situation and wrote back to brother George. Will proposed that Dave come down to Purdue and live with Will and his sister. There would be no expense for board and room, and Will would pay for the books and tuition "if you can spare him." George Ross saw a deal he could not refuse.

In the Big Arena

At age seventeen, George Ade entered Purdue University on September 10, 1883, already a "published writer" back home in the *Gazette*. Twenty-some years later, his essay "The Day I Arrived" told about Lafayette and Purdue during his first hours as a freshman:

> I remember that the sun was shining and the harvest fields on both sides of the Big Four [Railroad] line were dry and yellow, but I was not greatly concerned as to the weather conditions. My subconsciousness was trying to adapt itself to the overwhelming fact that I was about to venture into the Big Arena and fight for my life. The masterminds of the 19th century were waiting to discover me in the roadway and then crush me beneath the Juggernaut of infinite superiority. The high school lambkin was headed for the jungle where wild animals roamed.
>
> The train had come thirty miles and already I was homesick. Wedged between my feet was a glittering valise of the kind that will stand up unless the rain happens to strike it. In my left hand I clutched a worn copy of the *Annual Catalog and Register*. One section was charted with information for the guidance of those struggling toward the light. Board would cost $2.50 a week. With due economy as to the items of "laundry" and "sundries," the annual expenditures could be held down to $185—or say $200 a year when accompanied by riotous living. It seemed a lot of money to spend foolishly.

The courses of study were exhibited as towering pyramids, supported by brackets. The lower planes invited one to geometry and botany. The topmost heights up among the clouds, four years away, were marked Psychology, Analytical Chemistry and Political Economy. The more I looked at them the more evident it became that they were inaccessible. The cry of "Excelsior!" rose very faintly within my timid soul. My vision was not sufficiently prophetic to enable me to see myself in 1887 seated on the topmost pinnacle wearing a $30 Prince Albert suit and preparing a thesis on "Literature In the West."

The train rolled into the broad bottomlands of the Wabash [River], and I saw above the cornfields the clustered spires and massive walls of a great city. It looked like London, Paris, Vienna and New York welded together into one gigantic capital. To this day [1903], I never visit Lafayette without stopping to gaze at the Courthouse and wonder how it is possible to trim down a building to one-third its former size without destroying the symmetry. I looked down at the river and identified it as the Rubicon, after which the valise and I found ourselves in a multitude of thirty or more persons on a long platform on Second Street.

All of these persons seemed especially hardened to city life and indifferent to the trembling uncertainties of young persons from far distant points. The *Annual Catalog and Register* had given specific directions to govern one suddenly alighting from a train, so I stood on the platform holding firmly to my property and waiting for the next Turn of Fate.

Then Charlie Martin came into my life. Years may come and years may go, and memory may fail me regarding people and incidents of a quarter century ago, but Charlie Martin will always stand out in the solitary splendor of a landmark, silhouetted against a purple sky. Charlie drove an express wagon. He named a price for delivering my trunk to the dormitory, and said he would let me ride on the wagon. I had no trunk. He allowed me to substitute the valise. Why no trunk? Well, I had yet to pass my entrance examinations, and it seemed advisable not to stock up with all the shirts, underwear, and towels carefully set down in the *Annual Catalog and Register* until I felt sure that I could squirm through the portals and be enrolled on the heavenly list as a Real Freshman.

Anyone familiar with conditions on the Purdue campus in the autumn of 1883 will tell you that I should have brought the trunk. There was no possible chance of my *not* landing as a freshman. Along about that time any human being between the ages of fifteen and twenty, who ventured anywhere near Purdue's campus and showed the slightest symptoms of acquiring a college education was roped and dragged into the Registrar's office. A few "conditions" more or less cut very little figure. Purdue needed students, and needed them badly. Those on hand were to be treated kindly, and fed with a spoon as long as they gave reasonable evidences of human intelligence and came to recitations once in a while. In those happy days there was no merciless "weeding out"—no cruel and terrifying "flunk tests." The sword of Damocles was not doing business. The man who wanted to leave school had to commit arson or homicide, or something like that.

One commander had left and another was coming aboard. He had not been given time to organize his crew, set things to rights and get the ship back into her course. Purdue seemed to be wobbling, not to say floundering. The storms had buffeted, provisions were running low, and the hands had not been paid for months. Having offered these figurative allusions, I will get back to cold facts.

President [James A.] Smart and I arrived on the scene at practically the same moment. He came in a phaeton, and I came in Charlie Martin's express wagon. That day marked the turning point of the struggle to establish a school of technology in Indiana. Dr. Smart found a weakling and trained it into robust manhood.

The first great task confronting him was to build up the attendance. We lived by favor of the legislature, and the legislature had a way of dividing the total outlay by the enrollment, the result showing a per capita expense that was simply staggering. In order to reduce the per capita extravagance and smooth the way for shops, laboratories and more professors, the University needed more students. Profs stood at every entrance to the campus waiting to welcome them.

I was not acquainted with these facts. As we rode through the old boxed-in Main Street Bridge and across the narrow levee, with a boardwalk propped against one side of it, I felt sure that I was approaching the horrors of the Inquisition. I expected to be tried and found unworthy, and sent back home. At the foot of Chauncey Hill was a little cluster of wooden buildings. The long grade was sparsely bordered with dwelling houses. At the top of the hill was a lonesome drugstore, the only student rendezvous of the period. That part of the campus lying east of the carriage gate was then boarding houses.

"Yonder she is," Charlie Martin called as they reached the Purdue campus at the summit of Chauncey Hill. George Ade stepped out and, carrying his bag, trudged along a gravel walk to register. The University was only nine years old and, as Ade noticed, "the plaster was nearly dry" (Kelly, *Ade*, 49).

The old Main Building held the center of the campus, and seemed a trifle larger than St. Peter's at Rome. The other buildings were the Ladies' Hall, the Chemical Lab, the Engine House, that venerable ark known as Military Hall, and a neglected annex across the roadway.

Mr. Martin delivered me at the dorm. A soft-spoken prof with gold spectacles, a pink-and-white complexion and a complete set of auburn whiskers, took me by the hand and told me I was welcome, and suggested that I send for my trunk. He was afraid that if I went back to get it, they might lose me. He conducted me to a room on the third floor of the barracks where I met two Comanches from Sullivan, Indiana, who were to be my cellmates. He [the prof] pointed out a straw stack in a field to the west, and gave me some helpful suggestions in regard to filling the bed-tick. Then he led me to the Registrar and helped me to remember my full name, he also steered me to the Boarding Hall where I burned my bridges behind me and paid a month in advance.

George's room, one he considered a "chamber of monastic simplicity," cost fifty cents per week. Most freshmen, he noticed, wore their Sunday clothes. "The ready-made cravat was favored, and a full-sized Ascot was about the size of a lily pad," he wrote. "The horseshoe stickpin was regarded as a natty effect. The Derby hat with wide brim and low crown seemed to have been made in a foundry" (Kelly, *Ade*, 50).

George paid to take his meals—at two dollars and fifty cents per week—in the Ladies Hall. "When the waitress asked if you wanted fruit," Ade later wrote, "you got dried currants with here and there a stem and some gravel." He also wrote:

> Returning to my room in the dorm, I found awaiting me the two from Sullivan who informed me that the sterling drama *Fogg's Ferry* would be presented at the Opera House that evening over in Lafayette by Minnie Evans and Company, and that gallery seats were 25 cents each. As we went down the hill together, I began to feel almost like a Regular. Within a week I was leaning out of the window to pity the "fresh fish" Charlie Martin delivered every day.

Ade impressed his fellow freshmen about having seen the "awful good show" over in Lafayette. Before long, he knew every boy in the dorm and had collected a circle of friends. In his quiet, shy way, he showed an interest in everyone. His room became a rallying place for engrossing conversation. George had an engaging way of telling stories, often based on his uncanny observations of people and mannerisms in Chapel or in classrooms that the others missed. He merely stated what he had seen unobserved by others, in ways that brought laughter. He and his pals would sit around in stocking feet, playing cards and smoking.

"During my collegiate days I smoked cigarettes and a pipe," Ade wrote. "The Lone Jack and Marburg mixtures were popular in the 1880s. The favorite cigarettes were Sweet Caps [Caporals] and Richmond Straight Cuts" (Tobin 130).

During the months of George's "monastic" Purdue life, local events swirled all about. Some he noticed, some he did not. In both 1883 and 1884, for instance, September attendance at the Tippecanoe County Fair dropped noticeably. This was because organized temperance forces were boycotting the county's licensing of beer sales at the fair, hot weather or not. In November 1883, Purdue began rising in importance because of its weather station. W. H. Ragan was directing a statewide cadre of thirty-two volunteer observers who reported data to him at Purdue. Five Lafayette brothers named Cox, in December 1883, introduced the *Evening Call*. This Republican newspaper remained in business until 1905. At 4 a.m. on January 5, 1884, one of Ragan's devices measured minus twenty-eight degrees—the coldest reading since record keeping had begun at Purdue in 1880. A stronger newspaper, the evening *Courier*, estimated that about three hundred subscribers were using telephones. In February 1884, nine Lafayette partners put up thirty thousand dollars and opened a Brush Electric Lighting Company branch to sell incandescent lamps for homes. Later that year, Purdue started a School of Pharmacy.

George opted to enroll for courses leading to the degree of Bachelor of Science at Purdue. This allowed him to dodge higher math. Engineering types in his dorm helped him with math the first year. However, when he faced higher algebra in his third term and tried to fathom it without dorm help, his best mark was sixty.

Still, he came to be known as a hard worker during the first two years. Students who can do that, he observed, would be surprised at what they can get away with later. He proved to be good at drawing and history, and best in English composition and literature. He scored one hundred in each of three written literature tests. His essays ranked above average. In his sophomore year, he became one of the editors of a monthly, *The Purdue*, but stayed at that position less than a year. *The Purdue* printed one of his freshman essays, "Habit and Character." It began:

> The person whose qualities form the ideal character will be truthful and high-minded. He will respect others and yet maintain sufficient self-respect or individuality to resent insults or encroachments upon his rights. He will be ambitious when it leads to some noble end; generous and charitable when it helps a worthy cause. (Kelly, *Ade*, 53-54)

As a sophomore, Ade contributed pieces titled "Local News" to the monthly in January 1885, and "Romeo and Juliet" in May.

Purdue offered three literary societies—strong rivals—that met Friday nights for recitations, orations, and debates. One was named the Philoletheans, one for Thomas Carlyle, and the other for Washington Irving. George joined the Irvings and learned to detest the other two because many of them "lived in Lafayette and wore scarf-pins!" (Kelly, *Ade*, 55).

In George's senior year, *The Purdue* published his "Education by Contact" in December 1886. This serious and polished essay contained as excerpts:

> Few men possess a thorough knowledge of both men and books. Knowledge of the first characterizes the speculator and politician. A companionship of books develops the scholarly qualities. A proper knowledge of the two, men and books, fits a man for almost any sphere or capacity, disqualifying him for none...

> We can easily imagine...that the confident Bachelor, fresh from Commencement honors, is totally unfitted for *contact with men* in business and society circles. He may secure exemption grades for

four years and possess the unbounded regard of the spectacled professors and yet prove a boor in society and a mannikin in conversation. Such a man will be compelled to learn by hard experience, with men less considerate than his college mates, several simple rules of conduct. Perhaps he will never learn them.

The world does not request the college man to show his diploma and class record. It will judge him very largely by his actions when thrown into contact with men...

College organizations under the management and supervision of the students form a happy supplement to routine work. The old-fashioned literary societies should not lose their prominence in American colleges. They have taken hundreds of awkward country boys and made of them easy writers and forcible speakers. They tend to bring out the qualities of leadership, teaching one to be unassuming when victorious and to remain calm under defeat...

Athletic, social, scientific and other associations bring the student into various combinations with his fellows. The most successful institutions are marked by their presence. They dissolve class distinctions, bring the untrained into contact with the trained; the neophyte and veteran are thrown together. Their entire effect is stimulating.

The formation of steadfast friendship with congenial spirits is rightly judged to be the most potent factor in true education... Happy is he who has learned the beauty and worth of true friendship. The sweet sincerity of joy and peace, which I drew from this alliance with my brother's soul, is the nut itself, whereof all nature and all thought is but the husk and shell. (Hepburn and Sears, 181-182)

Ade also went on remembering his Purdue beginnings in "Only Forty Years Ago This Summer":

> We had a total attendance of about two hundred, including the Prep Department. Most of the men who did not live at their own homes nearby camped out in the old dormitory. The boarding house for the campus residents was in the Ladies' Hall. Some of us who were aristocratic took our food at this boarding establishment and paid the high rate of $2.50 a week. But the frugal souls organized a boarding club just across the road from the campus, and succeeded in getting through every week for something less than $2.
>
> There was no attempt to organize athletics. We had no football team, no basketball team, no track team and no gymnasium. Along in the spring a baseball team would be organized and it would play with local teams and possibly hook up once in a while with Wabash College. We had no fraternity houses and no recognized fraternities. The important organizations that divided the student body into factions were literary societies, and all the interest centered on them.
>
> There was no street railway to Lafayette, not even a stage line, and when we went skylarking to the city we either tramped across the old levee and through the tunnel-like bridge built of wood or else stole a ride from some farmer. There was one "dress suit" in the dormitory, and the owner of it was a subject of ridicule. We were much addicted to bandwagon rides out into the country and innocent parties pulled off at a minimum of expense. (*1923 Purdue Debris*)

George Ade's teacher of English composition, Anna Mont McRae, strongly influenced him. Among the class notes he saved for the rest of his life was one that read, "Concrete ideas render a composition beautiful by filling the mind with pictures. The abstract is dry and devoid of power over the imagination."

Another said, "A sentence may be constructed in accordance with the rules for concord, clearness and unity and still produce little effect. Something is wanting to fix the attention and sustain the interest."

Other notes reminded him of the importance of "fitting the words to convey the idea with force" and "to avoid use of newly coined words."

As the years passed and George adjusted to the life of a student away from home, going to the theater in Lafayette rated as his best weekend means of celebration. Admission to the second gallery in the stately brick and stone Grand Opera House cost only a quarter. "After a performance," George reminisced, "we went to the Globe Chop House where, for fifteen cents, one might get a small steak resembling a warped ear-muff, a boiled potato, bread and butter and coffee. After we had supped at our leisure and turned in our verdict on the play and the players, each one bought and lighted a fragrant five-cent cigar and then the jovial company went trooping back across the levee asserting in song that we had been working on the railroad all the livelong day, which was far from the truth" (Kelly, *Ade*, 57).

Besides his devotion to Opera House fare, George liked circuses. A top thrill was the traveling P. T. Barnum "Greatest Show on Earth" and its elephant named Jumbo. George could also be found in the second gallery at the Opera House for minstrel shows. Of all the offerings he saw during his student days, though, a light opera during his junior year topped everything prior. It was *The Mikado* with words and music by Gilbert and Sullivan. The lilting production opened new worlds to George. As he and his pals walked back to the dorm across the levee, Ade astounded his friends by how much *Mikado* he could sing from memory. In those days, Purdue had no glee club, no band, no drama club, no daily paper, and no athletic association. So George took no part in events beyond being a spectator and, at times, an amused and amusing commentator.

In his junior year of 1885-1886, George joined a Greek-letter fraternity. The Delta Delta Chapter of Sigma Chi rented a room over a store at Fourth and Main in Lafayette for meetings but supported no chapter house. George remained in the dormitory. Sigma Chi had won a legal battle, mostly against the rigid policies of former Purdue President Emerson E. White. The court had denied any state university the right to bar fraternity members from classes. George was proud to have been invited to join Sigma Chi and wore the biggest fraternity pin he could buy. Years later, when his fondness for Sigma Chi had multiplied many times over, he laughed at old snapshots showing his big pin as an example of what he called the "absolute yappiness" of his college days.

One future and famous Sigma Chi fraternity brother, cartoonist John Tinney McCutcheon, wrote in his autobiography:

> Along in my sophomore year one of the Sigma Chis was delegated by his chapter to look me over. It was the same youth whose profile I had been admiring from afar, and whose name turned out to be George Ade.

> Evidently George's report on me was favorable because I was invited to become a Sig. From that day began a relationship that remained one of the most valued throughout my life. The greatest asset Sigma Chi gave me was the friendship of George Ade. He was thin and tall and wore a sedate blue suit with tight spring-bottomed trousers that flared out at the ankle…

> "[Ade had] the most extraordinary memory. His experiences, his endless assortment of humorous stories, the words of songs and quotations—his grip on all these always astonished me. He remembered vividly common experiences we had—people we met and what they said—things that faded completely from my

memory. As a raconteur he was unrivaled." (McCutcheon, *Drawn from Memory*, 44-45)

McCutcheon was a "local" from a Wea Township farm home a few miles south of Lafayette. His father, a personable Civil War captain, livestock drover, and county sheriff, attracted friends. John T. McCutcheon reflected his father's graciousness, warmth, and charm all his life as an artist, writer, and traveler.

McCutcheon first met Ade in 1884, in Chapel, and he remembered how "an unusual face down among the sophomores—a refined, clean-cut, delicately aquiline face—stood out among the surrounding run of rugged, freckled, corn-fed features. Later I learned that the possessor of this cameo-like profile was George Ade. The name appealed to me as much as the face. He had three outstanding characteristics that made him an inviting subject for caricature—an unusual expanse of head behind the ears, a sweep of strongly marked eyebrows and a striking lack of abdominal fullness, described by realists as slab belly...Even my undeveloped instinct told me that here was an exceptional person" (Kelly, *Ade*, 61).

McCutcheon showed a knack for drawing. He began to illustrate for Purdue printed programs and publications. His work included caricatures of Ade. He and Ade became friends. After George invited John to become a Sigma Chi, the two became inseparable. McCutcheon continued:

> The Wabash River was in high flood. I don't know why we thought this would be a good time to go boating, but George Ade, Jasper "Jap" Dresser and I rowed up the old Wabash & Erie Canal channel and then, some miles up, portaged the boat over into the Wabash and started down with the current, a mad rush homeward. Darkness came on. We shot under the Brown Street Bridge and then through the gloom we saw we were headed for one of the stone piers of the Main Street Bridge. Frantically we used our oars and barely cleared it but did not see the tree that jutted out from the tangled mass lodged against the pier and overhanging the swirling water by only a couple of feet. We ducked and tried

to ward it off with our hands but the current yanked the boat out from under us. We were left dangling from the tree, our legs in the rushing water.

Finally somebody crossing the bridge heard us, and after a long time old Joker Hill came and rescued us. Joker Hill was the boatman at the end of the bridge, and we had chartered our craft from him. Later it transpired that he had first rescued his boat, thus detracting somewhat from the nobility of his heroic deed. (McCutcheon, *Drawn from Memory*, 46)

A Thanksgiving season treat for Ade and other theatergoers, in 1885, proved to be Lillian Russell starring in *Polly* in two shows in the Grand Opera House. The following April, Opera House patrons welcomed prizefighter John L. Sullivan and his touring "athletic troupe."

As his college days drew to a close, George Ade's library was growing. He bought books at a secondhand dealer's shop in Lafayette. His personal bookplate contained the warning "He who borrows and returns not is a kleptomaniac." Ade acquired *Gulliver's Travels, Decline and Fall of the Roman Empire, Popular History of the United States*, Dickens' *Bleak House*, Emerson's essays, and works of Shakespeare, Byron, Pope, Sir Walter Scott, Burns, and Thackeray. George read them all, too, even at times neglecting his assigned classroom work in math, zoology, and chemistry.

In his final Purdue year of 1886-1887, Ade led the Irvings and presided over Sigma Chi. He organized dances and picnics. He even took up with Lillian Howard, a blonde freshman from Lafayette. Nothing came of it, yet Ade's biographer decades later would write, "there is reason to believe that Lillian Howard was the one girl with whom George Ade would ever be in love" (Kelly, *Ade*, 63).

George's senior-year grades averaged eighty-nine—creditable for such a busy kid from a farm town. Purdue commencement on

June 9, 1887 honored Ade and seven other graduates. Each presented an "oration" or an abstract of a thesis. The others rendered far more technical presentations than George's "The Future of Letters in the West." In his effort, Ade predicted "the hub of the literary universe is about to shift from Cambridge, Massachusetts, to an indefinite region which includes Crawfordsville, Indianapolis, and Tippecanoe County, Indiana." After all, Lew Wallace's seven-year-old *Ben Hur* was becoming a classic, and other Indiana writers such as Edward Eggleston and Maurice Thompson had popular books to their credit. George also seemed to be thinking of future unknowns who would add to Indiana's literary glory. Ade confessed to spending weeks on that speech "rubbing out short words and putting in longer ones" (Kelly, *Ade*, 64). And he remained unsure of what he had accomplished by finishing Purdue. In an interview in 1902, he said after growing up in Kentland, "I went to Purdue, from which I graduated in 1887, and then my troubles began."

After his graduation, as Ade remembered it, he found work as a reporter for a short-lived Republican newspaper, the Lafayette *Morning News*. Ade said he was paid in stock and as little money as possible. In a letter half a century later, Ade expressed amusement and surprise that the inquiring writer had remembered his connection with the *Morning News* so many years before. Ade said the *News* was started so that there would be a Republican morning paper in Lafayette during the political campaign of 1888, "but it died before the campaign opened."

Answering another letter: "I never was a regular [typesetter at the *Morning News*.] I did a little typesetting just for practice. My job in the printing office was to run the job press, operate the roller on the old Washington hand press, address and fold the single wrappers and deliver papers to the post office. I was a kind of a 'devil' around the shop but never became a regular. I did write a few items for publication" (Tobin 203-204).

Just months after Ade finished Purdue, the school first fielded a football team. But Ade, who would describe those years as "a prehistoric era of pompadours, polkas, tight trousers, mandolins and Sweet Caporal cigarettes," came to love Purdue football so much that he "became a sophomore for forty years." He wrote that Purdue's first players were "tall, skinny boys who wore spectacles, and had the biceps of a sand hill crane." Albert Berg, a deaf-mute from Lafayette who had learned football in the East, came on as coach—for a dollar a day. Ade wrote that Berg's job was to "take charge of the halt, the lame, the blind, and the perniciously anemic to imbue them with stamina, courage and strategy. Any man who wished to play football could make the team by merely signing his name. [They] put down their names because they had read about Tom Brown at Rugby and wished to get a free ride to Indianapolis...Our athletes trained on pie and doughnuts" (Kelly, *Ade*, 68).

Ade called the Purdue team's season-opening (and closing) forty-two-point loss to Butler "a low comedy reproduction of the Custer massacre at Little Big Horn." But Berg, in a remembrance written in 1924, pictured the time more charitably:

> It was a fine bunch of boys that I coached in '87. On account of my inability to hear, my ability to talk only to a limited extent, and on account of [football] being practically new in this part of the country, my instruction was mainly by imitation by the boys of my own playing, and the way they caught on and improved upon it would have delighted and encouraged any coach. They were a willing and loyal lot, full of pep and college spirit, and the foundation, I am sure, was then and there laid for Purdue's subsequent gridiron success. (Lafayette *Journal and Courier*, November 20, 1924)

J. B. Burris captained Berg's team. Burris graduated from Purdue in 1888. He said he was chosen captain because, in the fall of 1887, he was the only man at Purdue who had ever seen a football game. He recalled:

Athletics at Purdue...came naturally to a bunch of old "dorm" hermits whose opportunity for exercise (except for the usual dorm escapades) was meager in the extreme. An occasional game of baseball in the spring during the middle of the 1880s played with some local nine was not an enthusiastic event. No means of recreation except short hikes up Happy Hollow, a row on the Wabash River or a cross-country foraging expedition were forthcoming.

In the fall of 1886 there came vague rumors that the game of football was being indulged in by three colleges of the state—Hanover, Butler and Wabash. Having a friend playing on the Wabash team [I] accepted his invitation and saw the game against Hanover at the old Athletic Park in Indianapolis.

During the fall a large round ball, similar to that [later] used in basketball had been kicked about the open space in front of the old [Purdue] dorm. No attempt was made at a game between teams.

Early in the fall of 1887 a few enthusiastic individuals called a meeting and an athletic organization was effected. At a subsequent meeting [I] suggested the colors old gold and black, borrowed from Princeton, and doubtless due to the fact that [I] was the only party present who had ever seen a game played, was chosen captain of the newly organized team.

Suits of bed ticking and brown canvas were made by a local tailor at a nominal cost, paid for from a fund mostly subscribed by occupants of the "dorm." Goals were erected on the open campus in front of the dorm and a mute, one Albert Berg, living in Lafayette, was engaged as coach at a price of one dollar per lesson.

This fellow had learned the game in Washington where he had attended school. Fancy, if you will, a mute coaching a football team! Also [imagine] football togs without shields, balloon tires, pads or protection fore or aft!

A game was arranged with Butler and on the morning of Oct. 29, 1887, the [Purdue] team with about 50 supporters boarded a Big Four train for Indianapolis. President [James] Smart came to the station, asking that we play the best we could and act like gentlemen. If winners, he said, send a message and he would come [and meet our train] with a band on return.

Clint Hare, an old Yale player, had coached Butler. William P. Herod, a Harvard man, was referee. The score was 48 to 6 in Butler's favor.

There followed an editorial from the November 1887 issue of *The Purdue*, the old college paper: "The reverse met with by the university football team in a recent intercollegiate contest should not in any way dampen the ardor of the athletic enthusiasts. While it is not to be denied that it was the worst kind of a defeat, when viewed in the light of existing circumstances it does not appear so bad.

"The team, as such, had practices for a week only, and that too when players were constantly being changed. The duties of the individual positions were not thoroughly understood and the men under limited amount of coaching did not fully realize the fine points of the game. The team certainly deserves the credit given them for the plucky manner in which they met such tremendous odds.

"This was their first game, and that too against the oldest team in the state. Everyone should feel satisfied that this much was developed: That we have the material for a strong team, men that are willing and enthusiastic in doing all they can in making Purdue a record for western college athletics."

The management of the *Morning News*, paying with job titles instead of money, at one point promoted George Ade to "assistant city editor." However, he was still the only reporter, still chased the Lafayette fire engines, and detected an economic end approaching. "The funds had dribbled away," Ade said. "The backers had fled, the editor had evaporated, the editorial writer had gone to Delphi to see his girl, the business manager was in retirement, the city editor had flown to Crawfordsville."

Only George and the foreman of the composing room were left. He wrote, "We held a brief funeral service just at midnight, then locked the dear departed in the cold forms, pooled our finances and went to an all-night beanery" (Kelly, *Ade*, 67).

"After the *News* flickered I went over to the *Call* and worked for 'Sep' [editor Septimius] Vater for practically nothing [eight dollars] a week," George continued. "I remember the Wise Saloon across from the Lahr House, even if I did not get over there very often. It was a tough dump" (Tobin 207-208). The *Call*, Ade said, "paid partly in meal tickets for a cheap restaurant that was a heavy advertiser."

Vater wanted George to write as many local names as possible into his *Call* stories. Through the rival afternoon *Courier*, George encountered John T. McCutcheon's brother George Barr McCutcheon. The latter worked under similar orders, from the *Courier*, that names make news. The two young drama fans found a common interest in a minstrel show comedian named Willis Sweatnam and his fictitious monologue characters. Before long, both the *Call* and *Courier* contained faked Ade and McCutcheon creations, borrowed from Sweatnam's acts, such as:

- "The widow Truckmuck is entertaining her cousin from Peru."

- "Lee Truckmuck returned from Chicago yesterday and reports a neat profit on his last shipment of yearlings."

- "The younger son of the widow Truckmuck is recovering from the scarlet fever."

"After a few months I went to work for a patent medicine concern," Ade said. "The owner, Harry Kramer, was a prosperous native who had many irons in the fire. I sold a cure for the tobacco habit and did well."

Ade roomed in the Stockton House at 634 South Street in Lafayette in his first post-college stop in life. Sisters of Holland Dutch descent—Gertrude and Lena Niemantsverdriet—ran the Stockton House. Ade continued seeing many shows, too, at the Grand Opera House barely a city block away.

Kramer owned a health resort where patrons took mud baths. He also ran a company that made and sold proprietary drugs. He offered Ade twelve dollars a week, later fifteen, to write ads, dictate letters, and handle mail as a "department manager."

"We sold to druggists at a time when a drug store was a repository for patent medicines instead of a combination of soda fountain, restaurant, beauty parlor, novelty shop and radio concert," Ade said. "The patent medicine business was not to be sneezed at when every prominent church worker and temperance advocate used about two large square-cornered full quart size bottles of 'tonic' every week. This useful remedy for whatever ailed you was compounded from No. 2 Pennsylvania rye whiskey, syrup and a small percentage of puckery bitters. Whisky, syrup and bitters—try to figure anything but a cocktail out of that! Yet no one ever said that the Deacon was a rum-hound or ever accused the druggist of being a saloon keeper" (Kelly, *Ade*, 69).

Another product was No-Tobac, Kramer's cure for the tobacco habit. Ade wrote a pamphlet containing testimonials about No-Tobac and got John McCutcheon to draw a cover. The cover pictured a Roman warrior sinking a sword into a part-serpent, part-alligator monster labeled Nicotine. Ade went on smoking Sweet Caporals while hyping No-Tobac and said that McCutcheon inhaled Richmond Straight Cuts while drawing and making five dollars for the effort. It is believed to be one of the first McCutcheon cartoons ever published.

By October 1889, McCutcheon had gone to Chicago for a job in the Art Department of the *News*. Back in Lafayette, Ade needed more things to write and more money for writing.

While visiting the Delta Delta Chapter fellows at Purdue, Ade suggested that the Sigma Chis produce a souvenir book to mark the University's fifteenth commencement in June 1890. They could sell advertising to pay for the publication. Ade persuaded McCutcheon to coax drawings from a couple of his artist friends in Chicago. A Sigma Chi named Paul Anders took bows for being the editor-in-chief of *A Souvenir*. However, according to McCutcheon, Ade wholly directed and largely wrote the project. Ade is believed to have composed the untitled ode to John Purdue, the University founder, who had died in the late summer of 1876:

> No gleaming shaft nor granite block,
>
> Nor sculptured pile of cold, insensate stone,
>
> No chiseled epitaph of empty praise,
>
> Marks his last resting place.

Himself without a home, he reared a place

Where Science might abide and Learning dwell;

Where Art should flourish long, and hold her court,

And grant to every worshiper his meed.

He sleeps—and tow'ring here above his couch

The products of his genius and his toil

Speak louder far than wrought or figured stone

Of life well lived and labor nobly done.

Ade further contributed poems titled "Picnics," "The Glorious Touchdown," "The La Grippe," and "The College Widow," plus a comic piece of nonsensical advice he called "Some Easy Lessons" and stories titled "The Dorm" and "The Annuals."

In "The College Widow," as matters would unfold, the seven stanzas contained the plot of one of Ade's most enduring literary works that became both a Broadway play and motion picture. The poem described the life of a college belle who, as her older admirers move on, accepts the attentions of younger ones:

(Stanza One)

When I was but a Freshman—and that was long ago—

I saw her first, but did not learn her name;

She was at a lecture, I believe, in the first or second row,

And the Junior with her seemed to be her flame.

He held her fan all evening and gazed into her eyes;

Thought I, "Now they're engaged, or soon will be:'

But afterward they quarreled, as I learned with some surprise,

When the faculty conferred on him G. B.

(Stanza Three)

O, charming college widow, I never can forget

The night when you put on my college pin;

I pressed your hand and told you that the act you'd not regret

And you said you'd stick to us through thick and thin.

I remember still the picnics and that moonlight promenade,

Just the night before I paid for my degree,

When we interchanged such sacred vows, and declarations made,

That we'd love each other through eternity.

(Stanza Seven)

She looked a little older, but her laugh was just as gay;

Beside her was a gallant Sophomore,

Who held her parasol aloft and gushed the self-same way

That I had doubtless done in days of yore.

I merely tipped my hat; I feared to introduce my wife,

For I knew that some remark might lightly fall,

Revealing to my better half a chapter of my life,

Which I'd rather she not suspect at all.

That spring George began receiving gushing letters about Chicago, not from any "charming college widow" at all, but from McCutcheon. The letters urged George to come. McCutcheon said his room had a double bed, so there was every reason for George to try working in the big town. In June 1890, when Kramer changed medicine company managers, George found himself out of work. So George informed McCutcheon by mail that he was now "at liberty" and would be willing to try Chicago and share that double bed.

A different breed of cat

In June 1889, when Dave Ross finished high school in Brookston, he wanted to go to college. However, his father, George Ross, considered college a waste of time. George Ross was not alone. Indiana Governor James D. "Blue Jeans" Williams once had chilled a college crowd when he opened a *commencement* speech by opining "eddycate a boy and he won't work!"

George Ross felt the same way. He insisted that Dave learn something *practical*. Dave had engineering in mind. Wasn't that practical? He wanted to go down to the Wabash River town known for years as Chauncey but renamed West Lafayette in 1888. There the teenaged Purdue University campus still struggled for permanence.

In 1889, Purdue amounted to eight buildings out in a field. The courses included agriculture and three forms of engineering—mechanical, civil, and electrical. In the debate with George Ross, Dave's Uncle Will, took Dave's side. Uncle Will offered to let Dave stay in his Lafayette home and walk a daily mile over to Purdue. It would save Dave and Dave's father about two dollars and fifty cents per week on room and board costs at Purdue. Uncle Will further offered to pay for Dave's tuition and books. With this much help, Dave's entire four-year Purdue education might cost George Ross no more than a hundred dollars.

Still, Brookston tongues wagged that Dave and George Ross quarreled over college. Some sided with George and hoped that the boy was not making a mistake. Uncle Will met Dave at the train station after the ride from Brookston. Some of Uncle Will's and

(Will's sister) Aunt Eleanor's Ninth Street Hill neighbors came by the house to wish Dave well. Purdue enrollment stood at four hundred sixty-some at the time.

It soon became obvious that, as another farm boy at Purdue, Dave Ross was going to be different from George Ade. Dave Ross was going to be "another breed of cat" as they said in rural Indiana. With his deep-set hazel eyes, thick, dark hair, and overhanging eyebrows, Dave was a serious looking lad. Lonely as he had always seemed, he still could smile. However, he was and would be no joke-spinning backslapper, no leader of dorm-party songs. Living with Uncle Will and Aunt Eleanor enabled Dave and his parents to save money but caused the boy to miss campus life and the friendships of which George Ade sang in his essay on "Education By Contact." George Ade had come to know his dorm mates by name in a day or two. Dave Ross had no such opportunity. George Ade became a Sigma Chi. No one invited Dave Ross.

Unlike so many country boys at Purdue, Dave was not powerfully built, either, and showed no talent for sports. He gravitated toward quiet boys like himself who preferred the background. Dave carried his lunch to Purdue, wrapped in newspaper by Aunt Eleanor. He ate with fellows from the country. One of them, Jack Kneale, rode in on horseback from a farm eight miles away. Kneale started studying electrical engineering but switched to pharmacy.

"Think of all the things they'll be doing with electricity," Dave said.

"I know," Kneale nodded, "but electric power will be controlled by big companies. I want to be in business for myself. I'll never own an electric street railway, a lighting plant or phone company, but I might own a pharmacy."

That sort of talk set Dave to thinking ahead. He, too, liked the thought of being in business for himself. Another event kept him thinking that way. It was an inspirational lecture titled "Acres of Diamonds" uttered by a Philadelphia minister, Russell Conwell. Conwell preached at Purdue about the sheer folly of people thinking that opportunities only exist far away. He cited many men who had struck it rich almost in their own back yard, saying:

> To be great at all, one must be great right here, now, in your own town. He who can give his city better streets and better sidewalks, better schools or colleges, more happiness and more civilization, he will be great anywhere. If you wish to be great, you must begin where you are, and as you are, right here, now. (Kelly, *Ross*, 28-29)

Dave remembered the lecture and the lesson. At Purdue, he made weak grades in subjects in which he would later excel. He barely passed Machine Design, yet even then showed talent for picturing complex machines in detail before drawing them. He made average Mechanical Drawing grades, too. But Dave's was a questioning personality and inquisitive mind. There was a growing tradition at Purdue for the undergraduates to try to "kidnap" the senior class president and keep him from going to his class's annual banquet. However, when Dave was invited to help in a kidnap he asked, "Why don't we want them to hold their banquet?" No one knew why.

Ross enrolled in an optional special course in civil engineering. Occasionally, as the class experimented, he would ask, "Why is it done *this* way?" The everyday student accepted the way things were always done without asking why. Dave's was one of the minds that thought that school and college success depended too much on the ability to be a clerk and neatly write down facts, ideas, or opinions from the teacher. Dave was poor clerk material, poor at recording what a teacher dictated.

In the first semester of Dave's freshman year, Purdue's newly revived football team coached by G. A. Reisner played three games. In its first home game ever—on a YMCA field in Lafayette—Purdue's team defeated DePauw thirty-four to ten. At Crawfordsville, Purdue defeated Wabash College eighteen to four but lost its finale at Butler fourteen to nothing in Indianapolis. A bitter Crawfordsville newspaper accused Reisner of recruiting non-students—

muscular policemen and boilermakers from Lafayette's railroads—in order to beat Wabash. The "Boilermakers" nickname stuck with Purdue teams.

In February 1890, Purdue opened its Electrical Engineering building. In July, federal census takers counted 35,078 people in Tippecanoe County, 16,243 in Lafayette, and 1,242 in West Lafayette.

In the autumn of Dave's sophomore year, the football team won two home games against Wabash and Illinois, and one game in Greencastle against DePauw, but lost other road games against Chicago, Michigan, and Butler. C. L. Hare coached the "Boilermakers" who scored an average of approximately twenty-eight points per game and held foes to about nine. Interest in football increased. One could tell by the size of the "home" crowds at the field in Lafayette.

By the end of April 1891, several of Dave Ross's closest kin embarked on a business venture. They platted high quality home sites on their partner James Reynolds's rolling pasture south of Lafayette's Kossuth Street. Their Highland Park Land Company filed articles of incorporation and raised twenty-one thousand dollars for working capital by selling 420 shares of stock at fifty dollars apiece. The stockholders included Reynolds, Dave's father George Ross, Dave's Uncle Will, Uncle Linn, and Uncle Linn's wife Lydia. For years, Uncle Will and Uncle Linn had saved their money while farming in White County. Reynolds, Will, and Linn were the Land Company's first directors. They took their time about planning, grading, piping, pouring concrete sidewalks, and paving streets in the once-pastoral acreage.

On November 14, 1891, teams from Purdue and Indiana played their first intercollegiate football game in West Lafayette. The event attracted twelve hundred spectators. Purdue led sixty to nothing when officials suspended play. To the delight of the growing numbers of football fans, new coach Knowlton "Snake" Ames's first

Purdue team won all four of its 1891 games against Wabash, DePauw, Indiana, and Butler. The team scored 192 points and held all four foes scoreless. As Purdue success and football popularity soared, a movement began to wave goodbye to Lafayette's YMCA field and put up a permanent set of bleachers and other amenities on the West Lafayette campus. Purdue opened such a venue and named it Stuart Field in 1892.

> The birth of Stuart Field was preceded by what might be termed a battle of The Old versus The New with Agriculture on one side and Athletics on the other...Then came recognition of the demand by patrons that athletic and physical training be afforded students by public institutions.

> This was the state of affairs in 1891: a football team had no regular place to play. Athletes and their supporters cast longing eyes at a plot of ground at the north end of the campus used as an agricultural experiment ground. Wheat experiments were being conducted on the plot at the time, and those in charge objected to such sacrilegious use of the ground as the students proposed. The continuity of valuable wheat experiments cannot and must not be disturbed, they said.

> Students petitioned the university board of trustees that a part of the campus be set aside for athletic purposes. Whereupon the trustees complied and voted to set aside a plot of eight acres north of the campus proper to be used as an athletic field. Thus a wheat field became an athletic field and Stuart Field was born.

> The trustees designated that the plot be known as Stuart Field in honor of the president of the board, Lafayette attorney Charles B. Stuart.

Work was completed on April 15, 1892. The field was dedicated the following day by a baseball game with Butler College. The field...did much to stimulate athletic activities at the university. In 1892 with funds derived from athletic fees, the Athletic Association constructed bleachers capable of seating about 800 persons. In 1898 the sophomore class provided a running track. The Class of 1898 donated upwards of $500 [for] a covered pavilion for the athletic field. This pavilion, seating about 600, was built in 1899. (Lafayette *Journal and Courier*, November 20, 1924)

Meanwhile, the men behind the Highand Park Land Company either had inside information or guessed right, because their investment benefited from a go-after-it spirit sweeping Lafayette. The results unfolded in a breathtaking sequence.

In the middle of June 1892, the Monon Railroad—crossing Indiana from Lake Michigan to the Ohio River—agreed to build maintenance and repair shops at a site off North Twenty-Second Street in Lafayette. The projected Monon Shops would employ up to one thousand men skilled in assorted mechanical trades and numerous boilermakers. The Shops would open with six hundred employees making an average of two dollars per day.

For the Land Company, this meant a boost in potential new homebuyers.

And there was more. In mid-June 1892, a Grand Army of the Republic committee met at Indianapolis and considered bids from Muncie, Warsaw, Cartersburg, and Tippecanoe County for the construction of an Indiana State Soldiers' Home. The committee's aim was to serve the aging and disabled Civil War veterans. Tippecanoe County won again.

These summer developments touched off boom conditions. The concept of "give in order to get" took hold. In the three years since natural gas service had begun and the Belt Railway had opened, seven factories had chosen Lafayette.

In October 1892, several events marked the four hundredth anniversary of Christopher Columbus' voyage of discovery. School programs, flag drills, and band concerts added to the festive season. The joy spilled over to Purdue. On November 1, Amos Heavilon, a Purdue alumnus who farmed in Clinton County, Indiana, gave Purdue land and notes worth thirty-five thousand dollars. Heavilon meant for his gift—the largest since founder John Purdue's one hundred thousand dollars and one hundred acres—to enlarge mechanical engineering shops, labs, and classroom space.

And during October and November 1892, Coach Ames led the Purdue football team to another undefeated season and a mythical "national championship." Playing at Stuart Field, the "Boilermakers" defeated Wisconsin, Michigan, Butler, Indiana, and Chicago and won road games against Illinois, Wabash, and DePauw.

In his senior year, one of Dave Ross's teachers proved to have special and far-reaching influence. He was Professor Reginald Fessenden, once an assistant to Thomas Edison. Fessenden headed Purdue's Department of Electrical Engineering and Physics and became a noted radio industry pioneer. However, he came off to many at 1890s Purdue as an absent-minded "character." They thought him crazy, at age twenty-seven, for predicting that one day a German would learn to take photographs through a wall, but Professor Wilhelm Konrad Roentgen, in his X-ray work, did so two years later. A decade before the Wright Brothers, Fessenden envisioned that one day men would fly. Classmates regarded Ross as strange because of his serious talks with Fessenden, but Ross liked Fessenden because Fessenden taught as an equal, not as an elite or superior professor.

On April 1, 1893—two months before Ross graduated from Purdue—the Highland Park Land Company put on sale 136 building sites between Owen and Kossuth streets west of Ninth. Highland Park would offer buyers paved streets and avenues bearing the names Central, Pontiac, Highland, and Shawnee, along with concrete sidewalks, storm sewers, shade trees, electric power, and purified, pressurized city water delivered to the homes in pipes.

The Company added twenty-eight lots during 1893. Lot prices more than tripled in three years.

Dave Ross finished Purdue in June 1893, receiving a Bachelor of Science degree in electrical engineering. Of forty-one engineers in the Class of 1893, he ranked in the middle. He served as corresponding secretary of his class and as business manager for a Purdue yearbook called the *Debris*. The student newspaper, in a series of senior class prophesies, predicted "Ross will electrify Brookston."

Ross survived typhoid fever instead. Dr. O'Ferrall (the younger, better educated doctor) prescribed outdoor, open-air work to speed Dave's recovery. With no post-graduate plans and no job offers, Dave regarded farm work as sensible a next step as any.

Chicago, here he came!

George Ade's bibliographer, Dorothy Ritter Russo, wrote in 1947 that "[Ade's] contributions to Lafayette newspapers have not been clearly identified, nor have his published advertisements for Harry Kramer's patent medicine company been found. His literary career, then, begins with *The Chicago Record*. He came to work in Chicago in June 1890. The *Daily News* changed its name to *The Chicago News-Record* in 1892 then, until 1900, the *Chicago Record*. The paper saw a prolific output from his mind and pen" (Russo, vii).

Ade himself has recorded that "in 1890, having risen to a weekly income of fifteen dollars [in Lafayette] I lit out for Chicago." McCutcheon met him at the train station and escorted Ade to the third floor hallway room they would share in a house on Peck Court near Michigan Avenue, later the site of the Stevens Hotel.

In some ways, McCutcheon saw a better future for George than George saw for himself at the age of twenty-four. McCutcheon recognized in Ade "a wonderful memory, an X ray insight into motives and men, a highly developed power of keen observation, four years of literary work in college. He had lived in the country and retained the most comprehensive impressions of country life. He knew the types, the vernacular and the point of view of country people from the inside. He had lived in a small town [Kentland] and acquired a thorough knowledge of the types and customs of that phase of life. He had learned college life after four years of observation [Purdue] and learned the life of the medium-sized town [Lafayette]. And with an intelligence great enough to use this knowledge he was ready to learn what a great city could teach" (Kelly, *Ade*, 77).

Now in the great city, George nervously tried out for a spot on the staff of the *Record* for twelve dollars a week. McCutcheon drew illustrations in the *Record's* Art Department. Ade took his entry-level weather-writing job seriously. After his first story, his work began making the front page. Chicagoans were sweating out a summer heat wave at the time. George asked people—even "nobodies"—how they were standing the temperature. He talked to hotel clerks about how the heat affected guests. He asked head-waiters how the heat changed what people ate. He asked draymen and liverymen how their horses were making out. When the forecast called for a cool-off, Ade wrote:

> The Chicagoan who places faith in the weather bureau put the heavy counterpane at the foot of the bed last night on the assurance that a cool wave with icicles in its hair and a claret punch in each pocket was approaching at a respectable gait...and would at least kiss its hand to us in passing.

Such freshness, thoroughness, and imagination caught on. One night in July, a telephone caller tipped the *Record* that an explosion had rocked the freight steamer *Tioga* in the Chicago River. George, the only reporter at hand, leaped to the sudden order to go find out about the story, which turned out *big*. A boiler blast had killed fifteen men. George called the office for reporting help. The *Record* rushed three more men to the *Tioga*, but George already had the story. The managing editor liked George's good judgment in asking for help and told the others to turn their notes over to George so that he could write the entire article. Ade's front-page account the next day earned general praise for being the best in Chicago. The *Record* raised him to fifteen dollars per week.

In August, George wrote to a friend back in Lafayette that "I like the job first rate and am getting some good hard newspaper experience that will be of advantage to me no matter what business I should ever go into...The streets are so full of cable-cars, hansoms, drays, express wagons, chippies, policemen and other public nuisances that a man doesn't know when he starts downtown in the morning whether he will get back at night or land up at the morgue" (Kelly, *Ade,* 81).

Chicago in the 1890s, having doubled its population in ten years, was home to more than a million people—more Poles, Swedes, Norwegians, Danes, Bohemians, Dutch, Croatians, Slovakians, Lithuanians, and Greeks than anywhere else in America. George learned about them all. His writing jobs took him into their lives, and to Irish picnics, German beer fests, strikes, inquests, police court trials, city council and county board meetings, charity balls, conventions, rallies, and sermons. By the end of 1891, George was the best on the *Record* and drew top assignments.

Among his jobs in the late summer of 1892 was a prizefight of national interest. The undefeated John L. Sullivan would face a former bank clerk from San Francisco named James J. "Gentleman Jim" Corbett down in New Orleans, Louisiana. Another assignment for Ade was the Columbian Exposition, commonly called the Chicago World Fair that opened in May 1893.

The *Record* assigned Ade and McCutcheon as a writer-artist team to fill two columns each day headlined "All Roads Lead to the World's Fair." Ade's job was to write what he saw. His work was not intended to have great or timeless news value. He was told to touch upon true-life incidents among the swarms of fairgoers. Ade found stories about the 365-foot Ferris Wheel, Buffalo Bill's Wild West Show, the great buildings, and a Sousa Band concert.

Ade and McCutcheon both reached the twenty-dollar-per-week salary level but tried to stay rooted in good sense. They did splurge by wearing thirty-five-cent chrysanthemums when Purdue beat the University of Chicago twenty to ten in football down in West Lafayette that fall.

The Columbian Exposition closed in October 1893. George returned to the *Record* reporting staff, but to his usual assignments he continued adding little stories of everyday people. "You can imagine what happened to my placid little yarns about shop girls and stray dogs and cable-car conductors," he said. "I would turn in a third of a column about a cooperative attempt to start a balky horse in Wabash Avenue. The copyreaders were instructed to keep every story down to the essentials. But they were helpless when they tackled something [of mine] that *had no essentials,* being unalloyed 'guff.'" The *Record* shortly gave Ade and McCutcheon the empty two-columns of post-Exposition space to use for their unique "guff." The editors marked their work "hands off" for copyreaders.

"I eventually became father of a department called 'Stories of the Streets and of the Town,'" Ade said. "I had to fill those two columns, which meant from twelve hundred to two thousand words a day." This feature and colleague Eugene Field's "Sharps and Flats" columns steadily raised the newspaper's acceptance.

By this time, Ade and McCutcheon each carried walking sticks on their daily hikes to work. "I became addicted to the walking stick habit all of my life, not because I needed support but because when I carried a cane I always knew what to do with at least one of my hands," Ade said. "Each of us usually spent ten cents every morning for a white carnation and tried to put a little brightness and sentimental decoration into the murky atmosphere surrounding us" (Tobin 197).

In his daily stories, Ade set a goal "to be known as a realist with a compact style and a clean Anglo-Saxon vocabulary and the courage to observe human virtues and frailties as they showed on the lens." He aimed to write about people as he knew them and tried never to caricature, stretch, or "embroider fancy situations." Ade and McCutcheon roved Chicago together. George called his daily writing "hand made" because he composed with a pencil.

Ade wrote about the problems of a streetcar conductor, small shops in the city, the search for a good boardinghouse, of storybook versus real detectives, junk shops, odd vehicles, sidewalk merchants and their wares, restaurant signs, a Pullman porter's story, and what occurs in the coroner's office.

The first of the "Stories of the Streets and of the Town" appeared in the *Record* on November 20, 1893, and the last on November 7, 1900. "Stories" became so popular that starting in April 1894, the *Record* reissued a booklet-size series of collections that it sold for a quarter.

The first of eight collections, all titled "The Chicago Record's Stories of the Streets and of the Town Copiously Illustrated," came out on April 1, 1894. It contained forty-two stories having first appeared in January, February, and March 1894 issues of the *Record*.

The second collection published on July 1, 1894 offered sixty-seven stories. The third issued from April 1, 1895 contained eighty-six. The fourth came out on October 1, 1895 with sixty-nine.

At one point, Ade and McCutcheon accepted expense-paid trips to represent the *Record* at a Midwinter Fair in San Francisco. The California jaunt ignited their interest in travel. Because neither ever had ventured far from Indiana soil, they dreamed up a plan to get to Europe. When they received ten-dollar raises to thirty-five per week, they pledged to save those bonus tens until further notice.

Meanwhile, Ade also became his paper's "assistant drama editor" and began writing reviews. This gave him free tickets to theaters and the chance to interview stage stars. It also added to his rapidly filling storehouse of people, especially the "characters" he found.

Ade and McCutcheon estimated that, by April 1895, they would have saved $520 apiece and could then start to Europe. They expected to quit the *Record*, but to their surprise, the *Record* wished to go on paying them in exchange for two illustrated travel articles each week they were gone.

Readers enjoyed the ensuing articles printed under the heading "What a Man Sees Who Goes Away from Home." In the articles, Ade avoided writing what he termed "guidebook stuff." His stories told what food cost in restaurants and the pay of performers in London variety shows and so on.

The two travelers spent about $1,800 apiece while visiting Ireland, England, Holland, Belgium, Germany, Switzerland, Italy, and France. Ade "began to see things from a new angle," adding that "the planet you are now visiting may be the only one you'll ever see. Even if you get a transfer, the next one may not have a Grand Canyon or a Niagara Falls" (Kelly, *Ade,* 120).

On April 1, 1896, the *Record* selected and reprinted a collection of the "What a Man Sees Who Goes Away From Home" stories. The paper attributed this work to an unnamed "Chicago Record Staff Correspondent in Europe." The collection contained sixty-four stories the *Record* had printed between May 20 and December 2, 1895.

Back home in Chicago, Ade began to sense that his readers might enjoy his "Stories of the Streets and of the Town" even more if they found familiar characters recurring. He started this approach in December 1895 when he invented a brash, good-hearted youngster he named "Artie" Blanchard. For this character Ade borrowed the colorful street talk and slang used by a real Art Department employee at the *Record* named Charlie Williams. "Artie" was designed to be a young man of sound morals, decent manners, and little flashes of wisdom. Before long, Ade pushed the idea further, creating likeable characters he named "Pink" Marsh and "Doc" Horne.

At one point, a Chicago foreign-language paper, the *Danish Pioneer*, commented, "We do not hesitate to compare George Ade with Dickens; indeed, he generally surpasses his great predecessor in his almost incredible power to give the most trivial things of life a new and fresh human interest" (Kelly, *Ade*, 122).

Early in 1896, Ade pondered a "moonlight job" offer of an extra twenty-five dollars each to write short books for children. A Chicago publisher wanted to put out six of them, each two inches square, to be sold as a set for one dollar. Over one weekend, Ade wrote and McCutcheon illustrated *Circus Day*. Ade then wrote another he called "Stories From History" about Christopher Columbus, George Washington, Abraham Lincoln, and others. However, the publisher wanted to promote a variety of authors for the series, so for *Stories From History*, Ade devised and used the pen name "John Hazelden." A Hazleton branch of his family tree inspired the pseudonym.

In late August 1896, both *Circus Day* and *Stories from History* appeared in a Little Folks Library series. The first bore the credits "Written by George Ade, Illustrations by John T. McCutcheon." The miniature history book said "Written by John Hazelden, Illustrations by John T. McCutcheon."

As early as May 1896, the Chicago publishing house of Herbert S. Stone and Company had wished to publish a book of the "Artie" sketches. Ade put together enough of them to make *Artie, a Story of the Streets and Town* for Stone to publish on September 24, 1896. Again, Ade and McCutcheon formed the creative team.

The book contained twenty "Artie" Blanchard stories printed in the *Record* between December 9, 1895 and May 30, 1896.

A tobacco company named a cigar for "Artie." The popular book also caused Ade to be "discovered" by William Dean Howells, foremost New York literary critic. Of *Artie* Howells wrote, "On the level which it consciously seeks I do not believe there is a better study of American town life in the West."

From the end of 1896 through May 1897, Ade produced the "Pink" Marsh stories about an African-American bootblack in a basement barbershop. In these yarns, Ade caught the talk and character of the sophisticated northern Negro. "Pink" told his stories in conversations with a fictitious Morning Customer. The Stone Company published a collection of twenty-one of them in *Pink Marsh* on May 22, 1897.

Ade's books impressed more than critics. Mark Twain wrote to Howells:

Thank you once more for introducing me to the incomparable Pink Marsh...My admiration of the book has overflowed all limits, all frontiers. I have personally known each of the characters in the book and can testify that they are all true to the facts and as exact as if they had been drawn to scale...It is as if the work did itself, without help of the master's hand. And for once—just this once—the illustrator [McCutcheon] is the peer of the writer. The writer flashes a character onto his page in a dozen words, you turn the leaf and there he stands, alive and breathing. (Kelly, *Ade*, 125-126)

Meanwhile, the *Record* siphoned more money—at a quarter a pop—out of its ongoing series of "Stories of the Streets and of the Town." The fifth collection appeared on July 1, 1897. It contained forty-three pieces reprinted from the *Record*. The sixth came out on July 1, 1898. The contents included forty-one stories. The seventh appeared on April 1, 1899 with fifty-five stories.

Next, Ade wrote stories about "Doc" Horne, a gentlemanly liar, and Horne's pals at the "Alfalfa European Hotel." The Horne stories ran in the *Record* through 1898. By June 29, Stone brought out *Doc' Horne*. The book contained twenty-seven chapters, rewritten in part from stories that had run between April 15 and June 9, 1897. For the last five chapters, Ade "wrote for the book, weaving a simple plot for the concluding chapters" (Russo, 30).

But Ade's work did not—as Mark Twain supposed—"do itself."

"I used to get desperate for ideas," Ade said. "One morning I sat at the desk and gazed at the empty paper and realized the necessity of concocting something different. The changes had been wrung through weary months and years on blank verse, catechism, rhyme, broken prose, the drama form of dialogue and staccato paragraphs. Why not a *fable* for a change? And instead of slavishly copying Aesop why not retain the archaic form and the stilted manner of composition and, for purposes of novelty, permit the language to be 'fly,' modern, undignified, quite up to the moment?

I [also] had learned from writing that all people, especially women, are fond of parlor slang. [So] in cold blood I began writing fables to make my columns go, but had no idea that those fantastic things would catch on the way they did" (Kelly, *Ade*, 136).

In saying "fantastic things" Ade modestly referred to "Fables in Slang," his runaway hit series of columns launched for the *Record* but also syndicated, reprinted, and read in many papers nationwide. "My first one [September 17, 1897] was about 'The Blonde Girl who Married a Bucket Shop Man,'" Ade said.

In the column, Ade made it obvious that he was just playing around. He hyphenated the syllables in the long words and capitalized the key words:

> Once there were two Sis-ters. They lived in Chi-ca-go. One was a Plain Girl, but she had a Good Heart. She was stu-di-ous and took first Hon-ors at the Gram-mar School.
>
> She cared more for the Graces of Mind that she did for mere Out-ward Show. Her Sis-ter was a Friv-o-lous Girl...
>
> The Friv-o-lous Girl who had naught to com-mend her except a Beauty which fad-eth, became Cashier in a Quick Lunch Es-tab-lish-ment and the Pat-ron-age increased largely. She chewed Gum and said "Ain't," but she be-came pop-u-lar just the same.

When Ade rewrote this little story he called it "The Fable of Sister Mae Who Did As Well As Could Be Expected." In the rewrite he dropped all the hyphens and made other changes but kept the plot.

> Luella was a good girl, but her features did not seem to know the value of Team Work. Her clothes were an intermittent Fit. She was a lumpy Dresser. She worked in a factory, and every Saturday Evening when Work was called on account of Darkness, the Boss met her as she went out and crowded Three Dollars on her. Sister

Mae was different. She was short on Intellect but Long on Shape. She became Cashier in a Lunch Room and was a Strong Card. Her Date Book had to be kept on the Double Entry System. She married a Bucket-Shop Man who was not Handsome but was awful Generous. Mae bought a Thumb Ring and a Pug Dog and the Smell of Cooking made her Faint. But did she forget Luella? No indeed. She took her away from the Factory and gave her a Position as assistant cook at Five a week.

Fables were supposed to end with a moral. The moral of this first one was: Industry and Perseverance bring a sure Reward.

Ade had liked the revision best, but the original had pleased his readers. "Next day," he said, "the score-keepers told me I had knocked a home run. The young women on the [*Record*] staff told me the piece was 'just killing'" (Kelly, *Ade*, 138).

Ade claims to have had no intention of writing other "Fables in Slang," calling that first one "simply a little experiment in outlawry." However, a month later another Fable appeared minus any Slang, then another without Slang, then no more until July 1898. Ade then devoted space to two columns clearly labeled "Fables in Slang." "It was a great lark to write in slang—like gorging on forbidden fruit," he admitted. "The bridle was off and all rules abolished" (Kelly, *Ade*, 139).

And yet Ade himself imposed certain rules: "I never referred to a policeman as a 'bull' because that word belongs in the criminal vocabulary, and mother and girls are not supposed to be familiar with the cryptic terms of yeggmen. I never referred to a young girl as a 'chicken.' The word originated in the deepest pits of white slavery. A young girl may be a flapper, a bud, a peach, a pippin, a lollypaloozer, a nectarine, a cutie, a queen, a daisy, even a baby doll without being insulted, but never a 'chicken.' There [also] are words of popular circulation that don't sound well in the mouth or look pretty in type. 'Slob' has always been one. Our fellow citizen may be a dub or even a lobster, possibly a mutt, but let us draw the line on 'slob'" (Kelly, *Ade*, 154).

Then Ade's book publisher closed in. The Stone Company gave up on him ever writing a novel the house could publish, but Stone now expressed interest in publishing a *Fables in Slang* book. "Closed in upon by frantic advisers," Ade narrated with tongue in cheek, "the harried young author began to write Fables in Slang with both hands. In vain did he protest that he was not a specialist in the easy-going vernacular, and that he wanted to deal with life as it is instead of verbal buck dancing and a bizarre costuming of capital letters. The friends told him to take the gifts that were falling into his lap, and not crave the golden persimmons that grow on the hilltops. So the crazy Fables became a glaring feature of our newspaper department" (Kelly, *Ade,* 139-140).

Before long, the *Record* asked Ade to finish and turn in the Fables a few days ahead of publication. It seemed that some papers in other cities had been reprinting them and now offered to pay for them if they could get and use them on the same day as the *Record*. Nothing was said about extra money for Ade.

The team—but never the friendship—of Ade and McCutcheon ended late in 1897, never to be resumed on the *Record.* A mutual friend who had risen to Assistant U.S. Secretary of the Treasury offered them and a Chicago *Tribune* man a chance to travel around the world on the government's new revenue cutter named *McCulloch*. McCutcheon and the *Tribune* chap went. Ade declined, because there would be "too many days at sea and too few ports." The ship arrived at the Philippines in time to join Admiral George Dewey's fleet at the Battle of Manila Bay. The coincidence drew McCutcheon into an important new career as war correspondent, author, and traveler.

Ade traveled, too, in 1898. He sent back travel stories from France, Switzerland, Italy, Austria, Hungary, Romania, Serbia, Bulgaria, Turkey, and Syria. The trip gave Ade new material for articles that appeared in the *Record* until the end of June 1899. While the Spanish-American War was going on in 1898, the *Record* asked

Ade to go and write about Spain. Ade replied that it would not be a good place for an American. "Pass yourself off as an Englishman" came the order. But Ade insisted, "I couldn't fool even a Spaniard into thinking I'm an Englishman. They would know I'm from Indiana" (Kelly, *Ade*, 133).

As a Chicago newspaper figure, Ade peaked when the *Record* began putting "By George Ade" on his stories in 1898. Meanwhile, he again ducked behind "John Hazelden" for thirty pieces he wrote to secretly help two friends launch a new Saturday paper, the *Evening Lamp*. The "Hazelden" efforts appeared in the *Lamp* between January 28 and mid-November 1899.

Shortly thereafter, Ade also helped Alfred "Alf" Ringling compile a *Ringling Brothers Circus Yearbook*, a record of one season on the road. In the book, Ade called the elephants "a ponderous pyramid of primitive pachyderms." The alliteration made Ringling beam, "You have struck the keynote of circus advertising!"

During 1899, Ade, feeling that he had "passed the limit of usefulness in the 'Streets' department," prepared to leave the *Record* and be "at liberty for an indefinite period." The *Record* management cordially asked him to reconsider. Ade consented to stay with the paper a little longer, but he still pledged to become a freelance writer by the end of his tenth year with the paper in early summer of 1900. He now was receiving top pay of sixty-five dollars per week.

The Stone Company brought out its first *Fables in Slang* collection in book form. The book contained Fables from the *Record* including the first one published September 17, 1897 and twenty-some others. *Fables in Slang* hit the bookstores in January 1900 and sold sixty-nine thousand copies that year. Ade suddenly became famous beyond Chicago. People of every taste, age, and profession talked about the book. A noted editor from Kansas told Ade in a letter that he "would rather have written *Fables in Slang* than be President" (Kelly, *Ade*, 144).

Jumping somewhat on the Ade bandwagon, the *Record*, in July 1900, brought out the eighth (and last) of the "Stories of the Streets and of the Town" collections. There were just thirty-six of them this time.

The Baltimore journalist and writer H. L. (Henry Louis) Mencken wrote that "those phrases [in Ade's *Fables*] sometimes wear the external vestments of a passing slang, but they were no more commonplace or vulgar at bottom than the 'somewhere east of Suez' of Kipling. They light up a whole scene in a flash. They are the running evidences of an eye that sees clearly and of a mind that thinks shrewdly...How easy to imitate Ade's manner—and how impossible to imitate his matter" (Kelly, *Ade*, 149).

Ade himself said the idea behind the Fables "was to tell the truth about what is going on and get a little fun out of the foibles and weaknesses and vanities of a lot of our neighbors without being brutal or insulting."

While readers from coast to coast chuckled at the *Fables* book, a New York publisher, F. H. Russell, proposed selling a syndicated series of Fables once a week to newspapers, the first to be released on September 30, 1900. The income seemed promising, so Ade felt justified in planning to spend some of it on a vacation trip to China and Japan and to visit his old friend and partner McCutcheon in the Philippines when he left the *Record*. At first only thirty-nine papers bought the syndicated Fables, but soon sales began to rise. Quality magazines sought rights to them, too, and the Fables would be a syndicate feature off and on for the next thirty years. Ade began depositing checks for up to one thousand dollars each week in the safest place he knew, his father's bank in Kentland.

In 1900, Ade thought that he would break away from Fables. "The idea," he wrote, "was to grab a lot of careless money before the reading public recovered its equilibrium and then, with bags of gold piled in the doorway to keep the wolf out, return to the consecrated job of writing long and philosophical reports of life in the Middle West."

He wrote Howells, however, that "four times I have given my ultimatum, 'no more of this sickening Slang,' and on each occasion Mr. Russell [publisher] has shown me the balance sheet and painted for me a picture of the mortgages being lifted from the old homestead in Indiana, and my resistance has become more feeble" (Kelly, *Ade*, 156).

Another penalty for Ade's growing fame came from having quips falsely attributed to him. A friend he knew as "Biff" Hall once sent a weekly letter from Chicago to the *Dramatic Mirror* in New York, putting in anecdotes he had picked up or invented. To end one letter, he wrote that Ade had been talking with a lady who gushed, "Isn't it wonderful how many bright people come from Indiana?" And Ade was supposed to have replied, "Yes, and the brighter they are the faster they come." Indiana papers published indignant rejoinders. Knowing that Hall had meant no harm, Ade did not embarrass his friend by denying the quote, but it took years for him to live it down.

On his trip to the Far East, when Ade stayed for some time in Manila with McCutcheon, the Philippine Islands started to interest him. He wrote a series of columns on "Stories of Benevolent Assimilation" that satirized America's imperialistic policies since winning the war with Spain and occupying the islands. From Filipinos, he heard stories regarding U.S. negotiations with the Sultan of Jolo, the main island of the Sulu Archipelago. Ade could see that this situation "had all the ingredients of comic opera and I believed that a good satirical musical play could be built around the efforts of our American civilizers to play ball with the little brown brother" (Kelly, *Ade*, 164).

Remembering *The Mikado* in Lafayette's Grand Opera House in 1885, Ade opted to use the lilting Gilbert and Sullivan approach to tell his own story in songs. He set to work on his first light opera.

Meanwhile, down on the farm

The fall of 1892 may have been great for Purdue football, but the spring of 1893 was a poor time to finish Purdue and hunt for a job. And for Dave Ross and anyone else, any year was a poor one to recover from typhoid fever. An economic depression had spread over the country, and engineers were being laid off instead of hired. After Ross had shaken the effects of the fever and had heard a doctor tell him to spend time outdoors in fresh air, Ross and his father talked over the situation. George Ross reasoned, "If you need to stay outdoors the thing to do is help manage the farm."

Dave replied, "I don't want to be just a boy helping around the place. I bet I could manage the farm all right. But I'd want you to stay in Brookston and not have anything to do with the farm at all."

George Ross had put a mortgage on the farm. He and his sickly wife both had required "doctoring." The thousand soggy acres frankly were not providing much of a living. The realities persuaded George to agree with Dave.

One of Dave's first moves as the farm manager was to increase the tillable acreage. He did so by convincing the three men on the White County Board of Commissioners and his farming neighbors of the value of his design for a drainage ditch. The ditch needed to be thirty feet wide and ten to twelve miles long. Such a ditch would enable Dave and other affected landowners to grow crops on their dried-out wetland.

The finished ditch did indeed dry out a lot of land, but snakes remained in the area where no man relished plowing. When Ross bought hogs to devour his snakes the neighbors could see that a Purdue education had done the youth no harm at all.

Next, Ross designed and built an odd-looking round barn. He did so knowing that, jibes and jokes aside, the round shape provided the most useful interior space and best resisted the high prairie wind. With more dried and snake-free fields planted with corn, his helping hands now faced a problem hauling it all to sell in Brookston. However, instead of paying to build storage space for the surplus, Ross spent much less to haul more corn faster. He paid the Indiana Wagon Company in Lafayette to build a conveyance Ross designed. The wagon was so big that it took four horses to pull it. But with the wagon, Ross's hired men could haul four loads of corn to a neighbor's one.

Dave gained admirers through his accomplishments. Voters elected him to the Brookston town board. One of his first ideas for Brookston was to replace the town's graveled or wooden plank sidewalks with poured concrete. To cut the cost, Ross applied his Purdue course in surveying. With this know-how and a few instruments, he charged the town no fee to figure the sidewalk grades for drainage. Ross also built a three-piece portable canoe. Each section measured four feet long. It was easy to hoist it into a horse-drawn buggy and haul it over to the Tippecanoe River for fishing or canoeing, just loosen or tighten a few threaded metal nuts and bolts.

Five years out of Purdue, in early 1898, Dave Ross and Jack Kneale, now his brother-in-law and now running a Brookston drugstore, decided to start a town telephone company. Other cities and towns were embracing the technology. It was Ross's first venture into business of his own. Within a few weeks, Ross and Kneale and a lumber dealer named Ira Boardman each had put up three thousand dollars. Ross borrowed his three thousand from his two helpful uncles in Lafayette and presided over the new Prairie Telephone Company. That spring and summer people could see the company president himself out setting poles and stringing wires with a hired crew. The company rented a room in town for its central equipment. Starting with one hundred twenty-five customers, the Prairie Telephone Company soon profited.

When Dave Ross finished Purdue, the era of the automobile had yet to dawn. In 1893, Henry Ford test ran a gasoline engine in Michigan. In 1894, Elwood Haynes, in Kokomo, Indiana, unveiled a gasoline-engine auto or "car." By 1900, magazines like *The Saturday Evening Post* advertised gasoline or electric cars for sale from many builders. In 1904, Ransom Olds' new company produced 5,500 Oldsmobiles. By 1905, more than 100 makes of cars gorged the market and twenty factories had rolled out 106,000 passenger cars. Eleven hundred trucks rumbled over graveled streets and dirt roads. Convinced by such numbers that motor vehicles were here to stay, Dave began reading about how cars worked. Sometimes, he visited repair shops to see the broken machines up close. When a car failed, Ross looked for *what* failed and *why*. He noticed that faulty steering systems, especially in loaded trucks, caused much accidental damage and injury.

By 1905, in his spare time, Ross sat at a drawing board designing better working parts. Common steering devices at the time called for small cogwheels at the lower end of a shaft. Most of the wear and strain came on two or three teeth in those cogwheels, and they would break. Ross saw a need to spread the stress over more area. Ignoring precedent, he tried making the *shaft* the stress-bearing surface instead of only the cogwheel. This approach proved much stronger in terms of metal endurance.

In April 1905, Ross applied for a patent on a differential gear—one that helped "drive" a car instead of steer it. In November, he applied for another patent for a speed-changing, or gear-shifting, device. On February 18, 1906, the U.S. Patent Office granted Ross his first patent. It was for a "Steering Gear for Vehicles." In April 1906, Ross designed a rear-axle differential (drive gear) with a reversing mechanism.

Now thirty-five years old, Dave wanted to start making and selling gears instead of routing snakes and bossing farmhands. He wanted to achieve something—besides run the family farm—to use his engineer's brain. A Purdue friend-turned-patent-lawyer helped Dave contact a factory man in Cleveland, Ohio, about his gear ideas. Dave nearly went to work for that man in Cleveland, but as he voiced these job prospects at home Uncle Will interrupted: "Dave, don't sign any contract just yet." Uncle Will thought that if Dave's gears were good enough for Cleveland to make they should be good enough for Lafayette.

Will and Uncle Linn had been laying away money both from farming and from converting that south Lafayette pasture into Highland Park home sites. Well-heeled, confident, and experienced salesmen, Dave's two uncles decided to organize a family company to make and sell their nephew's inventions.

In October 1906, Uncle Will became the president of the Ross Gear and Tool Company. Uncle Linn took on the secretary-treasurer duties. The brothers named Dave—the brains—the general manager. Jack Kneale joined as the only other founding investor. The company sold Dave what stock he could afford to buy with cash and gave him more shares in return for the use of his patents.

For its first factory Ross Gear bought a downtown Lafayette building from a company that made plumbing tools. At the corner of Ninth and Main, a Lafayette man had opened a car repair business in 1904, calling it an "auto hospital." A city directory had listed the proprietor, Frank Headson, as an "engineer." A year later, Headson was vice president of Headson Tool and Manufacturing Company in the same building. The company made and sold pipe cutters, wrenches, and other tools.

For twenty-four thousand dollars the Ross Gear partners bought the two-story-and-basement Headson building. Ross Gear started there with six employees, but within six weeks, thirty men were grinding and shipping gears for pay. Dave Ross went on improving his own as well as others' devices and inventing new ones.

Ross Gear began by making rear axles, universal joints, and differential and steering gears only for passenger cars. Months after selling the first steering gears, however, Dave Ross found ways to design, make, and sell better ones. Before long, Dave also designed and built a machine that could cut the crucial internal spiral grooves in the steel shafts of the company's most advanced gears.

A number of companies were hand-assembling trucks in those days. Those companies could—and were willing to—try installing new gears without disrupting an assembly line. Ross Gear's first order is said to have come from a man in Rochester, New York, who wrote in rhyme, "I don't know you and you don't know me. Send me a steering gear C. O. D."

Word spread, other orders arrived, and prospects looked bright. Some workers wanted to buy Ross Gear stock hoping to get "ground floor" rich, but Linn Ross counseled them: "The outlook seems good right now, but we don't know what's ahead. We wouldn't want anyone to lose through investing with us. If money is lost it will be ours." And for some time it looked as if those rejected worker-investors were lucky. Almost as many broken Ross gears came back with complaints as were sold, but the breakage traced more to weak metal than to design. Dave persuaded his uncles to start a department devoted to testing the effects of heat and load stress on metal—metallurgy—to reduce and prevent failures.

Competition grew. In Saginaw, Michigan, the Jackson, Church, Wilcox Company started making steering gears and other auto parts. And in 1907, a Purdue graduate engineer, George Gemmer from Williamsport, Indiana, and his backers founded Gemmer Manufacturing Company in Detroit. This started a business rivalry with Ross Gear that lasted for nearly half a century. In 1909, the Gemmer Company departed from screw-and-nut designs and started making gears based on worm-and-sector concepts. Within a year, the Buick Motor Company bought Jackson, Church, Wilcox; shortly thereafter, General Motors bought Buick.

During July and August 1908, the U.S. government granted Dave Ross patents for an axle, "compensating gearing," and a "change of speed device." Ross obtained three more patents in June, August, and November 1909, for what he broadly described as a "steering gear for vehicles," a "differential gearing and reversing mechanism," and a "differential mechanism."

By then, Ross Gear's customers included the Apperson Brothers Auto Company in Kokomo, Indiana; the Atlas Engine Works in Indianapolis; and auto makers in York, Pennsylvania; Hamilton, Ohio; Joliet, Illinois; Des Moines, Iowa; Chicago; Sioux Falls; and Cincinnati. One day, the mail contained an order for a steering gear for a *boat* on the Atlantic Coast. A Ross Gear engineer traveled to see the boat and design the gear. The post office delivered another letter to the Lafayette plant dated June 18, 1909 from Elkhart Motor Car Company in Elkhart, Indiana. This plant was building Elcars and Sterlings.

> We are in the market for a steering gear for a car selling at $900. We want a gear with the forward and back motion. Kindly give us blueprints and full particulars of a gear that you think will meet our requirements, and your best prices on these gears.

Two months later, Elkhart wished to buy fifteen hundred Ross gears. In July 1910, the Ross Gear board of directors raised Dave's salary to thirty-seven dollars and fifty cents per week, highest in the company.

In April 1912, Ross Gear began making steering and differential gears for trucks as well as passenger cars. Soon, the company announced plans to build a bigger factory. By that time, Dave Ross, age forty-one, was driving his own first car, a Westcott. Its maker,

Burton J. Westcott, had started in business in Richmond, Indiana, and later moved to Springfield, Ohio.

Dave obtained patents in April 1912 for two more steering gear designs, and Ross Gear became a tighter family affair. Uncle Will Ross died on January 28. Directors named Uncle Linn as president and treasurer and Dave's cousin Edward A. Ross (Uncle Linn's son) as secretary, director, and stockholder.

That summer, Purdue University built Smith Hall for dairy science studies with money given by William C. Smith of Williamsport, Indiana. Smith Hall became the ninth structure on campus to be funded by private donors, the first six tracing to John Purdue. In 1913, the school president, Winthrop E. Stone, also appointed Ernestine Shoemaker, an 1888 graduate and English faculty member since 1900, as its first Dean of Women.

During late summer, the Democrat mayor of Lafayette, a piano and music store proprietor named George R. Durgan, approached Dave Ross about getting into politics. Durgan, already in office ten years, had learned that a coalition of Republicans and Progressives had nominated Thomas Bauer to run for mayor against him. Bauer, president of Lafayette Box Board and Paper Company, would lead a "progressive" or Citizens ticket to overthrow all the Democrat incumbents. Ross's experience on the Brookston Town Board, his Purdue degree, and the good reputations of his Ross gears seemed to add credibility, if not votes, to Durgan's forces. At the Ross Gear plant a factory worker asked Dave to use his influence to get him out of jury duty. Dave demurred. "We're never too busy making gears to meet our community responsibilities," he lectured the man. He then practiced what he preached and consented to run on Durgan's ticket for the City Council.

On November 4, 1913, Bauer squeezed past Durgan by sixteen votes. A third candidate received seventy-seven. The city clerk race ended in a tie. The recount gave victory to the Citizens Party man by thirty-six votes. Citizens won six of the City Council's ten seats. A few weeks after he took office, Bauer came clean—he had been a Republican all along.

However, one of the four exceptions to the Citizens Party sweep was Dave Ross. He defeated a Citizens candidate—general contractor Robert Skinner Moore—307 to 287.

"Fables" and more

"When George Ade first showed signs of embarking in literary work," his pal McCutcheon wrote, "his father, a banker in Kentland, and his brothers, well-to-do landowners, predicted a future for him that would contain very little money. But when his 'Fables in Slang' were syndicated and the royalties began rolling in to his father's bank, the home folks were amazed. His brothers began buying land for George until he owned two thousand acres in the rich heart of the Corn Belt" (McCutcheon, *Drawn from Memory*, 44).

Helping those royalties roll in were two publishing houses, the Stone Company in Chicago and the R. H. Russell Company in New York City.

Stone issued *More Fables* in October 1900—nineteen more, to be exact. In October 1901, Russell produced *Forty Modern Fables*. Russell then brought out *The Girl Proposition* on October 13, 1902. There were twenty-two Fables in this book, but Ade was on the brink of another windfall that kept royalties rolling in for ten more years.

He finished his first stage play—a light opera, *The Sultan of Sulu*—in the room he had been renting with McCutcheon. Ade tried out verses for more than fifty songs before he kept twenty-two for performance. By train on April 24, 1902, Ade brought the Chicago Studebaker Theater's *Sultan* cast down to Lafayette to play it one night in the Grand Opera House. A railroad depot reception, testimonial dinner, and Purdue Band concert enriched Ade's homecoming. The *Sultan* underwent the usual tweaking during an eleven-week run in Chicago. On December 29, 1902, it opened in New York City at a theater on Thirtieth and Broadway. While he was in New York, Ade for the first and only time met his literary idol Mark Twain.

"[Twain] was greatly amused because a woman friend of his was trying to translate some of my 'Fables' into French," Ade recalled. "He didn't think she could do it. I told him that [a mutual friend] once gave me a sentence from Mark Twain I never encountered in his writings—*Bacon would improve the flavor of an angel*. I talked with Mark Twain only that once" (Tobin, 217).

The meeting resulted years later in Ade writing "One afternoon with Mark Twain:"

> For a good many years I had been waiting and hoping to meet Mark Twain. I think I had read everything he ever wrote. With great admiration and respect I had witnessed his "come-back" in the early nineties during which he repaid a mountainous debt as a matter of honor, not of personal legal responsibility.
>
> How unappreciative we often are, at the time, of the red-letter days in our lives!...What was in my mind at the time was the belief that he would live for many more years; and that, having met him on this occasion I would later visit him alone and at greater length...Beside his towering fame, my own stature was something like that of a child's mud-pie man, placed alongside the statue of Rodin's "Thinker."
>
> And thus it happened that I made no notes recording the details of the most momentous meeting of my life. I went; I saw and heard; I came away. The tragic events of the few remaining years of Mark Twain's life [he died in 1910] made it impossible for me ever to talk with him again...
>
> He stood alone on the porch waiting to greet. He wore a white or tan-colored suit, loose and comfortable looking. From the moment he took my hand in his firm clasp, he was the soul of kindli-

ness, cordiality and affability. I can recall only his eyes. I lack words to describe the calm, penetrating, unwavering grace he enveloped me with during the first few moments of our meeting. I was several inches talker than he, so that he must have looked upward into my eyes; yet I did not sense the difference in height. It seemed, indeed, as if he were looking downward on me...

He warned me that I was soon to be made the victim of a fantastic plan evolved by a woman of family acquaintance, to translate some of my "Fables in Slang" into French.

"She cannot possibly find any French equivalents for your specimens of American vernacular," he said, "but she is determined to make the effort and I am waiting until it is done so that I can watch some Frenchman go crazy trying to read it." (Lazarus, 199-200)

As newspapers across the nation printed series after series of Ade's "Fables," they went into more books until there were about a dozen collections, among them *People You Know* published by Russell on April 17, 1903. There were twenty-five Fables in that book.

On May 18, 1903, Russell published *The Sultan of Sulu* in a special book to celebrate the play's two-hundredth performance in New York City in June.

There followed a series of short, juvenile novels written by Ade for what was called The Strenuous Lad's Library series by Bandar Log Press. Seven such little volumes were advertised, but only three were ever published, and those in limited editions. The Press appears to have been Mexican, known also as "Progreso," located in Phoenix in the Arizona Territory.

Bandar Log issued the first in about July 1903, under the title *Handsome Cyril, or, The messenger boy with the warm feet*. An artist named Frank Holme made the book's woodcut figures. This "novel" ran for sixteen pages. Subscribers could buy all seven in the projected series for five dollars. There were 674 copies made of the first one. The material all had appeared before in the *Record* and would appear again in a collection titled *Bang! Bang!*

The second in the Strenuous Lad's Library series came out in October 1903. Its title was *Clarence Allen, the Hypnotic Boy Journalist*. "Progreso's" hand press in Phoenix stamped out 374 copies. The third volume bore the title *Rollo Johnson, the Boy Inventor, or, The Demon Bicycle and Its Daring Rider*. This book contained twenty-four pages when issued in January 1904.

Eventually, *Sultan of Sulu* stage performance royalties enabled Ade to acquire even more acreage east of Brook, Indiana, eleven miles from his Kentland birthplace. On that land, reusing his old pen name, Ade began developing a "Hazelden Farm" home, golf course, pool, and country club for neighbors. Why Brook? McCutcheon ventured this guess:

> A girl once remarked to him: "It is amazing how many bright men come from Indiana." George is said have answered: "Yes, and the brighter they are, the quicker they come."

> That line is clever enough to have been delivered by him. But when reported in Indiana it created such a furor that, to prove that he never said it, he moved [from Chicago] back to Indiana and made his home on Hazelden Farm near Brook. The friendly house, the swimming pool, the golf course and small clubhouse soon became famous. (McCutcheon, *Drawn from Memory*, 44-45)

During 1902, Ade finished writing a play he titled *Peggy from Paris*. This story told of an Illinois girl who returned for an American concert—after studying singing in Paris—using the name "Mademoiselle Fleurette Caramelle." There was a tryout for the play in South Bend, Indiana, before *Peggy from Paris* opened in Chicago on January 26, 1903 and in New York City on September 10.

⁓ ⁓

Shortly thereafter, Ade had another stage show prepared. He made *The County Chairman* a comedy of life and politics in a one-horse town of the 1880s. This play premiered in South Bend near the end of August 1903. Chicago audiences liked it so much that it succeeded *Peggy from Paris* in New York City.

The Saturday Evening Post published Ade's short story, "Getting Sister Laura Married Off," in 1903. The Russell people released *Peggy from Paris* and *People You Know*. McClure, Phillips and Company, New York, printed *In Babel*, a collection of fifty-some 1896-1898 Chicago sketches rewritten from the *Record*. *The Theatre* magazine, in June, published another piece Ade wrote in 1903, "Light Opera Yesterday and Today."

On February 9, 1904, Harper and Brothers in New York City printed *Breaking Into Society*. This book collected twenty-two of Ade's syndicated "Fables" published in the *Indianapolis Journal*.

Ade composed, but later cut out, a whimsical poem for use in Act II of a 1904 play he was writing that would be called *Sho-Gun*. The earliest printing of the poem was in the *Indianapolis Journal* on October 4, 1903. The title started as "A Bacteriological Love Story." The memorable verses showed up again, this time as "The Microbe's Serenade," in May 1906, in the *Indianapolis Journal*. The *Journal* said that Ade had "passed it out to his fraternity brothers last night at the Country Club" during a Sigma Chi annual state banquet. A biographer said that Ade "liked this piece so much he recited it at banquets, even handed out copies" (Lazarus, 230).

> A love-lorn microbe met by chance
>
> At a swagger bacteroidal dance

A proud bacillian belle, and she

Was first of the animalculae,

Of organism saccharine,

She was the protoplasmic queen

The microscopical pride and pet

Of the biological smartest set;

And so this infinitesimal swain

Evolved a pleasing, low refrain

"Oh, lovely metamorphic germ!

What futile scientific term

Can well describe thy many charms?

Come to these embryonic arms!

Then hie away to my cellular home

And be my little diatome."

His epithelium burned with love;

He swore by molecules above

She'd be his own gregarious mate

Or else he would disintegrate.

This amorous mite of a parasite

Pursued the germ both day and night,

And 'neath her window often played

A Darwin-Huxley serenade—

He'd warble to her ev'ry day,

This rhizopodical roundelay:

"O, most primordial type of spore!

I never saw your like before,

And though a microbe has no heart

From you, sweet germ, I'll never part;

We'll sit beneath some fungus growth

Till dissolution claims us both."

There was nothing whimsical about 1903 Purdue football, though. Oh, the team had been doing well enough, and the annual rivalry game against Indiana University was drawing big crowds. Years before, Purdue had won the first two games against "IU" by a combined score of 128 to nothing. Purdue won again six to nothing by forfeit in 1894, won twenty to six in 1897, and fourteen to nothing in 1898. Then fortunes changed. Indiana won seventeen to five in 1899, twenty-four to five in 1900, and eleven to six in 1901. Purdue won thirty-nine to nothing on Stuart Field in 1902.

In 1900, Dr. Winthrop E. Stone, in a report upon assuming the Purdue presidency, had commented with academic preciseness on this general success:

> In 1893 a number of citizens of Lafayette offered a handsome silver cup by Tiffany to become the property of the college that for three successive years should be the [football] champion of Indiana. This cup was won by Purdue and is treasured among its athletic trophies. From 1891 to 1899 Purdue has been the acknowledged champion of the state in football and during a portion of this time was unbeaten by an opponent, including the largest institutions of the west.

This prestige was probably due to the fact that Purdue was one of the pioneers in the game, and advanced more rapidly in a knowledge of the game than did its opponents. Of recent years this difference has been more nearly equalized and the advantages accruing to institutions with large numbers of students has come more prominently into evidence.

Purdue had won four games and lost two going into the 1903 match against Indiana on October 31. There would be three more Purdue games following. The Purdue and IU teams would play this game for the first time in Washington Park, near Thirtieth and Keystone in northeast Indianapolis. Athletic scheduling and financing matters at Purdue now were in the hands of Harry G. "Skillet" Leslie. Leslie was a bright and popular senior student from Montmorenci, Indiana, who had moved to West Lafayette. Leslie's junior class at Purdue had elected him their president. He had captained Purdue baseball and football teams in 1902, and pals chose him "student director" of a Purdue Athletic Association in 1903. He would play fullback for Purdue in the Indiana game and the remaining games that season.

On the day of the game, three Big Four Railroad special passenger trains left Lafayette carrying 964 passengers. Thirteen cars in the first train carried the football players, band, faculty, administrators, and fans. Rolling into northwest Indianapolis at twenty-five miles per hour, the first train abruptly smashed into seven heavily loaded coal cars mistakenly switched from a siding and standing on the main line. The thundering crash derailed the steam locomotive and tender full of coal, then crushed the first passenger car carrying mostly players, coaches, trainers, and a few high-roller businessmen who were team boosters. The screams and shrieks and shouts accompanied the impact that overturned the second car carrying the band and sent that car down an embankment while the third car rode up and over the first two. There followed a few seconds of shocked silence, then moans of agony and the flowing of blood. From the jolted safety of one of the rear cars, President Stone worked his way forward, stunned by the carnage.

Survivors from their rear seats and even some from the damaged forward cars joined good-hearted strangers who ran to the wreckage from nearby factories. They strained and lifted and struggled to find and recover the dead and injured. There were splintered bones. Blood dripped as from cracked water pipes. Smashed heads oozed blood diluted by what looked like yellow tapioca pudding. Sixteen aboard the train died at the scene and forty-some required hospital aid.

The Lafayette *Courier* for Saturday afternoon already had gone to press when the first telegraphed bulletin arrived. The paper did not print on Sundays. By Monday, November 2, the *Courier* at last printed, in alphabetical order, a "Complete List of Dead Compiled by Dr. Stone."

C. Coats, football player from Berwin, Pennsylvania

G. A. Drollinger, player from Mill Creek, near Laporte, Indiana

C. E. Furr, left guard from Veedersburg, Indiana

C. G. Grube, substitute from Butler [DeKalb County, northeast of Auburn], Indiana

Jay Hamilton, player from Huntington, Indiana

W. D. Hamilton, center from Beardstown, Illinois

Newton R. Howard, president of American Steam Laundry Company, Lafayette, a Purdue Athletic Association booster.

William Mailey, player from New Richmond, Indiana

Patrick McClair, team trainer from Tippecanoe [Marshall County southwest of Plymouth], Indiana

R. J. Powell, left end from Corpus Christi, Texas

B. Price, player from Spencer, Indiana

E. C. Robertson, assistant coach from East Helena, Montana

W. L. Roush, player from Gas City, Indiana

G. L. Shaw, player from Indiana Harbor [Lake County], Indiana

S. B. Squibbs, player from Lawrenceburg, Indiana

In a "Revised List of the Injured," the *Courier* alphabetized (Allen through Zimmerman) thirty-eight survivors' names, hometowns, and their conditions. Among them:

A West Lafayette physician, Dr. A. W. Bitting, being treated in St. Vincent's Hospital, Indianapolis for serious back and hip injuries and bruises.

The Purdue football coach Oliver F. Cutts, in St. Vincent's Hospital with a non-serious ankle sprain.

The Athletics Association student director Harry Leslie, senior fullback from West Lafayette, in City Hospital, Indianapolis with serious leg and jaw injuries.

Rescuers had pulled Leslie from the steaming, bloody, shattered wreckage, identified him, counted him dead, and carried him to a makeshift morgue. There someone chanced to see his right arm move. For months Leslie recovered in City Hospital from a fractured leg, shattered jaw, and side and internal injuries. He walked with a limp for the rest of his busy and distinguished public life.

Purdue and Indiana officials cancelled the football game. The *Courier* listed the most critically injured survivors as of Monday:

H. O. Wright, of Pendleton, Indiana, in St. Vincent's with a broken back, head cuts, and a fractured left leg.

S. V. B. "Sim" Miller, of Nineveh, Indiana, in City Hospital with both legs broken.

C. O. Tangeman of Fernbank, Ohio, delirious with head injuries that doctors feared could prove fatal.

T. Hendricks Johnston, of Evansville, Indiana, who "may die at any moment." He had contracted pneumonia after suffering severe head and chest injuries.

Lou Smith, of Lafayette, in City Hospital with head and back injuries. The patient had a "large hole in the right side of his back," the paper said, "and the physicians suppose that the projectile, whatever it was, penetrated the abdominal cavity."

The Monday *Courier* also described the grim scene at Purdue: "A half-masted flag, a dreary rain, a campus barren of students, a slow, mournful procession to the Fowler Hall chapel...[black] crepe evident everywhere and students stricken with heavy sorrow.

"Professor [Clarence A.] Waldo offered prayer at the close of the reading of the scripture by Professor [Emma] McRae in chapel, the ceremony beginning at 11 o'clock. The prayer touched the hearts of the assembled people, and tears coursed town the cheeks of students and professors alike."

President Stone spoke "with faltering voice":

> We must care for the heartsick as well as the wounded, which is our first duty...The faculty thought that it was fitting first to seek strength from God; learn what is best to be done and take steps to do that work...Some think mostly of the dead but ever since the disaster there has come, through the great confusion, people earnest and eager to offer aid.

> [Your surviving comrades] almost without exception are resting comfortably. Every hour there is new hope. All give promise of speedy recovery, but there are some exceptions...The best physicians, the best nurses are doing everything. There are four or five in serious condition.

The *Courier* reported that the catastrophe "has plunged [the entire state of Indiana] into deepest sorrow, and while the wound is more keenly felt in Lafayette and at Purdue, it is nevertheless felt all over the country, from which messages come pouring in filled with sympathy, devotion, anxiety and condolence."

Sunday had been "a day of woe here," the paper said, "and churches were filled with people who wanted to hear words of love and sympathy for the dead...and [the day] was one big 'Memorial Day.'"

Stone said the Purdue registrar, Alfred M. Kenyon, would maintain a bulletin board in the main campus building for further news and funeral arrangements.

Stone set up a temporary office in the Denison Hotel in Indianapolis. From there, he directed messages, visitors, mail, or gifts to the recovering survivors. Stone said no memorial service would be held for at least another week, and he would form a committee of faculty and students to arrange one.

Professor Stanley Coulter read messages of condolence from all parts of the United States, among them were resolutions from Indiana University and Northwestern University. The *Courier* of November 3 editorialized:

> Football at Purdue sounds like hollow mockery. It is certain that no interest can be taken in the game here this season, and it is doubtful if football will be a very great factor next year, when it is possible that the team will be reorganized.

> The fund started by the late N. R. Howard for the benefit of the Athletic Association amounts to about two thousand dollars, and it will be paid over to the Association at once. The Athletic Association was never in need of money as it is today, and the merchants of the city who have contributed to the fund started by the man who was killed in the wreck will have the satisfaction of knowing that the money has gone to a good cause.

> The Association had contracted to pay Cutts $1,500. McClaire and Robertson [also] were to have been paid. It cost the Association $600 to make the Indianapolis trip, outside of the unexpected expense incurred. The proceeds of the game at Indianapolis were to have gone toward erasing some of the obligations of the Association, but that and other big games of the season [against Notre Dame and two other foes] have been done away with, and there will be no further source of revenue.

The Association has been willing to refund money paid for tickets, but few have asked for it, and the in many instances debts have disappeared without being paid by Purdue. A transfer company in Indianapolis that was to furnish hacks to haul the players [from Union Station to Washington Park] presented a bill for $7. They were to have been paid $12 and $5 was paid some time ago. Without carrying the men to the game, they asked for the remainder.

The outlook for football at Purdue is very blue despite the fact that this had been looked upon as the great year.

By November 6, donations began arriving to raise fifty thousand dollars to build a Memorial Gymnasium. The gym would honor the train wreck dead. Word of the campaign spread in notices published in the *Journal*, the *Courier*, and the *Evening Call*. The stories stated that "no more fitting memorial could be raised and Dr. Stone has indorsed the movement."

Purdue conducted a service of mourning in Eliza Fowler Hall at 11 a.m. on November 11. "The spirit of the weather was in close communion with the drooping spirits of those who attended," the *Courier* reported. "Flapping in the furious wind were flags, half-masted and wet with dismal rain. There was no activity about the university; crepe hung from windows and over doors of neighboring houses."

Purdue reserved a section in Fowler Hall for families and near relatives of the deceased. On the stage sat faculty, trustees, and representatives from other colleges and organizations. Flowers, palms, and crepe adorned the platform. A choir of Purdue students sang "Lead, Kindly Light." Professor Waldo read scripture. Professor Coulter led a prayer, and President Stone spoke:

> We are cast down with the weight of a new and strange burden. Our hearts are sore. Pleasant recollections of the past are blurred with a dark shadow. Hope for the future seems almost vain...

> Purdue students are undergoing a training calculated to an unusual degree to impress upon you the power and unchangeability of the laws of nature. No other class of students is so well informed on this subject as you. In the natural course of events your life work will hereafter consist in directing and operating natural forces. In addition to this special training you are now brought face to face with an appalling instance of human disregard of these principles. It should be a lesson ineffaceably impressed upon your minds to be true to your responsibilities and to be honest in the performance of duty. (*Lafayette Daily Courier*, November 11, 1903)

The Marion County coroner in Indianapolis ruled on November 14 that a dispatcher in Kankakee, Illinois, had failed to notify the Indianapolis Big Four yardmaster that three "Purdue Special" trains would be arriving that morning. This was the "appalling instance of human disregard" to which President Stone referred. The coroner's ruling sent a new wave of regret Lafayette's way because the accused dispatcher was a native son. The *Courier* reported:

> The coroner also found that Engineer Shoemaker and Conductor Johnson were running too fast within the city limits, but were justified in believing that they had the right-of-way...[The coroner] makes his verdict public without recommendation to either grand jury or prosecutor, washing his hands of the affair.

By September 1904, ten months after the train wreck, the Lafayette *Journal* reported that Harry Leslie had recovered enough to manage Purdue's 1904 attempt to revive football. The paper called him "one of the most popular men at the university." Purdue put a team together. It defeated Indiana twenty-seven to nothing in Indianapolis. This concluded a purposely longer and softer Purdue football schedule. The team won nine times and lost three, but some of the wins came in games against "pick up" teams from the Purdue Alumni Association, from a certain North Division High School, from the Indiana Medical College, Beloit College, Earlham College, and Culver Military Academy.

Plays and more plays

Next from George Ade's creative mind, in 1904, came the completed *Sho-Gun*, a satirical drama about American commercial expansion. In this story a promoter from Michigan named William Henry Spangler lands on an island near Korea and starts trying to change commercial life. He meets characters named Sho-Gun, Hi-Faloot, Omee-Omi, Tah-Tah, Hanki-Panki, and so on. The M. Witmark Company in New York City published the two acts of *Sho-Gun*. After a few weeks in Chicago, *Sho-Gun* opened in New York on October 4, 1904. Dislodging *The County Chairman*, *Sho-Gun* stayed for one hundred twenty-five performances.

Ade then wrote a series of syndicated newspaper pieces under the running title "Old Stories Revised." In them he modernized the Rip Van Winkle, Enoch Arden, Vicar of Wakefield, Gulliver, and other legends. *Collier's Weekly* printed his essay "To Make a Hoosier Holiday."

Harper and Brothers, New York City, published two more collections. In 1904, *Breaking into Society* and *True Bills* contained reprints of a total of forty-five syndicated "Fables."

Ade named his next play *The College Widow*. He based it on, and gave it the same name as, his poem from 1900. "During the first three weeks after I entered my new home [Hazelden] and reveled, for the first time, in wide expanses of elbow-room and a real sense of proprietorship," Ade recalled. "I made up for lost time and turned out a play called *The College Widow*. It was approved by the public and never had to be revised and it did over two million dollars at the box-office before it went to the stock companies" (Russo 95).

The success of the play was in some ways phenomenal. It first was performed, in August 1905, in Boston's Tremont Theatre and taken later to London and even Australia. The actress Dolores Costello starred in a movie version. Warner Brothers named its 1930 talking movie *The Widow from Chicago* and titled a 1936 remake *Freshman Love*. Samuel French Company in New York City published the play on January 31, 1924.

By 1905, three of Ade's plays were running on Broadway—*Sho-Gun*, *The College Widow*, and *The County Chairman*. *Pearson's Magazine* printed Ade's timely article "How I Came to Butt Into the Drama" in November. It was timely because, at one point, Ade's Broadway play royalties alone exceeded five thousand dollars per week.

⁓ ⁓

In 1905, Ade created two more works for the stage: *The Bad Samaritan* and *Just Out of College*. But some critics considered *Samaritan* Ade's first setback in theater. "It was all wrong," Ade conceded after a while. "It had a bad title and people wouldn't come out to see it even the first night" (Kelly, *Ade*, 199). It went under after only fifteen shows in New York City.

Just Out of College made a better run in New York, toured for more than two years, and then became a motion picture. In that plot, young Edward Worthington Swinger falls in love with the daughter of a wealthy "pickle king." The "king" gives Swinger twenty thousand dollars if he will leave the daughter alone for three months and show sound business sense. With the twenty grand, Swinger buys a rival pickle business that the "pickle king" ends up having to buy to stay competitive.

By mid-June 1905, financial pledges at Purdue toward the Memorial Gymnasium had reached forty thousand dollars, of which fifteen thousand had come from the guilt-ridden Big Four Railroad. Purdue's Board of Trustees voted to budget twenty-five thousand dollars more to the campaign as soon as donations totaled fifty thousand. Ade pledged twenty-five hundred dollars. This pushed the campaign past fifty thousand and activated the Trustees' pledge of twenty-five thousand more. Lafayette contractor Joshua Chew won the job to build the gym in 1908, and Purdue dedicated it on May 29, 1909.

In the winter of 1905-1906, Ade sailed to Egypt. From that experience he wrote a series of syndicated travel letters for American newspapers. Then McClure, Phillips and Company, New York City, published those letters as a book, *In Pastures New,* in October 1906. Ade wrote "many were printed in a syndicate of newspapers in the early months of 1906. With these letters have been incorporated extracts from letters written to the *Record* in 1895 and 1898." Altogether, there were twenty chapters grouped into sections titled "In London," "In Paris," "In Naples," "In Cairo," and "On the Nile." Both Fable-less and largely Slang-less, the letters satirized the American tourist abroad. Vaguely copying from the character "Brown" in Mark Twain's *Innocents Abroad,* Ade created a "Mr. Peasley of Iowa" to be the protagonist for antics, comedy, and comments. In one sketch, Peasley declares:

> I can take a hundred pounds of dynamite and a gang of [Italians] and go anywhere along the Hudson and blow out a tomb in a week's time that will beat anything we've seen in Egypt. Then I'll hire a boy with a markin' brush to draw some one-legged men and some tall women with their heads turned the wrong way, and I'll charge six dollars to go in, and make my fortune. (Coyle, 134)

On June 16, 1906, *Collier's* published Ade's story "The First Night," and during the year, Ade dashed off a one-act play he titled *Marse Covington*.

At Purdue, students starry-eyed over stagecraft and endeavors dealing with the theater and performing arts formed the Harlequin Club in 1906. Ade became almost an immediate supporter with his talent, experience, reputation, and money.

Early in 1907, Ade's mother died. During that busy year, he guided his grieving father on a tour of California and Salt Lake City. Next, he finished writing *Artie*, a stage version of his eleven-year-old book. *Artie* as a play struggled through a short run in New York City and toured only for part of one season. Ade gave up on it as "one of our children that didn't live" (Kelly, *Ade*, 200).

Bobbs-Merrill Company, Indianapolis, published Ade's first and only long story, *The Slim Princess*, in May 1907. Ade had stretched it to novel length from its printing in installments in *The Saturday Evening Post* of November 24 and December 1, 1906, but book critics shrugged off this story as a burlesque of then-popular "Graustarkian" tales. In 1901, Ade encouraged John T.'s brother George Barr McCutcheon to publish the original *Graustark*. However, such plots of court intrigue, mythical lands, and American Youth versus Effete Old World Royalty dated back to Anthony Hope's *The Prisoner of Zenda* in 1894. Criticism aside, Ade converted the *Slim Princess* story to a play presented by the Indianapolis Dramatic Club in the spring of 1908. Two collaborators then made it a musical for Elsie Janis that opened in New York City early in 1909.

Ade paid a short but pleasant spring visit to Purdue for a program of readings. The honoree on May 22, 1907 was Evaleen Stein, forty-four, a Lafayette poet and children's author. Ade said that his and Stein's mutual friend James Whitcomb Riley had recruited the talent for the campus program in Fowler Hall. President Stone introduced Ade, Riley, Stein, and Hoosier novelists Meredith Nicholson and Charles Major. Ade read his essay "College Days."

There was a national convention of the Sigma Chi fraternity in August 1907 in Jamestown, Virginia. For the occasion, Ade wrote and recited a poem, "The Fountain of Youth."

Politics and partying figured in Ade's life in 1908 when he served as a delegate to the Republican National Convention. Later, U.S. Secretary of War William Howard Taft, the convention nominee, opened his presidential campaign in September with an address at Hazelden Farm. Ade and his hired help arranged for bands, fold-up seats in the front yard, and twenty acres of parking space for cars and buggies east of the house. There were two hundred luncheon guests and thousands of spectators. For those who came on trains for the rally, Ade provided horse-drawn hay wagons for rides from the Brook depot out to the farm.

Taft's was the biggest affair yet at Hazelden Farm. In *Drawn from Memory*, McCutcheon remembered how "the Sigma Chis, the Purdue Alumni, the Indiana Society of Chicago and many other organizations" also made merry at Hazelden Farm (McCutcheon, 45).

"These big parties," Ade told friends, "are a little hard on the lawn and shrubbery, but they're a great thing for the community."

After Ade wrote *Father and the Boys* in 1908, and it made the New York City stage, some reviewers called it the best comedy in town. The veteran actor and producer William H. Crane (1845-1928) played it for three years. *Father* was about how The Old Man gets the better of the Young Folks instead of the other way around. However, some complained that in this play Ade's characters were beginning to be "unoriginal." The play, one critic said, was "cluttered with stock types, obvious relationships, trite situations and tired witticisms. It has moments of freshness but they cannot redeem the comedy from the list of potboilers written by Ade since

The College Widow." Ade, they claimed, was "a fading playwright" (Coyle, 104).

Nevertheless, Ade wrote *The Fair Co-ed,* a stage play in three acts. The still- infant Harlequin Club tested it out in a Purdue show first. Having again re-worked that old, old *College Widow* plot, Ade called *The Fair Co-ed* "a kind of happy-go-lucky musical play." Witmark published *The Fair Co-ed* in November 1908.

By now, Ade's growing fame was raising his value as a Purdue alumnus. On July 1, 1909, with alumni support, he accepted prestigious membership on the Purdue University Board of Trustees by appointment of Governor Thomas R. Marshall.

A theatrical friend from Chicago named Charles Dillingham talked Ade into producing *The Fair Co-ed* on Broadway. Ade's first musical comedy since *Sho-Gun* opened on February 1, 1909 for a run of 136 performances. Its plot omitted an important football game scene from the original *College Widow* play script. However, one critic complained that "it never makes good on the sprightly promise of the first act; the humor is watered; the story collapses in the second act; the dialogue is often silly; the incidents uninspired; the lyrics banal and sticky...and even Ade's genius for observation is curiously limited" (Coyle, 106).

There was one other hostile response. Purdue President Stone seemed to have taken umbrage at the way Ade caricatured him—or *appeared* to be spoofing him—in the *College Widow* character of the "college president."

Ade finished another play in 1910 and titled it *U.S. Minister Bedloe.* In this story, Bedloe from "Springfield U.S.A." becomes U.S. Minister to San Quito, in a mythical Central American republic of Caribay. Bedloe has just landed when a revolution breaks out.

Bedloe opened in Chicago but never reached New York City. "I knew it was a goner ten minutes after the curtain went up," Ade groaned, "but I had to stay there all evening while the blood slowly froze in my veins" (Kelly, *Ade*, 201).

Ade's last full-length play, *The Old Town*, opened January 10, 1910 in New York City and remained for 171 performances. It marked the end of Ade's ten-year run as a big-time playwright. Ade did write a short play—*The City Chap*—for the Harlequin Club for performances on March 28-30, 1910. H. Remick and Company, New York, published the script later that year.

Out at Hazelden Farm, Ade laid out a golf course consisting of nine approach-and-putt holes. He intended it for weekend guests, but he sensed that it did not seem neighborly to limit its use to special pals, so Ade formed the Hazelden Country Club with about forty members from around Brook and Kentland. When he enlarged the course in 1913 and made it one of the better nine-hole layouts in Indiana, the Country Club membership rose to 150. Ade said:

> I began to try to play golf in the 1890s...I remember that every fellow was trying to use a "cleek" and some of us had "baffies," and the mashie was usually described as a "lofter."

> I remember that as late as 1913 when I laid out my first long course I had Tom Bendelow help me. He was well known as a pro and a designer of courses and was plenty capable but a lot of country courses were being opened about that time and the clubs out in the country could not afford to pay for blueprints and expensive construction and Tom would lay out a course in one day. He would pick out a likely spot for No. 1 tee and put a stake in the ground and mark it then walk out until he thought he had come to a good place for a cross bunker and he would put down another stake and then go ahead and mark another bunker and then decide where to put his green and where to put the traps around it. As his services came to $25 a day the country clubs seldom kept him longer than one day because after he had given them a rough

sketch and a few directions they were ready to begin work on their course. (Tobin, 188-189)

Ade each day visited a barbershop in Brook, shaving himself only on Sundays. He knew the barbershop was a good place to hear what the neighbors were talking about. His nephew-by-marriage, Jim Rathbun, his farm manager, held that job for thirty-five years. The morning mail became a highlight of Hazelden life. Stacks of letters arrived from readers or theater patrons who were strangers, but Ade felt duty bound to answer. "Early to bed and early to rise," he used to say, gently poking fun at farm life, "and you'll meet very few prominent people" (Kelly, *Ade*, 230).

Finding rest, semi-retirement, and rejuvenation in his forties in the friendly fields around Hazelden Farm, Ade worked on more book collections, magazine stories, and syndicated newspaper yarns. He elevated his involvement in the affairs of Sigma Chi and the fun-loving, irreverent Indiana Society of Chicago. He took long trips and basked in Florida winters. Ade sailed much of the way around the world. He touched Hong Kong, India, and Europe with Orson "Ort" Wells, a wealthy friend since their Lafayette days. Years later, when asked whether he ever met the noted actor Orson *Welles* (different spelling), Ade revealed:

> He was named after me and Ort Wells. Ort and I were on a West Indies trip with Mr. and Mrs. Dick Welles of Kenosha [Wisconsin.] We became very friendly. Mrs. Welles said she was expecting a little stranger and if it turned out to be a boy she would name him after us or *for* us, take your choice. In due time we received word that the baby was a boy christened George Orson Welles. We did not suspect that [he] would turn out to be a celebrity. (Tobin 209-210)

A rare publication titled *I Knew Him When* showed up in December 1910 as a souvenir, limited to one thousand copies, of the annual dinner of the Indiana Society of Chicago. The Society credited the presswork to A. D. Winthrop and Company, Chicago. There was a subtitle, too: "A Hoosier Fable Dealing With the Happy Days of Away Back Yonder by George Ade," with cartoons by McCutcheon, Kin Hubbard, and other Hoosier talents.

Then there appeared *Hoosier Hand Book* that dated to June 1911 for the members and guests of the Indiana Society of Chicago. These people rode on a special train down into Indiana from the Dearborn Street Station in Chicago on June 23. *Hand Book* contained humorous and factual data about places between Chicago and Indianapolis, such as Whiting, Hammond, Dyer, St. John, Cedar Lake, Lowell, Rose Lawn, Fair Oaks, Rensselaer, Monon, Monticello, Delphi, Rossville, Frankfort, Kirklin, and Terhune. The Society published *Hand Book* with the subtitle: "A Compilation of Facts and Near-Facts concerning Objects of Interest Along the Monon Line between Chicago and Indianapolis, garnered for the use of members and guests of the Indiana Society of Chicago."

The Society leaned upon Ade again on December 11, 1911. For the membership the Bobbs-Merrill Company, Indianapolis, produced *Verses and Jingles* for a dinner in Chicago. Ade's part was Volume IV of twelve called "The Hoosier Set." Most of these contributions from Ade had been published before, including material from his Chicago *Record* days in 1893 and his "Fountain of Youth" poem from 1907.

Early in the twentieth century his fans considered George Ade one of the best-known writers of humor and drama in the United States. In the relative quiet of West Lafayette, he was a Big Man on Campus at Purdue as well. It helped any organization—the Purdue Trustees, Sigma Chi, the Purdue Alumni Association, or any other—to have a link with George Ade's name.

Purdue alumni began calling themselves an "Association" in 1912, but already, in 1911, they were emerging as a strong entity. At the end of Purdue's annual Gala Week just before commencement in June 1911, the Alumni Association made known it would co-sponsor an "air show." An "aeroplane" would fly to Stuart Field, which was spectator-friendly with its bleacher seats and parking spaces for horses, carriages, buggies, and a few newfangled motorcars.

Tippecanoe County's aviation history began on that June day barely seven and one-half years after the Wright brothers' first flight late in 1903. Many advances in aeronautics were taking place by the spring of 1911. Employees of Glenn Curtiss's Herring-Curtiss Aeroplane Company factory in Hammondsport, New York, were building and selling spindly but roaring loud "aeroplanes," recruiting and training pilots, and touring at air shows scheduled by the Curtiss Exhibition Company.

On May 17, the Lafayette *Journal* revealed that, with the Purdue Alumni Association, the paper would co-sponsor the city's first "aviation exhibition." It would take place on Tuesday, June 13. The level grounds and grandstands of Stuart Field still served as the home turf for Boilermaker football games. In its advance blurbs, the *Journal* disclosed that aviator J. A. D. McCurdy would fly a Curtiss and Wright biplane with a sixty-horsepower, eight-cylinder gasoline engine. Follow-up stories raised hope that a second pilot and biplane and as many as three mechanics might show up, too. Railroads scheduled excursion trains so that the curious could see the air show. The sponsors decided to charge fifty cents for seats in the Stuart Field bleachers. Car owners would pay a dollar for parking places. On June 12, the paper reported that C. C. Witmer, rather an unknown, would fly the second biplane.

Newspapers ranked the Aviation Day crowd the "greatest in Lafayette history" even though it did take place in *West* Lafayette. Converging hordes of horses, wagons, buggies, bicycles, motorcycles, and cars jammed West Lafayette's narrow streets. An estimated seventeen thousand people crowded about Stuart Field, some clinging to telephone poles or perched in trees. About seventy-five hundred of them occupied the stadium proper, overflowing the bleachers built to hold five thousand. Drivers parked an estimated two hundred fifty automobiles—as much a novelty as "aeroplanes" in 1911—all about the premises. Purdue's *Debris* yearbook proclaimed:

> The aeroplane exhibition was a splendid success. Thousands of people saw for the first time machines able to convey man through the air, circling about, and finally coming to earth again. (Topping, 165)

George Ade's name, fame, and money helped the Sigma Chis, too. "The Sweetheart of Sigma Chi" was being penned at Albion College in Ohio in 1911. There was a Delta Delta chapter house of Sigma Chi on Waldron Street near the Purdue campus. Edward J. Wotawa, a senior science major, wrote the music for a "Purdue War Song" in 1912. James Morrison, a science sophomore, composed words leading to renaming the war song. Wotawa, student director of the Purdue Glee and Mandolin Club, dedicated the new song to the Glee and Mandolin Club's members. Wotawa and Morrison published "Hail Purdue" in 1913.

Writing plays and playing politics was not all the ammunition in Ade's arsenal. His syndicated articles printed in the newspapers in Chicago, Indianapolis, and elsewhere continued to bring chuckles, especially to college types who had endured events like one described in February 1912 in "The Night Given Over to Revelry." Here are a few excerpts:

> All those who had Done Time at a certain endowed Institution for shaping and polishing Highbrows had to close in once a Year for a Banquet. They called it a banquet because it would have been a Joke to call it a Dinner....

To insure a Riot of spontaneous Gaiety the following Organization was effected: Committee on Invitation. Committee on Reception, Committee on Lights and Music. Committee on Speakers. Committee on Decorations. Committee on Police Protection. Committee on First Aid to Injured. Committee on Liquid Nourishment...

The Frolic was to be perpetrated at a Hotel famous for the number of Electric Lights. The Hour was to be 6:30 Sharp...Along about 7:30 a Sub-Committee wearing Satin Badges was sent downstairs to round up some recent Alumni who were trying to get a Running Start, and at 7:45 a second Detachment was sent out to find the Rescue Party. Finally at 8 o'clock the glad Throng moved into the Main Banquet Hall...

Beside each Plate was a blond Decoction named in honor of the Martini Rifle, which is guaranteed to kill at a Distance of 2,000 Yards. The compounding had been done in a Churn early that morning and the Temperature was that of the Room, in compliance with the Dictates of Fashion.

Those who partook of the Hemlock were given Courage to battle with the Oysters. These came in Sextettes, wearing a slight Ptomaine Pallor...

Luckily the Consommé was not hot enough to scald the Thumbs of the jovial Stevedores who had been brought in as Extras, so the Feast proceeded merrily, many of the Participants devoting their spare Moments to bobbing for Olives or pulling the Twine out of the Celery...

The Fish had a French Name, having been in the Cold Storage Bastille for so long. Each Portion wore a heavy Suit of Armor, was surrounded by Library Paste and served as a Tee for two Golf

Balls billed as *Pommes de Terre*. It was a regular Banquet, so there was no getting away from *Filet de Biff Aux Champignons*. It was brought on merely to show what an American Cook with a Lumber-Camp Training could do to a plain slice of Steer after reading a Book written by a Chef...

Between the Rainbow Ice Cream and the Calcareous Fromage a member of the Class of '08 who could not sing arose and did so. Then each Guest had to take a Tablespoonful of Cafe Noir and two Cigars selected by a former student who had promised his Mother never to use Tobacco...

Along about Midnight the Cowards and Quitters began crawling out the Side Doors, but most of the Loyal Sons of Old Bohunkus propped themselves up and tried to be Game. Before 1 o'clock a Member of the Faculty put them on the Ropes with 40 minutes on projected Changes in the Curriculum. At 1:30 the Toastmaster was...getting ready to spring the Oldest Living Graduate.

Protected by all the Gray Hair that was left to him, he began to Reminisce, going back to the Days when it was considered a Great Lark to put a Cow in the Chapel.

The Toastmaster arrived home at 3 a.m. and aroused his Wife to tell her it had been a Great Success.

MORAL: If they were *paid* $3 a Head...no one would attend.

The more time and thought Ade devoted to the Purdue students and alumni, however, the more he detected a sullen, unspoken resentment of President Stone. Campus affairs and Stone's grip on them kept pulling at Ade's conscience, and so did politics.

The lifelong Republican broke away from the regulars and hosted a rally at Hazelden Farm for Theodore Roosevelt's Bull Moose Party in 1912. There was even some talk of Ade running for Governor of Indiana that year.

Out in New York City, Doubleday, Page and Company selected thirty-three of Ade's syndicated newspaper stories from 1910 and 1911 and published *Knocking the Neighbors*. The Company next began preparing for an *Ade's Fables* collection.

Ade gave Sigma Chi funds for a new Purdue chapter house that fronted on 202 Littleton Street in West Lafayette. The "Sigs" had outgrown their house on Waldron. The rear of the new house looked east across the Wabash River valley and North River Road with front-door access from Littleton. For the architect, Ade engaged William Mann, Purdue Sigma Chi, Class of 1893. Working from Chicago, Mann also had designed Ade's 1905 Hazelden home at Brook and the Lafayette Country Club that overlooked Durkee's Run in south Lafayette in about 1909.

Ade's was the talent behind "A Picture Book for Purdue Sigs" that came out in 1912 apparently to inspire "Sigs" to support the new chapter house project.

In September 1913, when his father, John Ade, turned eighty-five, George arranged a celebration at Hazelden Farm. "We had a ball game," George said. "My brother Will could not circle the bases because he was stiffened up with rheumatism so father ran for him" (Kelly, *Ade*, 215). On April 28, 1914, the venerable John Ade attended the Indiana Republican Congressional Convention in Valparaiso. He even chaired the Resolutions Committee and helped draft a platform, but as he sat in the convention hall listening to someone else read his committee's report he fell dead. Even at that sad moment George held warm memories: "He and my mother were what they were, which was plenty good enough for this speckled world" (Kelly, *Ade*, 215).

Ade's Fables featured McCutcheon's art when it appeared in April 1914. The book offered fifteen syndicated fables from the *Indianapolis Star*.

In 1915, the three-year-old Purdue Alumni Association and the Stone Administration began to tangle more openly over athletics and regulation of student enterprises. Stone riled the sports crowd when he fired a promising football coach named Andred "Andy" Smith. In the football seasons of 1913, 1914, and 1915, Smith's teams won an acceptable twelve games, lost six, and tied three. To alumni, Stone compounded the mistake of firing Smith by hiring Cleo O'Donnell whose teams won only five games, lost eight, and tied one in two seasons. Worse, Stone yanked intercollegiate sports from the control of students and alumni in the Purdue Athletic Association and placed it under a new Department of Physical Education that Stone dominated.

No record shows Stone's motive for this change. The 1903 train disaster in Indianapolis may have been a far-off factor. Professor Oliver F. Cutts had coached the 1903 and 1904 football teams. But starting in 1904, Stone had picked Cutts to be the director of the new Department of Physical Education. Either Cutts or Stone or both then named a new football coach for 1905. He was A. E. Hernstein. His one team chalked up six victories, one loss, and one tie.

Before Cutts, R. W. Rusterholz had been presiding over the Athletic Association. Its affairs had been in the hands of students—like director Harry Leslie who graduated in 1905—with faculty help. There was much work for Cutts to do to put the various sports on a sound basis and establish a financial system.

It pleased Stone that Purdue could brag about having six baseball diamonds, six football fields, ten tennis courts, a quarter-mile running track, a straight track, and five thousand seats at Stuart Field. Stone supported intramural sports, believing them to be part of the educational maturity of every student.

But then more changes rumbled. Stone replaced Cutts with Hugh Nicol, and Nicol replaced Coach Hernstein for 1906 with M. E. Witham. Nicol enjoyed eight years of reasonable success, but Witham proved to be a flop. His one football team in 1906 scored only five points all season in losses to Chicago, Wabash, Notre Dame, Wisconsin, and Illinois. Coach L. C. Turner replaced Witham for 1907 only to lose five more. F. Speik succeeded Turner for football in 1908 and 1909, his teams winning six and losing eight. A coach named M. H. Horr followed Speik, winning eight, losing eleven, and tying once. Then Andy Smith coached three years.

Yet Hugh Nicol did stabilize Purdue sports. Born in Scotland in 1858, the peppy little Nicol had played major league baseball for American teams including the Cincinnati Reds and St. Louis Browns. He was a speedy five feet four inches tall and weighed one hundred forty-five pounds as a player. However, his tenure as Purdue athletic director appears to have ended in dissension. An unnamed and undated newspaper item printed probably in early December 1914 reported:

> Alpha P. Jamison will succeed Hugh Nicol as athletic director at Purdue. The athletic board made the announcement tonight [Dec. 7] and it is understood Jamison will accept.
>
> The new director is a Purdue grad and was a noted football player for four years. He was quarterback on the famous team that won the western championship.
>
> After graduation in 1895 Jamison accepted a faculty position and about 10 years ago was elevated to a professorship in the mechanical engineering department. He resigned a year ago to go into business.
>
> Jamison is popular with students, faculty, and alumni and the athletic board's selection meets with general approval. While on

the faculty, Jamison was admired by the student body because of his tendency to look on college questions from the student viewpoint.

> It is believed that Jamison will make an ideal director of athletics and that he will work in absolute harmony with all the coaches. Head football coach Andy Smith is greatly pleased with the appointment. Nicol has retired and possibly will accept a position at some other college.

This article, however, proved to be wrong in its speculation. Purdue records contain no mention of Jamison ever having accepted the directorship. Instead, he appears to have remained treasurer of his wife's family's business, the venerable Ruger Baking Company in Lafayette.

Purdue records show instead that President Stone re-hired Professor Cutts to be the adult/faculty athletic director a second time, during 1915-1918. Nicol stayed in West Lafayette and engaged in concrete block sales for a time. Four years later, Nicol and a partner, Harry Ruger, vice president of the bakery, conducted business as "manufacturer's agents" with an address on Main Street. When Nicol died in 1921, his obituary said he was Purdue athletic director "1906-1916," both dates being close, but wrong.

More anti-Stone resentment simmered over matters pertaining to the Student Union building idea Stone had espoused since 1902, and to the Purdue Marching Band, *The Exponent* newspaper, and *Purdue Alumnus* magazine. While playing for a student director's baton at Stuart Field football games, the Band had become popular and grown to more than fifty musicians. In 1904, Stone hired Paul Spotts Emrick to be the Band's faculty director.

Ade sided with the students in this matter, too. He believed that students and alumni should have a greater voice in forming Purdue policy. There began to be whispers of firing Stone, but he seemed to ignore—or at least remain above—alumni interests and concerns. Stone discerned too much emphasis on extra activities at Purdue, too much, as he put it, "multiplication and exaggeration of every conceivable form of amusement, distraction and recreation in connection with student life" (Topping, 180). As early as January 4, 1915, Ade addressed a blunt letter to "My dear Dr. Stone" about what Ade perceived to be "the scrapping between the coaches and the Athletic Director":

> I believe that the final and proper solution will be to have the general control vested in a Board in which the faculty, the alumni and the undergraduates will be equally represented. I do not believe that the alumni representation should be members of the faculty. They should be men of sufficient age and experience to permit them to stand as a kind of buffer between the intemperate zeal of the undergraduates and the restraining conservatism of the faculty. I believe you will find out that in colleges that have adopted this plan of control the faculty and alumni usually work together to correct and modify the too-ambitious projects of the students. I believe this Board should select a good coach for each department of sport and that it should have a capable business manager who has no connection with the work of coaching. The plan of having one Athletic Director and giving him supreme control might work out all right if you could accomplish the miracle of getting a man who would command the loyal affection of the students and win a large majority of his games...

> I can well understand that faculty members often become discouraged when compelled to abide by student legislation, but we must remember that the men in college average more than 21 years of age and are supposed to be ready to go out and manage important business affairs, and I believe the modern policy will continue to be to give the undergraduates certain legislative powers, even if they do muss things up once in a while...

I think that even in Yale and other eastern schools, where student control is very strong, the faculty would always have the power of a kind of Supreme Court if it cared to assert it. (Tobin 57-58)

Made for the movies

Away from the rising tempers at Purdue, George Ade's name began to appear in motion picture credits. A Chicago company bought rights to a series of his syndicated "Fables" to make into short "picture plays." When asked to put a price on them for the motion picture rights, Ade said he would "be glad to consider any insulting offer." Between 1914 and 1917, Essanay Film Company made sixty-some of Ade's newspaper "Fables" into ten-minute comedies. Co-founders George Spoor (the S) and Billy Anderson (the A) were the S and A in Essanay. The men ran studios in Chicago and in Niles, California, for about ten years. Just how insulting an offer—if any—Spoor and Anderson ever made to Ade is unknown.

Ade's movie work, largely unnoticed by his biographers and bibliographer, began in June 1914 when Essanay released *Two Pop-Up Fables* and one that Ade both wrote and directed, *The Fable of the Brash Drummer and the Nectarine*. A young and unknown actor named Wallace Beery played the lead in *Drummer* when it first reached theaters on June 17.

By December 1914, Essanay had turned out twenty-seven more versions of "Fables" at about weekly intervals. The series ended with *Two Dinky Little Dramas of a Non-Serious Kind.* Released on December 30, this one also starred Beery with Ade directing. Ade's directing probably took place in Chicago. On October 19, 1914, a feature-length film came out based on *The County Chairman*. The Famous Players-Lasky Corporation in California produced the film. The production company's president, Adolph Zukor, started with a Famous Players Film Company in 1912.

Essaney released *The Fable of the City Grafter and the Unprotected Rubes* on January 2, 1915, setting in motion another busy year in which about forty of Ade's Fables became movie screen shorts guided by Ade's knowledge of the characters and story lines. Lubin Manufacturing Company, having filmed on location in Pennsylvania, released a silent one-hour version of *The College Widow* in May 1915.

On May 24, Essanay used Beery, Francis X. Bushman, and others in its cast for a full-length *Slim Princess*. On July 7, the Universal Studio released *Betty's Dream Hero*. This was a play for which Ade was credited with having written scenarios. Less than a week later, Rolfe Photoplay Incorporated turned out a film drama based on *Marse Covington*. The Frohman Amusement Corporation, in August 1915, produced and distributed *Just Out of College*. In business between 1915 and 1920, Frohman engaged both in production and distribution. The actor Lon Chaney played in Universal's *Father and the Boys* released on December 20, 1915.

The Purdue Alumni Association re-nominated Ade for the university's Board of Trustees on June 8, 1915, but before another year had passed, Ade resigned in disgust. For his departure Ade blamed a last-straw episode that had occurred on April 24, 1916, that night the Purdue Harlequin Club staged Ade's review "Around the Campus" for only a lukewarm crowd.

Five days later, Ade also quit as a Trustee. In a letter, Ade asserted that, under President Stone, Purdue was being committed to a course of mediocrity. Ade believed that graduates from Stone's repressive leadership could not be expected ever to hold more than routine jobs. "You can't teach a bird to fly," Ade reasoned, "by tying it to a limb" (Kelly, *Ade*, 238). On August 6, 1916, Ade further explained his resignation in another letter, this time from Hazelden Farm:

No college club could afford to pay what an author counts on receiving in royalties from any sort of success. The work I have done for Purdue has been not only *gratis*, but I have followed it up with plenty of hard coin. (Tobin, 61)

However, Ade enjoyed productive days in 1916 in his writing and movie work. Essanay, Vitagraph Company of America, and the Chicago Sport Comedy Company treated moviegoers to more screen versions of Ade's huge body of writing. Essanay released another seventeen "Fables." That series started with *The Fable of the Two Philanthropic Sons* on January 12, 1916. On April 17, Vitagraph turned out a fifty-minute feature titled *Artie, the Millionaire Kid*. A Chicago Sport Comedy short in October bore the title *The Fable Of the Kid Who Shifted His Ideals to Golf and Finally Became a Baseball Fan and Took the Only Known Cure*. Essanay stretched one of its "shorts" beyond ten minutes when it produced *The Fable of the Throbbing Genius of a Tank Town Who Was Encouraged by Her Folks Who Were Prominent*.

On May 4, 1916, the Indiana Historical Commission, Indianapolis, celebrating the centennial of statehood, published a collection of writing by Hoosier authors that Ade had selected and introduced. The work bore the cumbersome title *An Invitation to You and Your Folks from Jim and Some More of the Home Folks*.

As the years passed, Ade's routine away from Purdue became one of financial security, settled ease, and comfort. Trusted, reliable help and plenty of friends surrounded him at Hazelden and his five other working farms. Ade enjoyed ongoing success with motion pictures, too. Between September and December 1917, the Essanay people released another dozen short "picture plays" based on "Fables."

Ade still escaped Indiana winters by going south. On March 11, 1917, while in Belleair Heights, Florida, Ade wrote to one Purdue chum:

> I have not been at Purdue for about a year. I felt disgusted with Doc Stone and most of the Faculty and [felt] thoroughly discouraged because of the lack of any real spirit or enthusiasm among the students. After devoting many weeks of hard work and a considerable sum of money to putting on the Annual [1916 Harlequin] Show, it did not seem to me that the students were grateful or even interested. A man's only reward when he tackles a college job is the knowledge that the boys are with him, so I have been off of Purdue ever since. I have made no definite plans for returning at any time although I still have the kindliest feelings in the world for the Sigs. As for Doc Stone I wish him everything he wishes me and I could not say anything rougher than that. (Tobin 62-63)

In his Purdue history, published in 1988, Robert W. Topping rated Ade "among the most vociferous alumni. He served briefly [1918-1921] as editor of the *Purdue Alumnus* magazine and aired his opinions about the perceived faults of Purdue under Stone. Ade felt Stone stifled student and faculty spirit and initiative. Ade started a one-man campaign among political powers and legislators to have Stone fired. Ade was Stone's most formidable antagonist. Ade dabbled dangerously in behind-the-scenes Republican state politics in which he was nominally influential. To a stable, conservative and rather monolithic Purdue administration he was something of a gadfly. Ade did not like Stone and did not believe Stone liked him" (Topping, 178).

In a letter to former Governor Samuel Ralston in 1919, Ade tried to rally support to persuade the Purdue Trustees not to renew Stone's presidency. At one point in that letter, Ade wrote:

> I am taking an awful chance in writing this because I don't know what you think about Doctor Stone of Purdue. What I think about him cannot be set forth in this letter as I do not wish to violate the federal statute against sending profane matter through the mail. (Topping, 179)

The debate still simmered over athletics. Unless they were a natural part of the general sports program Stone showed little respect for intercollegiate rivalry, but Ade felt that beating rivals generated student body spirit and loyalty. His combat with Stone added to the reason Ade quit the Trustees. After Ade left the Trustees, he kept nipping at Stone. "Though [Ade's] manner was gentlemanly and restrained," Topping wrote, "he continued his insistence that Purdue should become a livelier, more imaginative school—such as it no doubt had been when he was a student" (Topping, 180).

Ade contended that there were two extremes in the polemic that had developed at Purdue: "Those who believe that Purdue is being put into a category with the penitentiaries at Michigan City and the Plainfield Reform School, and the grim disciplinarians who cannot see beyond the campus's iron fence and who say that any who argue against any established policy are misinformed mischief-makers and enemies of the University" (Topping 180).

"Life at Purdue," Ade would summarize later, "had been just one misunderstanding after another. The alumni had been estranged, student morale had deteriorated—even the faculty had begun to feel the effect of Stone's ways. Stone had one solution to every problem, "sterner discipline and more hours of work." Ade complained that Stone liked only those athletic coaches who "did not cost much money" and could be hired so long as they were "obedient and respectful—regardless of whether they knew anything about coaching." Ade felt that alumni wanted everything that would "make Purdue men and women *proud* of their school…a revived loyalty to the school and its associations" (Topping 181).

However, the target of Ade's wrath was the one man whose attainments and supporters as Purdue's president had been many. No one argued much with Ade's appraisal of Stone's leadership style, but then no one questioned Stone's dedication to or interest in or overall value to Purdue.

During Stone's presidency that began in 1900, private donors had built Eliza Fowler Hall in 1903 and Smith Hall in 1913. Purdue had started a Department of Home Economics in 1905, a Department of Education in 1908, a School of Chemical Engineering in 1911, and the first phase of building a Library. Gifts of land and on-campus construction enlarged and improved the School of Agriculture and its Experiment Station in 1909. The Memorial Gymnasium opened in 1909. There followed acquisition of the Moses Fell Farm in southern Indiana in 1914, the building of greenhouses on campus in 1915, and the Davis Forestry Farm gift in 1917. A veterinary science building went up in 1916 and a biology building in 1917.

When the United States entered World War I, Stone provided steady yet careful, morally sound, and disciplined leadership. Purdue organized a Student Army Training Corps in a contract with the U.S. War Department. Purdue housed, fed, and trained soldiers to be auto and truck mechanics, radio operators, and even concrete workers. Temporary buildings went up in wartime on some of the Stuart Field space: barracks, equipment sheds, a garage for trucks, a recreation building. Enrollment rose by fourteen hundred. In 1918, a Purdue Armory on University Street replaced a wooden structure built in 1874. The latter had been a social and cultural center, gym, drill hall for Reserve Officer Training Corps cadets, and site of the first commencement in 1875.

World War I cost Purdue sixty-seven dead. More than four thousand faculty and students served the U.S. military. Purdue renewed its stalled campaign for private funds to build the Student Union that Stone had championed. Stone would be nobody's pushover.

Ade had no personal political ambitions, yet his Republican Party connections pulled him into certain "war work" for the State of Indiana during the term of Governor James P. Goodrich. For the Indiana Council of Defense Ade directed wartime news releases. He occupied an office in the Indiana Statehouse in Indianapolis. So much war propaganda flooded Hoosier newspapers that it was impossible to print it all. Ade condensed it into a daily column. He wrote a series of pamphlets, too. They were intended to instruct the public as to how various age groups could help the war effort. In September 1918, Ade sponsored a golf tournament at the Hazelden course to raise money for the Red Cross. The event sold, at patriotically inflated prices, permits to carry the clubs of several famous professional players and raised more than five thousand dollars.

In early November 1918, days before the end of the war, Ade helped arrange publication of *Marse Covington*, the one-act play he had written in 1906. The play re-emerged now as a project of the Commission on Training Camp Activities, Department of Dramatic Activities Among the Soldiers. Ade also composed a number of new one-act pieces, among them *Nettie, The Mayor and the Manicure,* and *Speaking to Father*. But then a habit-changing illness set in.

"For many years after I took up the writing game I smoked whatever was readily obtainable with a preference for a mild Havana cigar of the Panatella shape," Ade said. "[But] in November 1918, just as I got through with some war work and the Big Trouble was ended, I was put flat on my back for a month by an attack of illness. When I tottered back to my usual haunts I learned that I had retained a modicum of my normal thirst, but had lost all desire to smoke. I would light a cigar or cigarette and take a few puffs at it and experience a sense of disappointment and discontinue the effort. I love to see others smoke and select cigars and cigarettes with great care for my friends who have not enjoyed the misfortune of being cured" (Tobin 130). It is unclear whether Ade's "attack of illness" at age fifty-two referred to the influenza pandemic that spread throughout Europe and the Americas and caused twenty million deaths during 1918-1919.

During and for a while after World War I, Ade wrote and mailed news bulletins to Purdue students in the armed services and began serving as Editor of the *Purdue Alumnus* magazine. Editions of the *Alumnus,* nearly all monthly, had been coming out since 1911. As editor Ade helped initiate three new surveys of Alumni Association members. The canvasses sought answers to:

1. How to stimulate a free interchange of opinion among local Alumni groups and compare plans to reorganize and improve them.

2. How to learn from alumni officers from other Midwestern universities the causes and extent of indifference and apathy on the part of four-year graduates, and the best plans to revive interest.

3. What kind of publication Purdue Alumni prefer, what they want to read in it, and if there is a "slack interest" in alumni enterprises, why so?

On February 24, a 'Committee of Ten" represented the Purdue Alumni Association in a sort of summit with the Purdue Trustees. In this meeting Dave Ross and George Ade barely missed getting acquainted. Both Ross, Class of 1893, and Judge Henry H. Vinton, Class of 1895—a close friend of Ade's—sat with the Committee of Ten. But for nearly three years Ade, having resigned in disgust, had left the Board of Trustees and, therefore, was absent.

As a sort of bottom-line, those at the summit agreed that the Trustees needed the active help of the Alumni. The Committee of Ten in turn pledged "continued, undivided support" of the Board and to the University" (*The Purdue Alumnus*, April 1919).

On July 4, 1919, Ade threw a postwar homecoming party at Hazelden for World War I veteran soldiers and sailors. An estimated fifteen thousand attended. Ade's experience of some fifteen years as a host caused him to comment:

> Fried chicken alone will make the party a success if the springers have been dispatched and dismembered on the morning of the

day before, soaked in cold water and finally rolled in flour and fried slowly in sweet country butter and served moist and piping hot...Real gravy can no longer be found except in the country. We serve huge receptacles of genuine gravy in which the giblets jostle one another. The partakers are not only permitted to drown the mashed potatoes and blot up the overflow with the highly absorbent country biscuits, but are actually urged, in a nice way, to do so...

If I had to select an All-American menu for a large cluster of people out in the country in the summertime, it would run about as follows: fruit cocktail (if compounded by local experts with no hotel experience); fried chicken prepared by women over thirty years of age; bona fide gravy; cole slaw, made of fresh young cabbage; country biscuits, lined up in rows; cakes and cakes and cakes; pie, made of fresh fruits; regular ice cream; coffee, milk or iced tea." (Kelly, *Ade*, 224-225)

The July issue of *The Purdue Alumnus* contained this bit of commentary that bore the tone and subject matter, albeit unsigned, of Editor Ade:

The alumni cannot keep track of all the inner details of instructional work at the University. They cannot brood over certain problems which may be moving about under the surface of the campus. If an important department takes a bad slump, they may come to know about it in time. But they can, and probably will, if they are entirely alive above the shoulders, continue to take a long-range interest in football, baseball, basketball, track athletics, the Harlequin Club, the musical clubs, the band, the daily paper, the annual, the frat houses, the Junior prom, the fetes and carnivals and May-Days and so on.

When an old-timer makes inquiry, he doesn't say, "For Heaven's sake, tell us how the boys are getting along in Animal Husbandry and Pharmacy." No, what he asks is: "Have they got a real team this year? Can they lick Chicago?"...

We believe we know what we are talking about.

We believe that the student activities should be accepted as beloved members of the family and not treated as bothersome stepchildren...Take away from student life the many-sided relationships growing out of organizations that some people seem to regard as accidental and frivolous, and what would remain? Only bare walls and cheerless drudgery. Without student activities, the only difference between Purdue and a Correspondence School would be that Purdue undergraduates would not have to write letters.

If the student activities are here to stay, why not set aside for them a little more kindliness and tact? Why should there be a shortage of the spirit of friendliness? Whatever is worth doing at all in the name of the University is worth doing well. An army won't get anywhere even with willing soldiers if the General is sitting off in his tent guarding his personal prerogatives.

Let's get together—alumni, ex-students, students, faculty, friends, everybody—and bolster up the weak places in the complex organization known as Purdue University. (*The Purdue Alumnus*, July 1919)

The reasons behind it are long forgotten, but in 1919, enough hostility existed between Purdue and Indiana Universities over athletics that relations broke down. They did not meet in football in 1918 or 1919. One of George Ade's unsigned editorials in the January 1920 *Purdue Alumnus* contained this report:

> The editor had ready a wise prediction that the time had about arrived for Purdue and I. U. to bury the hatchet and become, once more, "friendly enemies." Just when the editorial was in type, along came word that the prophecy had been fulfilled ahead of time and the feud was to be forgotten and next year Indiana was to play Purdue [in football] at Lafayette on November 20th. So get ready for Homecoming on that date...November 20th is a little late in the season but the Indiana game will certainly prove the best possible attraction and if both teams continue the improvement which they were showing at the close of this [1918] season, there will be a real mix-up on Stuart Field.

Hand-made Fables from Doubleday, Page and Company, Garden City, New York, illustrated by McCutcheon, came out on March 18, 1920. The book contained thirty "Fables" that *Cosmopolitan* had published during 1915-1918

In early 1920, Ade wrote an essay he titled "Chapter Houses." Evidently, he composed it for circulation among Purdue's Sigma Chi alumni. The national *Sigma Chi Quarterly* reprinted it in May 1920.

Then, after nearly a three-year hiatus, Ade enjoyed a revival of his motion picture work. On July 19, Goldwyn Pictures Corporation released a re-make of *The Slim Princess*. It starred actress Mabel Normand in a fifty-minute version classifed this time as a "comedy-drama." (Essanay called its shorter treatment in 1915 mere "comedy.") Victor Schertzinger directed the Goldwyn treatment, and Ade and Gerald Duffy wrote scenes and dialogue. Next, Goldwyn made and released, on November 27, 1920, a remake of *Just Out of College*.

For months after the war Ade also helped on several advisory committees. "Promoting things," he said, "brings one into pleasant association with cheerful people" (Kelly, Ade, 236).

Peace and War

Dave Ross took office for four years on the Lafayette City Council in January 1914. He also went right on running Ross Gear and Tool Company as its general manager, inventing things related to that job, and piling up salary and stock certificates.

As a City official Ross pushed for better pensions for Lafayette police and firemen, for improved fire protection, and for a stricter building code. It made sense to him for the City to merge three little old fire stations into one really modern, central building of brick and stone that housed the best trained men and the most modern equipment. He went out and walked smelly alleys and urged City minions on to better trash pickups. He campaigned for good sanitation and clean neighborhoods. "Few cities in the country have a greater per capita wealth than Lafayette," Ross said. "Why not make this city beautiful?" (Kelly, *Ross*, 64).

The year 1913 had brought on the use of radio. Ross's old Purdue professor, Reginald Fessenden, made the news. Radio was evolving from 1890s Italy and the inventions of Guglielmo Marconi (1874-1937). It would take nearly thirty years to become something all people could use, but that day was drawing nearer. Radio first had touched Lafayette in January 1903. Jeptha Crouch, owner of the Lafayette Stock Farm, received a message from his brother, George, who was aboard a trans-Atlantic ship en route to Europe to buy horses. George had arranged to beam that message to New York City by wireless then to Jeptha via the wires of Western Union telegraph, a linkage then known as "Marconigraph."

Then in 1906, Professor Fessenden—long after his Purdue days—first sent human speech instead of dots and dashes from Brant Rock, Massachusetts, to ships in the Atlantic. Fessenden is believed to have conducted some of his early wireless research at Purdue in the Dave Ross 1890s days. Electrical engineers, in the meantime, had learned how to make vacuum tubes to send, hear, and amplify radio signals. These advances spurred the public sale of radio equipment and spare parts to hordes of eager hobbyists known the world over as hams.

Purdue electrical engineering ("double-E") professors Raymond Schatz and David Curtner built a transmitter and receiver for World War I U.S. Army trainees to use in 1918. The first day it worked Curtner sang "K-K-K-Katy" into the microphone and out into the airwaves. "Radiophone" sending and receiving kept making friends the world over after the war.

Double-E Professor Francis Harding persuaded Purdue to build and license a daily broadcasting station. The station could be an educational, news, and entertainment medium for the public, Harding believed, and could be a training lab for double-E majors.

By 1922, efforts involving Harding, Schatz, Curtner, and others led to Purdue starting Indiana's first licensed radio station with the call letters WBAA. With twenty watts of power and its federal license dated April 4, WBAA debuted at nine p.m. on April 21, 1922 with a program about Arbor Day. The third floor of the double-E building housed the primitive studio.

Working as Ross Gear plant manager during 1915, Dave Ross collected patents for two steering gears and a steering arm. That fall there was a renewal of serious City Council talk about merging Lafayette and West Lafayette. Merger made management and economic sense to Dave Ross, but such talk came to nothing. There were not enough Dave Rosses.

In 1916, Ross obtained patents on a differential mechanism and three steering gear designs. In Europe, entire nations warred without America's involvement. Yet on June 23, 1916, war nerves pushed artillery Battery C of the Indiana National Guard into girding for duty near the Mexico-Texas border. Lieutenant R. W. Levering of Lafayette commanded the one hundred eighty men. Purdue "just in case" started recruiting a Battery B for the National Guard. The men of Battery C left for Texas on July 7.

During the summer of 1916, the Ross Gear Board of Directors raised Dave Ross's pay to two thousand dollars per month, the highest in the booming company.

For Ross, the money from factory salary, stock, and patents was piling up. His uncles had done well in real estate, and Dave saw the same opportunities. He wished to have some quiet "country place" to visit when stress in the city wore him down. He wished for land, woods, hills, and water. He found the right land for sale in Shelby Township along the Wabash River west-southwest of Lafayette. He bought fifty-nine acres from John Noll on December 27, 1916. Thirteen months later—January 30, 1918—he acquired one hundred eight adjoining acres from a seller named McKinsey. Ross's hilltop place in Lafayette at 506 South Seventh Street became merely his winter home. The Shelby Township land contained level fields, woods, ravines, and a bluff-top view of the Wabash River. Ross called the place "The Hills" and on it chose where he could build a home.

As he began improving the ruggedly beautiful area his inventive nature again surfaced. Saying to heck with common sense, he built a barn on a steep hillside. Ross reasoned that one could drive a manure spreader under the windows on the low side and fill the spreader without having to do any lifting. Then to prevent erosion on a steep, curving driveway down to the river, Ross designed and installed V-shaped, concrete dams spaced twenty feet apart to divert storm water to an underground drain tile.

Ross turned architect for his three-story, twelve-room home at "The Hills." He designed a fireplace with a copper hood that directed heat to parts of the upstairs instead of out the chimney. As the home took shape Ross invited friends out for the country air and his home cooking. Overnight guests learned certain quirks about Ross. He rose each day at 6:30 a.m. He loved having recorded music—later commercial radio music—going from the crack of dawn. He enjoyed card games and other entertainment. However, he was not to be disturbed if he retired to a workshop or drafting table where he might flesh out sudden brainstorms.

When he hired and moved a tenant-caretaker and his family to "The Hills," Ross bought the caretaker's children a Jersey cow if they would take care of it and learn to milk it. He joked: "Since I'm a bachelor I naturally understand children. There's nothing so good for children as having regular daily duties. That's one great advantage of bringing up kids in the country" (Kelly, *Ross*, 80).

Ross, in 1917, received patents for an electrical current generator and spark distributor and for a way to oil steering gear-rocker shafts in cars and trucks. He was perfecting amazing instincts and sensitivities to machinery, something like a doctor. He could watch a machine run and spot flaws; feel its vibrations and discern problems; hear it going and head off trouble; and even smell it and sense trouble with its bearings or ignition and know what to do.

In April 1917, as Congress voted the United States into World War I, Purdue urged its students to enlist in the army in return for credit for any courses they were taking. Readying for war included local meetings on food growing and military recruitment. Ten thousand people attended a downtown Lafayette parade on April 9. Recruiting rallies and war bond sales drives began.

On May 7, 1917, the Lafayette *Journal* reported a patriotic moment at the Ross Gear plant. The three hundred workers stopped making gears long enough to hoist a huge outdoor American flag. Curious Heath Street neighbors watched and listened. Two uniformed military men blew bugles. A nine-man rifle squad fired three rounds as the flag went up, opened, and flapped atop an eighty-foot pole. Dave Ross served as master of ceremonies. A Purdue professor described World War I as "a contest of force, brains and science for the freedom of mankind." The work of the mechanic in preparing war materiel and of the farmer in producing food to feed the armies were as important, the speaker said, as the work of soldiers on the firing line. The speaker discussed the role of trucks, armored cars, and ambulances in modern warfare. Ross Gear workers' hands were making the gears that were driving and steering many of them. A man sang "Old Glory." Another rendered "Indiana." Ross Gear decorated its factory floor with four-by-six-foot American flags and draped two larger ones over the plant entrance.

On November 6, Ross and his Democrat friends celebrated easy wins in the 1917 City elections. Former mayor Durgan, ousted by those Republicans-in-Citizens-clothing in 1913, won the job back and prepared to start his fourth term. Democrats won every other City office and all ten seats on the City Council. Dave Ross defeated Republican hardware dealer James Jamison by ninety-one votes in the Fifth Ward and took office for four more years. The Lafayette *Courier* commented that Ross "ranks among the city's most substantial businessmen...His best recommendation is his record as a member of the City legislative body where he has always fought for the interests of the people" (Lafayette *Courier*, November 7, 1917).

Lafayette and Ross Gear were riding an uplifting wave of progress. In mid-February 1918, local contractor and Purdue alumnus Alva E. "Cap" Kemmer and his men began work on a ten-story limestone building. It would stand in downtown Lafayette at Third and Main for the fast-growing Lafayette Life Insurance Company. Next door to the east Will and Linn Ross financed construction for offices of a three-story stone Ross Building. It looked like the tall Life Building's little-boy son.

At midnight on April 2, 1918, a state liquor prohibition law took effect. The law closed hundreds of Indiana package stores, saloons, and breweries like the Thieme and Wagner and the George Bohrer plants in Lafayette.

Three weeks later, Purdue dedicated its Armory, and in it the next day began teaching automotive mechanic courses to five hundred Army men. In mid-June, the Lafayette City Council urged patriotic types to plant vegetable gardens to boost the wartime food supply. Citizens tilled and raked about four hundred acres into forty-five hundred private plots. Purdue's School of Agriculture helped with seeds and advice about soil, planting, fertilizing, harvesting, and food preservation.

During 1918, Purdue housed, fed, and trained five thousand enlisted military men in technical courses. Twenty-five hundred students enrolled in the Student Army Training Corps. In the fall of 1918, the nation's Fourth Liberty Loan bond drive set a goal of more than three million dollars' worth of sales in Tippecanoe County. The success of the 1911 Purdue Alumni Association air show came to mind. Local backers of the war bond drive planned, on September 26, to procure four army planes from Indianapolis. The planes would "bomb" Lafayette. The pilots would drop bond-sale leaflets and land on a Purdue farm west of the campus. High wind and engine trouble cancelled the "bombing" stunt, but the county beat its bond sale goal anyway—by ninety-eight hundred dollars—on October 20.

During World War I, the Ross Gear plant turned out steering gears for military trucks. The company contracted with the U.S. War Department to cut, grind, polish, and ship a thousand gears for what the military called "Army Truck Type B." Government and civilian business for Ross Gear also grew in wartime. The company Directors, in December 1918, rewarded Dave Ross with a twenty-five percent raise. That brought his monthly pay to twenty-five hundred dollars.

At Purdue, the University dedicated the new Biology Building. On November 11, telegraph messages brought good news from France. An armistice had ended World I. Railroad locomotive whistles tooted in Lafayette. Church and school bells clanged. Factories closed for a day in celebration. Thousands cheered around Lafayette's courthouse square. There were two parades with pounding drums.

But Dave Ross stayed at his drawing board. In 1919, the government granted him a patent for a machine that could cut internal threads in metal gears. At Ross Gear, he insisted on two policies:

    1. Every key employee should have an understudy who can take the job.

    2. It's more important to get a job done than for anyone to get credit.

As business grew the factory became crowded. That is why Uncle Linn Ross, in 1919, presided over the start of Fairfield Manufacturing Company. The Fairfield men began making rear axle and transmission systems for heavy trucks in a corner of the Ross Gear plant. When a building became available two miles away on Earl Avenue, the Rosses moved Fairfield. There they started making gears that propelled both light and heavy trucks. The left-behind Ross Gear workers still focused on gears that helped drivers steer.

Purdue football had fallen into hard times. The school had fired Coach "Andy" Smith after his 1915 team won three of seven games. Coach Cleo O'Donnell fared no better. His teams in 1916 and 1917 won only five times. "Butch" Scanlon came on, and it took him three seasons to win seven times. Sports-loving alumni grew restless.

During 1920, Dave Ross's new patents included a steering gear design for Ross Gear in February and one for speed reducing transmission gearing for Fairfield in November. Business and other interests persuaded him to get out of Lafayette politics, but before leaving the City Council, Ross agreed to take one new job "for the public good." He agreed to chair the Purdue Alumni Association committee, still struggling to get enough donations to build that Student Union on the West Lafayette campus. Purdue wanted to raise five hundred thousand dollars. The Class of 1911 had started the drive, but by 1917, the proceeds had grown to fewer than eighteen thousand dollars. In the patriotic air of World War I, Purdue shifted the purpose from *Student* Union to *Memorial* Union to honor Purdue's World War I dead and dying. That helped a little.

Trouble is, when Ross joined the effort to get money and pledges from fellow alumni, some of them rich and famous, he met with a lot of whiners. "Give us a winning football team for a change," they said, "and we'll talk about giving money to Purdue." They had a point, to which Ross had been paying little attention, but it made more sense the longer he pondered the issue. It had to do with *Purdue Pride*. Since 1911, Purdue had won thirty-one football games, lost thirty-two, and tied six. Not much of a fan of college sport, Ross now considered how to reply to the whiners.

Dave Ross, in 1921, enjoyed one of his most productive years ever for getting patents. In January, June, and October he received six—three for steering gears, one for a steering wheel design, others for a gear grinding machine, and a means of dressing grinding wheels.

Early that year the Purdue Alumni Association persuaded the Indiana General Assembly to amend state law so that the Alumni could recommend three of the Governor's appointees to the Purdue Board of Trustees instead of one. Harry Leslie, now a member of the Indiana House of Representatives, helped pass the law. When the law took effect, fifty-year-old Dave Ross, on July 1, became the first Trustee to be appointed that way. Trustee membership also added a touch of clout to Ross's fund-raising efforts for the Memorial Union.

The win-or-else mindset among alumni football fans clearly slowed fund-raising, but Ross reasoned, "If enough people say that about athletics our success is assured—we have something to talk to them about. Every one of them has stuck his head in a noose. We can shame them into doing their part" (Kelly, *Ross*, 69).

Before long, Ross was visiting rich alumni in big cities and laying a gently worded guilt trip on any who wanted to talk football:

> Look, you have had great success since you left Purdue. Is what you accomplished on account of football or other forms of training you got there? Surely you're a big enough boy now to know that athletics isn't everything. Shouldn't you get out of knee pants? What about putting your name on this sheet of paper and make a decent pledge toward the Memorial Union? (Kelly, *Ross*, 69)

While Ross was at it, he also spoke his mind to certain other people in high places at Purdue. "It's time we administrators, Trustees and alumni look ahead and think about land for dozens of new buildings that the university will need," he said.

"Look ahead ten years?" someone asked.

"No, I mean *fifty* years," Ross replied (Kelly, *Ross*, 70).

His Purdue colleagues began to recognize that this relative unknown—Dave Ross, Class of 1893—had "horse sense," foresight, and the ability to get things done.

Ross visited Purdue alumni groups through the Midwest to present the Memorial Union plan and to solicit support. As a result of such efforts, alumni met their goal.

From his string of inventions, mostly for automotive gears, since 1906, Ross had earned a fortune, which grew yearly. But in 1921, he was starting to see ways to use his wealth to help Purdue. Yes, he came across as a folksy, amusing character from the country, but he voiced fresh ideas about education, farming, housing, and government. One idea was to use Purdue scientific research as a *teaching tool*. Let industry bring problems to Purdue. Let Purdue professors and students solve the problems and *teach* while students *learn* along the way. In that arena alone, Ross influenced American education, but his interests widened as Purdue's own problems arose. His brilliance and vision blossomed in helping find solutions.

At Purdue, however, the summer of 1921 turned abruptly tragic. Since 1906, President Winthrop Stone had enjoyed mountain climbing. It had begun with a summer vacation trip to British Columbia. In the years that followed, he had joined various climbing clubs in the U.S. and Canada and scaled high peaks. World War I had pinned him in his Purdue office. However, in early July 1921, after a routine meeting with the Board of Trustees, Winthrop and his wife Margaret Stone left for a climbing vacation in the Banff region west of Calgary, Alberta.

On July 15, the two began to scale Mount Eon. That peak rose 10,860 feet along the Alberta-British Columbia border. At about six p.m. on Sunday, July 17, the Stones had struggled to within fifty feet of the top. Stone in the lead called down to warn Margaret of loose footing he had come upon in the rocks. She shouted back to inquire whether he was near the peak. "I see nothing higher," he called.

At war with Purdue

Even after World War I ended, George Ade's ongoing battle with Winthrop Stone reached no armistice. On May 20, 1919, Ade wrote to alert Indiana Governor Samuel M. Ralston to a "crisis at Purdue" about electing a new president. Ade maintained that the Trustees were "about equally divided" on the subject. Many, Ade wrote, believed that Stone by "hard and dictatorial methods" and other faults "has been a blighting influence at Purdue instead of a help." Ade urged the governor to ask other Purdue people to verify the situation and he, Ade, would be "only too glad to tell you everything I know" (Tobin, 71-72).

There were happy days, too. Ade entertained hundreds of guests at his Hazelden Farm picnics. His estate stood now as a showplace and a Mecca for writers and stars of the stage, screen, politics, and sports. For a number of years prior, Ade had been planning and hosting the annual picnics. From the surrounding townships large numbers of youngsters came to devour hot dogs, fried chicken, and ice cream, to compete in contests and vie for prizes. Ade filled the home with souvenirs from around the world and with mementoes from notable people.

In the fall of 1919, Ade kept campaigning for administrative reform at Purdue. On October 17, in a letter from Hazelden, he wrote to Dave Ross, the fellow alumnus he had almost met. Ade briefed Ross about both the Purdue "crisis" and a personal political "fix" he wished to dodge. The "fix" loomed because Republicans had asked Ade to sign a letter of endorsement for Warren McCray, from Kentland, as a candidate for Governor of Indiana:

There are certain reasons why I should sign such a letter. Mr. McCray is my brother-in-law...We have not been in political accord at all times in recent years and there has been a coolness between us [and yet] if I refuse to endorse him my refusal will be attributed to petty reasons and small local jealousies.

My refusal is based upon the fact that when he became a Trustee at Purdue [1917-1918] he was an ardent supporter of Dr. Stone and his policies, without giving the alumni a chance to state their case. He declared emphatically to friends of mine in Kentland that Dr. Stone was altogether in the right and that I was altogether in the wrong...Several weeks ago Mr. McCray asked me to give him my support. I told him that I would not make any attempt to prevent his nomination but it would be impossible to line up Purdue alumni in his support since it was believed that he was outspoken in his support of Dr. Stone and in his opposition to the alumni. He replied that he was not committed to any support of Dr. Stone and would be glad to get further information and would be guided more or less by my judgment in the matter. I do not attach much importance to those vague promises because he put himself on record long ago regarding the Stone issue.

Ade informed Ross that he expected McCray to be nominated. He also expected the Democrats to name John Isenbarger, a Purdue Trustee since 1918, to oppose McCray. "If so," Ade wrote, "I will be in a devil of a fix. If I support McCray I will have to throw down our best friend on the Board [Isenbarger] and I am more interested in Purdue University than anything else in Indiana. If I support Isenbarger I will have to desert my party and oppose the man who married my sister and I will be given credit for being actuated by small and selfish motives... (Tobin, 74-75).

Ross's response to the letter and solution to Ade's "fix," if any, is unknown.

In 1920, McCray won the Republican nomination and the election for Governor. Ade's sore feelings toward Stone remained unchanged.

Aside from all that—perhaps a welcome refuge for Ade—Doubleday, Page and Company, New York City, published a collection titled *Hand-Made Fables*. Ade also composed magazine fiction and articles in those years of semiretirement and editorship of *The Purdue Alumnus* magazine.

As early as January 1919, Ade had written "A Timely Message" for a *Purdue Alumnus News Letter and War Bulletin*. And in the January issue of the magazine itself he had contributed "The Flag—The Salty Seas—The Yankee Sailor." In the next five years, Ade wrote seventeen articles, editorials, or speeches that reached *The Purdue Alumnus* pages.

As editor, Ade used its pages to snipe away further at President Stone, sometimes in editorials signed "By George Ade," other times "By the Editor," as he did in an "Observations at Random" essay published in the January 1920 issue:

> In the December number of THE ALUMNUS Dr. Stone found occasion to say:
>
> "The constant multiplication of diversions and 'activities' among college students has reached the point where even the most liberal-minded of college and university authorities feel that great inroads are being made upon scholarship. Recognizing to the utmost the necessity for recreation and diversion among students one cannot help but feel that these things have gone to excess in our American colleges and that here at Purdue they are becoming one of the several factors which are operating against the realization of the best results in teaching."
>
> If Dr. Stone is finding fault with only the "activities" which are put under way for "recreation and diversion," the organized

alumni could hardly take reasonable exception to anything in the above paragraph.

Perhaps the alumni and Dr. Stone have pleasantly disagreed in the past because of a failure to get together on the definition of student "activities."

But when it comes to a consideration of the Student Union, of the athletic teams, of the daily paper, of the *Debris*, of Home Coming or Gala Week, or the Band, or the musical clubs, or the dramatic clubs—we cannot regard these sample activities as insignificant, even when compared with the most serious plans of the instructional departments...

Perhaps the difference of opinion between the administration and some of the bothersome alumni, regarding undergraduate privileges, has been due to a misunderstanding as to the real meaning of "activities."

Dr. Stone suggests that the student enterprises which jazz up all the machinery of the curriculum are devoted to "recreation and diversion."

The student "activities" for which the alumni have been pleading may carry with them some incidental "recreation and diversion," but primarily they are intended to unite the student body in loyal support of their *alma mater*, strengthen the community spirit, cultivate initiative, teach the value of team-work, make the college four years a sentimental journey as well as a hill-climb and give the young people that important training which comes only from many-sided contact with people of brains and ambition and sweet human qualities.

The alumni (years out of college and far removed from the campus) have not been lying awake nights worrying for fear the boys and girls at Purdue will fail to get their proper "recreation and diversion." They may be depended upon to find it, in one way or another…

The complaint of the alumni has been that the activities which seemed to them important, and almost essential, have been tripped up and reprimanded and put on half-rations and reminded of their imperfections until some of them have voluntarily walked across the levee and jumped into the Wabash River.

Their experiences in business and professional life have led them to believe that the "all-round man" who has initiative and ambition and some of the qualities of leadership enjoys a decided advantage over the mere "grind" who was spoon-fed at the University and did not mingle freely with other human beings.

You cannot improve the mental habits of a young fellow by hiding his dancing pumps. (*The Purdue Alumnus*, January 1920)

Topping's research led him to write that Ade's overall onslaught against Stone was "terrible to behold." The attacks mainly occurred in Ade's private letters, but Stone, Topping said, "resisted it with grace" (Topping, 181). The onslaught abruptly and shockingly ended a thousand miles away and eighteen months later. The Stones had paused high on Mount Eon. Margaret had called ahead to ask whether Winthrop had reached the peak more than two miles above sea level.

"I see nothing higher," he had replied.

Suddenly, loose rock slid away beneath his boots, and he fell nearly 1,000 feet to his death. Winthrop Stone was fifty-nine years old. Dazed beyond belief, Margaret inched back down to a narrow rock shelf, from which she could safely go nowhere else. Stranded there for nearly a week, she survived on a trickle of water from the rock wall. A rescue party led by a Swiss Alpine guide found and carried Margaret down to the base of Mount Eon for treatment by a doctor and nurse. She suffered from bruises and exposure. Margaret urged someone among the rescuers to telegraph her husband's Purdue secretary, Helen Hand, about the tragedy.

Once he heard the sad news, Joseph D. Oliver, President of the Purdue Trustees, telephoned Lafayette from his South Bend home to ask Henry Marshall to "look after matters at the university until [we can take] other action." Marshall, a Trustee only since February 1921, already chaired the Executive Committee.

The heavy-hearted Trustees met on August 4 and appointed Marshall Vice President (and later acting President) of Purdue until Stone's successor could be found. Oliver appointed Marshall, James W. Noel of Indianapolis, Dave Ross of Lafayette, Perry Crane of Lebanon, and himself to a search committee.

In Canada, the recovery team found Stone's crumpled remains on August 5 jammed between the sides of a seventeen-foot-deep crevice. The team climbed up to the peak of Mount Eon. There the members built and photographed a rock cairn and crowned it with Stone's ice axe and a box containing a sheet of paper inscribed:

> This monument was built in tribute to Dr. Winthrop E. Stone, President of Purdue University who on July 17, 1921 with his wife virtually completed the first ascent, reaching a point not more than fifty feet from this spot. Dr. Stone's axe crowned this monument. (Topping, 183)

President Stone's death shocked all connected with Purdue. Margaret Stone had to be escorted back to Indiana for Winthrop's funeral on August 13. Many an eye quietly turned to George Ade for reaction. He waxed diplomatic:

> Like everyone else who knew Dr. Stone intimately I am much grieved to learn of his death. We all recognize his great devotion

to the university and its interests and realize at the same time that the university has suffered a loss that will be hard to repair.

"Stone belonged to the nation," Topping would write years later. "He was much admired and respected in the national circles of higher education management and the world of scientists and scholars. Tributes to Stone poured in from all over the country" (Topping, 183).

Some viewed Henry Marshall, fifty-six, as a crusty, opinionated conservative, but his savvy business knowledge worked well for Purdue in this crisis. He stayed in the background and handled Purdue's affairs smoothly. He and Professor Stanley Coulter, president of the faculty, worked well together. Marshall stayed out of academic affairs. Both men helped in the candidate search.

One other Purdue man besides Ross and Ade had been detecting the hunger for Purdue Pride. He was that first band director, Paul Spotts Emrick. Emrick hit on the idea of beating on a really, really, really *big* drum to draw attention to his Purdue Marching Band. Members of Lafayette's Lodge 143 of the Benevolent and Protective Order of Elks pitched in to help Emrick get the money. In August 1921, Emrick paid eight hundred dollars to the Leedy Manufacturing Corporation in Indianapolis to make such a drum. In those days, the size of steer hide available for drumheads limited the dimensions of a drum. The huge hides located for use on this drum were said to have come from Argentina. When introduced in the 1921 football season as "The World's Largest Drum," it made the desired splash and remained a crowd-pleaser before interruption in 1940. The finished drum—its diameter in the range of ten feet (but kept secret by Purdue bandsmen) and its width of nearly four feet—weighed about three hundred pounds. In parades or on football fields, four designated bandsmen had to roll it around on a wheeled carriage while two drummers ran alongside pounding away on both skins. The drum with its uniquely deep boom served as a sort of heartbeat that kept the musicians in step.

⁓ ⁓

In May 1922, the Purdue Trustees elected Edward Charles Elliott, forty-seven, former Chancellor of the University of Montana, as Purdue's next president. Years later, Topping compiled a helpful summary:

> President Abraham Shortridge managed to get the doors of Purdue University open and classes started. President Emerson E. White answered the question of what Purdue was going to be. President James Smart picked up the school's tempo and made it a widely recognized engineering school. President Winthrop Stone balanced the academic scale and insisted on scholarly standards of high order. Elliott's charisma and administrative brilliance carried Purdue far beyond the wildest imaginings of his predecessors. (Topping, 185)

Elliott first met with the trustees on May 16, 1922. He asked for unanimous approval, an indefinite term, salary, moving and business travel expenses, a month of vacation, a residence suitable as a home yet large enough to meet a president's social demands, and an expense account. The trustees saw no problem.

Elliott formed a team around him that included Robert Bruce "R. B." Stewart, a brainy young money man; Trustee Dave Ross with great ideas, vision, and generosity; Agriculture Dean John Harrison Skinner; and Engineering Dean Andrey A. Potter, a Lithuanian-born graduate of the Massachusetts Institute of Technology. Topping wrote:

> This remarkable coterie steamed undaunted into the battles against ignorance. The Elliott-Ross-Stewart team was one of the most noteworthy, perhaps phenomenal, combinations of administrators in higher education. Certainly their impact on the direction Purdue traveled in the 1920s and 1930s is indelible. (Topping, 193)

Together at last

Dave Ross had learned in his Memorial Union fund drive that Purdue alumni wanted sports success, especially in football. They yearned for Purdue Pride. But Ross, in truth, thought far more strongly about research projects and quality teaching. He admitted that good football teams did add to a school's prestige and did inspire more alumni to give. He would need to feel out the new president, Elliott, about it all and go from there. Ross also wished to sound out Elliott about a long-range campus Master Plan. It would take money, land, and a planner.

During 1922, Ross obtained four more patents on his designs for three steering gears and one differential gear, all in September. To make his work more lucrative, the Ross Gear Directors released him from handing over any more patents and voted instead to pay him for them.

As Ross mulled over some ideas about expanding Purdue, the judge of Tippecanoe County Superior Court, Henry Vinton, came to mind. Ross had met and liked Vinton when they were members of the Alumni Association's Committee of Ten and had known him as a lawyer and judge in regard to Ross Gear and Fairfield matters. Vinton had been an 1885 Purdue science graduate, a lawyer since 1887, a judge since 1901, and a warm Purdue friend of George Ade, that wealthy and famous bachelor writer from Brook. When, in early 1922, Ross asked Vinton for an introduction to Ade, it took

Vinton by surprise. "You mean to say that two Purdue alumni as well known as you and George Ade aren't already friends? I'll be glad to introduce you, but that isn't necessary," Vinton said. "All you need to do is telephone George and tell him you want to see him. He'd be delighted." But Ross wanted a meeting in Vinton's courthouse chamber. Vinton made the call. Why sure, Ade said, and drove down the next day. He had heard good things about Ross and was pleased that they would meet at last.

They shook hands and small-talked. The talk covered farm life, old Purdue professors and literary clubs, the Board of Trustees, President Stone's death, the pros and cons of personal wealth, Republicans and Democrats, the bachelor life, and so on. Ross told Ade about gears and patents. Ade told Ross about writing "Fables" and other pieces for the movies. Ross asked to drive Ade out to where he had something to show him. They drove for ten minutes to a hilly, gullied old farm beyond the northwest corner of the campus. There they crawled through barbed wire and started to walk.

"I'm becoming a little curious to know what you're up to," Ade remarked.

"Just wait, you'll see," said Ross.

Ade noticed that Ross was soft-spoken, seemed to have a sense for the dramatic, and did not want to spoil an effect by tipping off anything too soon. They climbed a steep hillside covered with burdock and fennel. They walked over a stretch of high, level ground gouged here and there by little gullies. Shortly, they came upon a great hollow scooped out by Nature.

"Here it is," Ross announced.

"Here is what?"

"Here is where we [Trustees] will put our Purdue recreational field and stadium. You'll notice that much of the work of grading and providing a hillside of just the right slope for a stadium grandstand has already been done [by Nature.] It's about the same size as the ancient stadium of Athens. I had a man look up the dimensions. There isn't much difference."

Ade nodded. "Interesting. I was *in* that old stadium at Athens in 1898, and this *does* look to be about the same size."

"The contour here that makes it good for a stadium and grandstand would require expensive grading for housing," Ross said. "So it can be bought at a reasonable price. I have an option and can get sixty-five acres for a little under forty thousand dollars. All we have to do is buy it before the owner finds out he has a stadium on his premises."

"Just how does all this concern me?" Ade asked.

Ross chuckled. "The fact is I've been wondering if you'd be willing to join me to help finance the whole thing. How would you feel about that?"

Ade peered around appraising the landscape and building a stadium in his mind's eye. "Well, I've tried to take the lead in promoting worthy [Purdue] projects a time or two. I've said, '*Come on, boys, let's do this.*' But I never had much luck in getting others to follow. To help someone *else* would be a great relief. So my answer is yes. I'll be glad to go along with you" (Kelly, *Ross*, 72-75).

Then and there the two men who had newly met formed a partnership to go with their friendship. Ross was fifty-one years old, and Ade was fifty-six. They agreed to share equally in buying the land with the hope that one day the stadium would be built. "We must do it while we're still alive to see some games played in it," Ade said. It seemed to Ade to be a fine way for two old bachelors to "pay their fines to society" (Kelly, *Ade*, 239-240). Ade put an amusing creative writer's spin on that meeting with Ross a few months later in a message written for a Purdue Alumni Association dinner:

> After I arrived there [Ross] re-enacted a famous scene of which you may have heard. He took me up on a high mountain and tempted me. I had not the resisting powers of the One who resisted the original Satan and I fell. From the start I was just as enthusiastic as Dave. (*The Purdue Alumnus*, October 1922)

Any number of Purdue histories overly simplify the matter by saying that Dave Ross "got an option on an old dairy farm" for the site of the stadium. The fact is, the first Ross and Ade meeting appears to have dated to March or April 1922 when weather and ground conditions would allow them to walk the site. There followed a complicated series of large and small land deals. They involved the father-son real estate team of Robert Harding ("R. H.") Shook and Charles W. "Charlie" Shook. The two had started the Lafayette-based Shook Agency in 1915. The deals, some involving purchases, some simple swaps, took place among the Shooks, the dairy farm owner Frank Tilt, adjacent land owner Milton Sammons, and others.

Indications are that the stadium site, or part of it, tramped by Ross and Ade that day had belonged to a third party, identity no longer clear, who had sold it to the Shooks who in turn sold it to Ross and Ade. Meanwhile, Ross seems to have acquired other land from Tilt and Sammons and traded it, or some of it, to the Shooks for a fuller stadium site. Then parts of the old Tilt and Sammons properties, in the hands of the Shooks, became part of West Lafayette's "Hills and Dales" subdivision north of Stadium Avenue and east of Northwestern Avenue. The wheeling and dealing all had the long-range effect of promoting logical growth north and west for Purdue, and north for the City of West Lafayette.

An Indianapolis planner and urban design consultant named Lawrence V. Sheridan laid out the sixty-nine lots in Hills and Dales. The Shooks recorded Sheridan's plan with Tippecanoe County government in October 1923. Some of the street names, now past eighty years old, long ago became familiar—Ravinia, Chelsea, Bexley, Forest Hill, Ridgwood, Carrollton, Northridge, and Crestview. The first home went up on the northeast corner of Northwestern Avenue and Meridian Street. The superintendent of West Lafayette's public schools, Frank Burtsfield, persuaded his school board to invest in fourteen undeveloped Hills and Dales acres bounded by what Sheridan had marked as Ravinia, Grant, and Meridian for a future school site. For years that purchase appeared to be leading to a "Burtsfield's Folly," because it lay untouched for so long in such a remote area. Today it is the site of the West Lafayette Junior/Senior High School.

Many "housekeeping" deals, some merely quit claim deeds, had to take place to "even out" the shapes of some lots in Hills and Dales because of the several land buyers and sellers involved.

After he met Ross, George Ade returned to Hazelden Farm to his many daily routines. He spent months working with his actor friend Tom Meighan on full-length silent movies. *Our Leading Citizen*, a lighthearted political satire, marked the first time Ade had written more than titles for the screen. Meighan played "Lazy Dan" Bentley, a lawyer who would rather be fishing. *Back Home and Broke* came out later in 1922. This featured another performance by Meighan as rags-to-riches Tom Redding.

In Eliza Fowler Hall in early October 1922, Ade presented a Purdue convocation address about his remembrances of the Indiana poet James Whitcomb Riley (1849-1916.) Both the *Journal and Courier* of October 7 (Riley's birthday) and the *Purdue University Bulletin* in January 1923 reprinted Ade's talk. The newspaper headlined the speech "James Whitcomb Riley, As George Ade Knew Him and Estimates the Great Poet's Worth."

Single Blessedness and Other Observations from Doubleday, Page and Company came out on November 18, 1922. In a foreword, Ade wrote "in this book you will find, possibly disguised and altered, certain dissertations which first found their way to the public through the columns of *The American Magazine*, the *Cosmopolitan Magazine, The Saturday Evening Post*, the *Century Magazine* and *Life*. Also there is some miscellany first exhibited in private and now put into type for the first time" (Russo, 89). Among Ade's "dissertations" were "Babies," "Broadway," "College Students," "Looking Back from Fifty," "Vacations," "Oratory," "Musical Comedy," "Christmas in London," and "Golf."

During the winter of 1922-1923, the editors of the coming edition of the Purdue senior yearbook—*The 1923 Debris*—asked Ade to write about his freshman year in 1883. Ade of course complied—from his winter home in Miami Beach—and began "Only Forty Years Ago This Summer" with the words:

> I am sitting down in Florida to write an article for the *Debris*. Outside, the sun is shining brightly and a warm breeze is moving the palm trees, and the golfers are flitting about in their knickerbockers and there is no work in the atmosphere.

> Summoning all my scant knowledge of mathematics I succeed in discovering that it is just forty years ago this September that I matriculated at Purdue. It is hard to realize and harder still to admit...

> We had a total attendance of about two hundred, including the prep department...

> We are proud of Purdue, but it is not the school that we knew long ago. Possibly we find an inward satisfaction in the belief that we helped to lay the foundation of the great community which is illustrated and described in the present [*Debris*] volume.

Another silent movie based on Ade's work titled *Woman Proof* came out in October 1923. The Famous Players-Lasky Corporation also released it as *All Must Marry*. In this movie, Meighan played Tom Rockwood who got a traffic ticket while looking at a pretty woman. Other notables in the cast—with fame in their futures—included Louise Dresser and Mary Astor. The movies each brought Ade royalties of about forty thousand dollars.

In late December 1923, the Samuel French Company, New York City, published the texts of three of Ade's old one-act plays, *The Mayor and the Manicure, Nettie,* and *Speaking to Father*. Ade had written them as early as 1914. In the case of *Mayor*, the Indianapolis Dramatic Club had performed it during 1917-1918. In 1919, Ade had permitted its performance for a benefit for the Actors' Fund of America. Ade's bibliographer Dorothy Russo later noted that the National Broadcasting Company asked for permission to "televise" both *Mayor* and *Father* in May 1939, in the earliest days of the TV medium. Ade's response to the requests is unknown.

When he was young, a tall, slender athlete named Nelson Kellogg had run two-mile races for University of Michigan track teams. Kellogg in his day had been the best two-miler in the Midwest. After graduation he gained experience both as a college coach and athletic director. In 1919, he left the University of Iowa to be the Athletic Director at Purdue. As his predecessors Cutts and Nicol had found out, it was no easy job.

They all had faced problems that differed from other schools in the Western Conference or "Big Ten." Purdue was one-third to one-half the size of big state universities like the ones in Illinois, Michigan, Ohio, Minnesota, and Wisconsin. To have only one man eligible for sports against schools that had two or three was a ratio that dimmed Purdue's hopes of winning much. Purdue enrolled only students in agriculture and engineering—none in liberal arts, commerce and business, law, or medicine. Ag schools like Purdue enrolled scant talent in football or other sports. Ag students nearly all came from the Kentlands and the Brooks and the Brookstons where they played few, if any, high school games, and players never worked with good coaches in any fundamentals. Engineering class loads were heavy. The slide-rule-carrying students might labor in shops, labs, and classes from eight a.m. to four p.m. Rounding up a football team for practice from that material in that setting was difficult.

Purdue by now had gone through football coaches "Andy" Smith, Cleo O'Donnell, Arthur Scanlon, and for one year, a Native American Lakota Indian named William Lone Star Dietz. Dietz's team lost six of seven games in 1921. Those coaches all knew football and how to teach the game. They worked hard, but the Purdue job overwhelmed them. Another factor was that so few Indiana high schools played much football before the 1920s.

When Kellogg reached Purdue, he, like Dave Ross, saw the need for expansion. Kellogg drew up plans for a football stadium north of Stuart Field along West Lafayette's Seventh Street. President Stone's death and other factors caused Kellogg to shove expansion talk to the "back burner." But then Dave Ross began inflaming the Trustees with his long-range thinking, and the new President came on board. The Trustees began to see better uses for the Stuart Field land and the need for a Master Plan that might—just might—include a better stadium.

Interested more in growth than sports, Ross and the Trustees asked Kellogg to find a good place for athletics when Stuart Field had to go. Kellogg recommended that rugged old farm to the northwest.

For the 1922 season, Kellogg—with Trustees' approval after Stone's death and still in the absence of a president—hired as football coach twenty-nine-year-old James M. "Jimmy" Phelan. Phelan had been a three-year starter at Notre Dame before flying as a pilot in World War I. His first Purdue team in 1922 lost five times and tied once in a seven-game season. It won two games out of eight in 1923. But then the progress began to set in.

Walter Scholer

Dave Ross went right on working on the idea of a Master Plan for Purdue. He had his man in mind for the job of drawing it up, too. The man was a thirty-year-old Lafayette architect named Walter Scholer. A native of Jay County, Indiana, youngest of a Swiss immigrant couple with three daughters and ten sons, Walter had come to Lafayette in 1919 to work in a firm that became Nicol, Scholer and Hoffman. These architects had done some work for Purdue as early as 1920. Their firm stayed intact until Scholer left it to start his own in 1925.

"It was my good fortune," Scholer said, "to meet with the [Purdue] people, some of the Trustees like Dave Ross and Henry Marshall, and it fell to my lot to begin to do work at Purdue. It really started in 1922. That is, the idea [for a Campus Plan] started in 1922—not the actual work."

> Dave Ross called me up and said he would like to pick me up in his car if I would be on the corner of Third and Main. He wanted to show me a farm he and George Ade were about to buy. It was a dairy farm pretty much of a dilapidated looking place, too, with some barbed wire fence around it. But Dave Ross could see the hollowed out place where a stadium might be built without much excavation...

> This led to the campus Master Plan. Dave said he wanted a pen and ink sketch showing how a stadium might look connected to the rest of the university. I agreed to make it, and as I got work-

ing on it, thinking about it, I wondered what I was going to do? I mean, you could show the stadium, but the university was then all south of [the biology building.] It was a cornfield. I asked Dave what I should show in between those areas and he said, "Well, just show some buildings. Simple." It bothered me more than it did him. (Scholer, 9-10)

The Purdue Trustees held their first meeting, the minutes of which mention anything about a Master Plan, on March 14, 1922. Scholer recalled:

After a general discussion...Mr. Ross offered the following motion:

"I move that the Building Committee be empowered to get a survey of the buildings of Purdue University." Mr. Noel seconded the motion then made the following motion. "I move further that the Building Committee be requested to submit plans and specifications for heating and lighting systems for the campus, and the estimated cost [and] I move that the Building Committee be empowered to submit a comprehensive plan of the grounds as to driveways, buildings, shrubbery and pipes." (Scholer, 11)

Meanwhile, by 1922, Ross and his alumni committee had collected more than $800,080 in payments and pledges for the Memorial Union. Using $400,000 worth of uncollected pledges as collateral, Purdue borrowed $200,000 more by issuing ten series of $1,000 notes, twenty notes in each series, paying six percent interest, with one series maturing each year for ten years. For starters, Dave Ross and Henry Marshall each bought twenty thousand dollars' worth of notes. Purdue scheduled the Memorial Union groundbreaking during Commencement Week in June 1922. Ross turned the ceremonial first spade full of dirt.

George Ade that spring accepted multiple responsibilities. He served as Executive Secretary of the Purdue Alumni Association, Chairman of the 1922 Gala Week Committee, Editor of the *Purdue Alumnus* magazine, and "three or four other titles." Confessing that this made him "hardly capable of writing unbiased comments concerning the wonderful reunion of grads, former students and other boosters last month," he wrote "My Impressions of Gala Week" anyway for the July *Purdue Alumnus*. Among his comments:

> Each year the pilgrimage to Purdue becomes more and more a sentimental journey...After a man has been out of college for thirty-five years a visit to the Campus arouses emotions which are more or less tinged with melancholy. The old grad is happy to meet a few of his long-ago associates, but all the time he feels himself checking up, rather sorrowfully, the appalling list of absentees. Unless the program for returning visitors offers a real entertainment instead of didactic gloom, a so-called Gala Week may easily take on all of the merry aspects of Decoration Day in a cemetery. I believe and shall continue to believe that alumni who come to Purdue during Commencement Week need not be solemnly reminded as to their "responsibilities" in connection with the University...In recent years the policy of the Alumni Association has been to provide diversion and good cheer...The policy has justified itself and should be continued. (*The Purdue Alumnus*, July 1922)

Members of the Purdue Alumni Club in Indianapolis were among the first to welcome President Edward C. Elliott. A dinner took place in the Lincoln Hotel on September 6, 1922. That night Purdue's former acting president, Trustee Henry Marshall, revealed what had been printed in the program as "The Secret." The secret was that Ross and Ade had bought and would give Purdue the sixty-five acre farm. Marshall rated its topography "ideal for a new stadium" with room also for at least three baseball diamonds, tennis courts, and possibly a nine-hole golf course.

Illness caused Ade to miss that dinner, so Judge Vinton read Ade's written message about the gift of land:

> For several years the University has wished to own a sixty-five acre tract lying somewhat northwest of Stuart Field and almost directly north of the built-up residence district just west of the Campus. This tract was once a dairy farm but it consists largely of undulating clay hillsides with a border of timber at the west and the Morehouse concrete road cutting through it along the east side. Because of the hilly character of this tract it has never been opened as a subdivision although West Lafayette has built very closely up to it.
>
> Mr. Ross went out and looked over this tract...He climbed to the highest part of the ground where there is a magnificent view of the Campus and West Lafayette and the distant city of Lafayette, and he looked about him and regarded the almost mountainous character of the scenery and he made an important discovery. He discovered that an all-wise Providence, knowing that some day Purdue University would be built on the table land just below and would be in need of an athletic field, had made all the necessary preliminary arrangements. In other words, some glacial drift, probably a hundred thousand years ago, had hollowed out that great hillside and excavated it for a Purdue bowl and it had been waiting all these centuries for Dave Ross to come along and discover it.
>
> It was months ago that Dave...began looking for ways and means to acquire that tract and he kept the secret of his discovery pretty much to himself. The few friends that he called in to confirm his judgment...were highly enthusiastic. They could not help but be. Dave conferred with Mr. Marshall, then with other members of the Board, and found them willing to vote for a purchase of the property. They offered to call a special meeting of the Trust-

ees. This was along in July of this year. By that time Dave had secured from the owner a definite option on the entire tract, the purchase price to be, with a clear title, $39,000.

The more Dave studied the whole proposition the more strongly he felt that taking over this tract and planning and building the bowl should be an alumni proposition. He wanted to have a hand in the actual work and began looking around for someone who would join him in giving the big project a fair start. The honor fell upon me...

We went ahead and bought the property and it is now in our name. It is not entirely paid for, but that is a detail which should worry no one but the bank. It is our intention to turn this tract over to Purdue and there will not be many strings attached. There will be a very definite understanding, however, that the natural amphitheater crowning the tract will, as soon as possible, be converted into a modern bowl or stadium sufficient to take care of the largest crowd that might be attracted to Purdue by a football game or a pageant. At this time Dave and I cannot be very definite as to the plans for building the bowl or the entire financing of the proposition. We are going to do all we can to help carry out the whole understanding. We are selfish enough to hope that when the bowl is completed and dedicated our names will be associated with it in some way.

Fortunately we have two of the shortest names in existence and if they are to be hyphenated, the combination will be Ross-Ade and we will call the amphitheater a "bowl" instead of a "stadium." The name of Ross should be first because the whole project was conceived by Dave and he has carried out all of the business details and made possible the whole enterprise. I welcome the opportunity to make this public announcement of our plans because I want you to know that the big idea belongs to Dave, and I am simply trying to go along with him. (*The Purdue Alumnus*, October 1922)

President Elliott stood and led the applause. Elliott then said he had "no personal policy for the leadership of Purdue except that of remembering every working hour that I am the trusted servant of the people of Indiana as they are represented by a devoted and far-seeing Board of Trustees...I have no policy save that of keeping the faith with all of those such as Dave Ross and George Ade who have the faith in the destiny of Purdue." He continued:

> Be assured that I am a firm believer in collegiate athletics. I cannot, however, either as President or as a citizen, lend aid to any plans for college sport that make a sport of the college.
>
> I have been studying the plans devised and put into operation by the Alumni Association for the promotion of athletics in the University. It is indeed personally gratifying to be able to say here tonight that these plans bear the stamp of men who are jealous of the good name of Purdue University. They want teams that win. But those teams must be made up entirely of men who are professional students and amateur athletes and not composed in any part of men who are amateur students and professional athletes.
>
> Purdue and Purdue men will, I am confident, contribute a full share towards the solution of the present difficult athletic problem. That problem is big; but Purdue is bigger. And whenever the goddess of victory crowns a Purdue man or a Purdue team, that man and that team can look the world in the face with a clear conscience and accept the reward with clean hands.

Dave Ross then rose to do a little selling. A Purdue Athletic Association would be formed, he said. It was to be a legal fund-raising and tax-sheltering brainstorm of R. B. Stewart, the new Elliott staff's young financial whiz. Ross said if this Athletic Association could sell 300 life memberships at $200 each—it would raise

$60,000—then he would give an additional ten thousand dollars toward stadium construction.

Within an hour 228 alumni wrote checks or signed pledges for $45,600. Life members, among other perks, would get preferred seats in the new stadium.

Athletic Director Kellogg responded to the alumni dinner news with a signed article in *The Purdue Alumnus* saying, in part:

> The gift is the first gun in a campaign for a new and improved athletic field. The campaign will not be completed, of course, until the field is ready for occupancy by the various athletic teams... Lying as it does within two blocks of the present field [the gift] opens at the University's very door a tract particularly suited for intercollegiate sports...In the southwest corner running north and south will be the football stadium enclosed by the running track with a 220-yard straight-of-way. This in turn will be surrounded by the concrete stadium of which the larger half will lie in the natural gully which will be excavated to the proper size. It is estimated that the use of this gully will save about one-half the cost of the stadium.
>
> The level ground along Northwestern Avenue and along the south edge of the field will give ample room for tennis courts, a varsity baseball diamond with its necessary grandstands; at least two other diamonds for the second team and freshman varsity, and the necessary practice football fields. The northern half of the property is diversified enough so as to give opportunity for a golf course, probably of nine holes.
>
> The new tract will take care of all outdoor intercollegiate sports and in addition will furnish opportunity for the entire student body to take part in tennis and golf.

I think at this time it [also] is well to put before the alumni the future needs of the Athletic Department which are divided into three parts: (1) The outdoor intercollegiate activities which will be amply taken care of by the new field; (2) the outdoor intramural activities, for which there is no room on the present field and which will have to be taken care of elsewhere; and (3) the indoor activities which have completely outgrown the present Gymnasium.

While it is not possible for the alumni to finance the new Gymnasium and the new intramural grounds, it is possible for them to bring the necessary amount of pressure upon the Board of Trustees and the Legislature of the State to furnish adequate facilities.

I express my sincere thanks to Mr. Ross and Mr. Ade for the magnificent way in which they have come to our support. I find it the one thing which has renewed my hopes for future successful athletic teams at Purdue.

When the Purdue Trustees met on November 3, 1922, they passed Dave Ross's motion that President Elliott and Henry Marshall be appointed to hire a "competent architect." The architect would draw a long-range plan for the main campus, the agriculture campus, and the empty land in the proposed "Ross-Ade recreational field." Given those marching orders, Elliott and Marshall invited Walter Scholer to draw it all up (Freehafer, 10). This was the first time that Scholer began to figure in Purdue University's future.

Since hiring Elliott, the Trustees also had needed to acquire a home for the new President and his family, a place suitable both for entertaining and rearing four children. The Trustees at first rented for the Elliotts a house at 500 University Street in West Lafayette but kept looking for a permanent location. In July 1923, Purdue paid $44,400 for a vacant yet more imposing hilltop home at 515 South Seventh Street in Lafayette. This home was but a short walk from Ross's "winter home" in the city. Shortly thereafter, Ross and bachelor physician Richard B. Wetherill, a sometimes donor to Purdue's Department of Chemistry, bought a vacant lot next to the Elliotts' home for twenty-five hundred dollars and gave it to Purdue to add to the President's land (Freehafer, 11).

Before long, Elliott made it an almost daily habit to hike from his Lafayette home over to his campus office about two miles away. The route took him over streets and sidewalks down a hill, through downtown Lafayette, across the concrete Main Street Bridge at the Wabash River, then up State Street hill to the West Lafayette business "village," and a few more level blocks to the campus.

"Occasionally," Topping learned, "Elliott also walked home along the same route at the end of the day. Frequently he turned down offers of rides from friends and acquaintances. He enjoyed the walks because they were a substitute for earlier times with his sons prowling the Montana mountains on ten- to fifteen-mile weekend hikes" (Topping 192).

During 1923, in his Ross Building office, Scholer labored over the Purdue Trustees' order for a Master Plan. When finished with one, Scholer tried to describe it for the trustees but came up short.

"Dave Ross, after the meeting, told me I did a darn poor job of explaining a good thing," Scholer recalled. Ross was nearly twenty years Scholer's senior. "He thought that I—like so many people technically educated self or otherwise—could not tell in a fluent manner what it was all about. He helped me an awful lot by that remark, and Dave didn't spare words when he was talking to me" (Scholer, 10).

Scholer's first Master Plan purposely showed no dormitories for women, because Purdue did not own land being considered for dorms. "At that time Dave Ross was battling [property owner] Dick Russell in the courts, and I think it took seven years to get that land," Scholer said. "Dave didn't want to be presumptuous and show something [on the Master Plan] that the courts hadn't settled yet. Dick Russell owned land way back [to the west.] Purdue finally got it, but it took, as I recall, seven years. Eminent domain. Purdue sometimes had trouble with that" (Scholer, 21).

"Dave [next] wanted a 'bird's-eye view.' We would call it an airplane [aerial] view now but it was a bird's-eye view then showing how this [spread-out campus] all hooked up. I made a small sketch showing an extension of the north and south drive [Marstellar Street]. I extended the center line of that north to a mid-point on Northwestern Avenue and then, bisecting that same line, formed a common point with an avenue [Stadium] going out [west] to the recreational field and the dormitory areas [under consideration.] It was just a happenstance, so there was the framework" (Scholer, 17).

The U.S. government issued six more patents to Dave Ross between January and October 1923. They involved designs for a steering wheel hub and spoke, a hydraulic steering gear, a road shock regulating device for steering gears, an anti-rattling bushing, bevel gear transmission, and variable-speed transmission gearing.

George Ade, during the same months, still busily recalled the days gone by and finished that "Only Forty Years Ago This Summer" piece about his freshman year at Purdue—the writing job he had started in Florida—for the *1923 Debris*.

> Looking back after all these years I am sure that we [in 1883] were what the modern youth would designate as "yaps." But we had a lot of fun, and cultivated a real community spirit, and were very loyal to the University, and quite sure that it would turn out to be something important some day. We were on more intimate terms with our instructors, and there was probably a closer feeling of fellowship than there is today.

If you could have seen West Lafayette and Purdue as we saw it in 1883—a straggling settlement of houses and a few lonesome brick buildings out in a field—you would understand why we old-timers come back to the campus awed and dazed and tongue-tied and oppressed by a sense of our own unworthiness. We are proud of Purdue, but it is not the school that we knew long ago. (*1923 Purdue Debris*)

Under laws then in effect, Purdue could not sell bonds to get cash to turn the old farm into a stadium and playing fields. Purdue had to rely on state appropriations or gifts to provide buildings and facilities. So the cash gifts from Ross and Ade would pay for only part of the project, and this raised problems. For a solution, President Elliott (with R. B. Stewart's shrewd coaching) suggested to Ross and Ade that a separate *corporation* be founded. It needed to be controlled by the University. It could then sell bonds and retire them and prevent putting any financial burden on Purdue. The Trustees agreed with the scheme. Therefore, a Ross-Ade Foundation came into being.

In November 1923, Ross and Ade, to speed the stadium project, offered an additional ten thousand dollars each if 300 more alumni and friends of Purdue would buy life seats in the stadium for $200 each. A letter about that proposal went out to a thousand alumni. The letter invited the thousand to a dinner in the Home Economics Building on campus. More than 400 attended. Ross and Ade made their new offer. They explained that a minimum of $80,000 more were needed to build the stadium that would cost between $150,000 and $160,000. The result was the subscription of 173 more life seats (totaling $34,600.) This, with the newest cash gifts from Ross and Ade, made a total of $54,600. The diners also each pledged to solicit five to ten others to raise the rest of the needed funds. All understood that the Ross-Ade Foundation was set up because, as a private corporation, it could borrow money while, as a state institution, Purdue could not. All told, alumni and friends eventually bought 201 of the "life seats" raising $40,200.

The diners took votes to organize the Ross-Ade Foundation "to promote Purdue's educational purposes" by taking steps to "develop the physical welfare of students and acquire and disburse funds to carry out its plans." The assembly chose a nine-man board of directors for the Foundation:

• Three members of the Ross-Ade Foundation: George Ade, J. R. Safford of Chicago, and J. E. Hall of Indianapolis.

• Three Purdue administrators: President Elliott, Athletic Director Nelson Kellogg and the student president of the Memorial Union, R. H. Watson.

• Three Purdue Trustees: Dave Ross and Henry Marshall, from Lafayette, and James Noel, of Indianapolis.

The Foundation Directors elected Elliott president, Marshall vice president, and Jack E. Walters, general manager of the Memorial Union, secretary. The Directors also voted to reserve ten lifetime seats in the stadium for Ross and Ade to use.

Then they chose a consulting construction committee. The choices, all "Purdue men," were Engineering Dean A. A. Potter, Scholer's architect partner Charles W. Nicol of Lafayette, and A. B. Cohen of New York.

With the Ross-Ade Foundation leadership in place another useful gift arrived. It was a deed for three West Lafayette city lots. Professor George Spitzer in Purdue's Horticulture Department gave the land on the north side of what would become Stadium Avenue. Designers and builders eventually used those lots for south entrances and drives to the stadium. Still later, the lots became the site of the men's dormitory known as Cary Hall and, eventually, Cary Quadrangle. Spitzer Court, the courtyard within the Quadrangle, remembers the donor couple.

Even before Purdue broke ground for the stadium, Dave Ross envisioned a field house containing a gym, pool, indoor tennis courts, and equipment. "Purdue should not want athletics to consist too largely of spectators," he said (Kelly, *Ross*, 76).

Scholer did not get the stadium architect job for good reason. "There were not too many stadiums of that type built at that time," Scholer said. "A firm in Cleveland planned most of the college stadiums in the country. Dave Ross had the say-so and...I agreed with him that stadium design was a special line that we [Lafayette architects] had no experience in, and so the Trustees appointed this firm in Cleveland" (Scholer, 23).

The Ross-Ade Foundation Directors next met on December 15 and decided to get going with stadium building. The Directors engaged the Osborn Engineering Company of Cleveland to be the architects and engineers. The Osborn draftsmen drew plans and solicited and reviewed competitive bids for the work. The job went to low bidder Alva E. "Cap" Kemmer, the Lafayette contractor and building supply company owner, Purdue alumnus, and Boilermaker supporter and friend.

Ross-Ade

For George Ade the year 1924 combined looks both backward and ahead. The Samuel French Company in New York City published his *Father and the Boys* on January 24. The comedy-drama dated back to about 1908. A motion picture version already was in the talking stage. Fox would put it on a screen—with sound—in 1931 and title it *Young As You Feel.*

In March, the Samuel French people published the eighty-two-page script of *The County Chairman.* Ade wrote the comedy-drama in 1904, and the Purdue Harlequin Club played it in 1911. The Samuel French Company also printed *Just Out of College*, Ade's three-act light comedy.

For a while naming the promised new stadium became a problem. Ade embraced the idea of "Ross-Ade Bowl," but it was not going to be a bowl, it was going to be an open-ended stadium. Besides, Dave Ross disliked people who "gain immortality the cheap way" by having their name on a public building. Yet, having already consented to naming the Ross-Ade Foundation, Ross let his name be used with Ade's again. They settled upon "Ross-Ade Stadium." The slopes would be horseshoe-shaped, open at the south, rounded at the north, and thus technically a stadium rather than a closed-in "bowl."

"I like that idea," Ade said of the choice. "In fact, I'm utterly shameless about it. Ross and I are old bachelors and will not have any children." He then added with a wink: "It is even doubtful if we'll have any *grandchildren!* Students who come here a few years from now will know nothing about a fellow named Ade who wrote Fables in Slang and plays, but if my name is linked with Ross's on the stadium, they'll be tipped off that someone named Ade was identified in some way with Purdue University. I'd like that. Ross's name should come first since it was his idea and he did most of the work of putting it over. Luckily our names are short and euphonious together. Ross-Ade Stadium sounds good to me" (Kelly, *Ross*, 75). Ade did worry just a little that "Ross-Ade" sounded like a soft drink like lemonade or orangeade or, years later, Kool-Aid. But "Ross-Ade" it became, and "Ross-Ade" it remained.

At their meeting on April 9, 1924, the Purdue Trustees heard Dave Ross "strongly recommend" that Scholer's Master Plan be made public and that Indiana's ninety-two County Agents be given copies of it to show people what Purdue hoped to accomplish. Ross also moved that President Elliott procure a table and a glass cover for the original Master Plan and a frame with glass for the bird's eye view version of it. "[Elliott] had a table built," Scholer recalled, "and the plan went under a half-inch thick glass that the Trustees met around in old Fowler Hall, second floor" (Scholer, 22).

Then Ross requested Scholer to make a larger copy of the plan that could be traced and copied on oilcloth. Ross called this eight-foot-long roll his "bed sheet." On it Scholer colored existing campus buildings gold and marked the proposed future ones black. Ross would unfold this sheet and thumb tack it on a wall at meetings. Audiences could understand it from across a room.

On June 2, 1924, Kemmer put his overall-clad men to work on the stadium Some wore clodhopper boots and wide brimmed hats or pith helmets to ward off heat from the high June sun. The clanking iron wheels of steam shovels churned up plumes of brown dust. Their stacks belched black smoke while the shovels dug into the tough clay to reshape the hill. Kemmer installed electric floodlights so that work could go on in the cooler night air. Excavation of 45,000 cubic yards of mostly clay during the hot weather complicated the job. The men poured 5,000 yards of concrete. In an eighteen-day stretch, they spread 100,000 square feet of loam eleven inches deep, then seeded it with Kentucky bluegrass for the playing field.

The finished stadium extended 675 feet long and 425 feet across from top wall to top wall. There would be east and west grandstands, each longer than the 100-yard playing field. The grandstands would be connected by a round, sloping north end without—but ready for—more concrete, steel, and seats. The level, open south end would provide the entrances from and access to public streets. About fifty carloads of cinders and 250 loads of sand, gravel, and other material had to be wheeled in, spread, and graded. The work force ranged from 180 to 300 men. In five months, the Kemmer people built the stadium with bolted-in wooden bleacher seats for 13,000 fans, and groomed the playing field.

Athletic Director Kellogg scheduled four home football games for Coach Phelan's third Boilermaker team of 1924. Purdue played the first three home games, against Wabash, Rose Polytechnic, and DePauw, at the thirty-two-year-old Stuart Field. Kellogg saved the final game on November 22 against rival Indiana University for the dedication game for Ross-Ade Stadium. A photograph of the finished stadium taken from a low flying Army airplane showed the tidy, scraped, and smoothed landscape around the gleaming white concrete stands facing the well clipped playing field. The goalposts had been whitewashed. Empty land extended south from the stadium entrances toward a few West Lafayette homes and Purdue campus buildings. Beyond the stadium to the east the aerial photo showed, past Northwestern Avenue, the first winding streets and a few scattered homes and trees in what became West Lafayette's stylish Hills and Dales Subdivision.

The picture from the airplane illustrated the spirit of the progressive times. On January 16, 1924, Purdue had mortared into place the cornerstone on its Electrical Engineering building on Northwestern Avenue. On February 18, West Lafayette's Town Board had voted for a reorganized Police Department, motorized vehicles and equipment for the Street Department, and several new street names. In mid-March, a Lafayette Merchants and Manufacturers' Association had favored annexing West Lafayette to create one city. Association members also backed removing downtown Lafayette railroad grade crossings and building a central railroad depot. None of those futuristic ideas came to pass.

On March 27, 1924, at a public meeting in the red brick West Lafayette High School on Fowler Avenue, people had chosen April 1 for an election. The voters would decide whether to scrap *town* status and *town board* government and become a fifth-class *city* run by an elected mayor, clerk-treasurer, and city council. The outcome had been close, but the people had voted 651 to 642 for city status subject to an election of officers on May 27.

Between May 1 and 3, Purdue marked its fiftieth anniversary with Gala Week concerts and lectures. Guests included eighty-year-old Harvey W. Wiley, a popular young bike-riding, student-friendly, baseball-playing professor on the original 1874 faculty. Purdue now boasted 3,234 students and 323 faculty members. Purdue Librarian William Murray Hepburn and History Professor Louis Martin Sears already were at work writing the book to be titled *Fifty Years of Progress*.

At the request of the University, both Ade and McCutcheon as notable alumni took part in the celebrations. A pamphlet tied with silk cord contained Ade's spoken tribute titled "Purdue Fifty Years Old." McCutcheon illustrated printed copies of the speech with a drawing "If John Purdue Could See Us Now." Ade distilled his remarks into six paragraphs:

> We have always thought of it and talked of it as a "new school." Plenty of ambition and a glowing future, but a shortage of traditions and ivy. We who were on the campus during the first decade,

when the so-called University was a faltering infant and the cube-shaped brick buildings stood lonesomely apart and only a straggle of students could be detected on the campus—we who remember the gibes and jeers of the other Indiana colleges, and the prophecies of failure, and the faintheartedness of our friends in Lafayette, we can hardly believe that we have come to the semi-centennial and that our beloved *alma mater* has become a great cluster of rugged citadels and, best of all, a triumphant vindication of all who believed in it away back yonder.

Engineering, the applied sciences, and scientific agriculture are no longer the timid stepchildren of the educational world. A good many years ago Indiana University, DePauw, and Wabash began to admit that a university may have standing and influence even if it does not specialize on the dead languages and oratory. Purdue alumni and ex-students have migrated to the four corners of the world and have made good. That is the most important fact that we are called upon to celebrate on our fiftieth birthday.

John Harper took his degree in the old Military Hall in 1875. Some of the Lafayette people came over to attend the novel ceremony and John Purdue was on hand to witness the small beginning of his pet enterprise and give some fatherly advice. He was rugged, plain spoken, choke-collared, practical—very much of the old school. He had large hopes for Purdue. He said, that day in 1875, that he rather expected that some day or other Purdue would be one of the "most useful high schools in Indiana." He did not dream that some day the school bearing his name would crown all the hills of West Lafayette, and be respected and honored from sea to sea.

Perhaps John Purdue is looking down from somewhere and making note of the miracles that have been accomplished in his name. What we wish is that he could be here during semi-centennial week, accompanied by... all the other patriarchs and builders of the local community, so that they might rejoice with us over the working out of a great plan which they knew in its infancy...

Purdue is almost as large as Princeton and it is several times the size of influential old schools that have made luminous history.

We who belong to Purdue have a right to be content with all of the physical aspects of the University, the curriculum, the teaching staff, and the working plans. Our part is not to advise those in authority, but to keep alive a spirit of loyalty to the school as a whole, to glorify the past and help build for the future. "Bully for Old Purdue!" means something now. Fifty years old and going strong! (*The Purdue Alumnus*, May 1924)

Later in the year, Purdue put into operation a key part of the Master Plan. It was a central, coal-fired power and heating plant with a towering red brick smokestack two hundred and fifty feet high.

At Hazelden Farm in late October 1924, George Ade hosted his biggest crowd ever for a political function. His friend—lawyer and financier Charles G. Dawes (1865-1951)—made the closing speech of his campaign for U.S. Vice President. He won. And out in New York City the Samuel French Company published the texts for four of Ade's more successful plays-turned-movies—*The College Widow, The County Chairman, Just Out of College,* and *Father And the Boys.*

Ade also finished writing an article for the homecoming game program in Ross-Ade Stadium and called it "A Short Story about the Stadium." It appeared on page nine. Meanwhile, Ade was receiving accolades from readers of his unusual new essay in *Cosmopolitan* magazine. Ade titled the piece "The Yankee's Prayer." He wrote in a form that Protestant churchgoers in post-war America could relate to:

> Help me to get things straight. Give me an outlook on the whole world. Open my eyes to the truth regarding the material wealth and the golden opportunity of my native land, but strike me with swift punishment if I roll my r's in speaking the word "great" or feed the vanity of my ignorant neighbors who think that the U.S.A. has become a symbol of perfection.

> Help me to understand that the comforts and luxuries and pleasant accessories of modern life abound in my bailiwick because my friends and I have moved into a new country in which there is much recent wealth to be divided. Teach me to modify my sense of importance with an humble thankfulness.

> Save me from delusions regarding continued and abounding prosperity. Give me the wisdom to preach against wastefulness.

> Incline me to avoid boasting, but keep me from being an idle weeper or a mere faultfinder. Let me read history aright and learn that a people seldom can be made happy and prosperous by involved and ponderous legislation. Assist me and my associates to look to ourselves and not to Congress.

> Give me patience and tolerance and the strength to brace myself against sudden and hysterical and gusty changes of popular feeling. Let me not construe the rule of the majority into a fool axiom that the majority is always right. Cause me to bear in mind that in every age of which we have record, an unpopular minority advocated measures which, later on, were accepted by the majority.

Protect me against labels and memberships and binding obligations which will submerge me as an individual. Save me from being enslaved or hampered by catch phrases. May I never take orders which will make me a coward in the sight of my conscience. Let it not be said of me that I "belong" to a political party.

Lead me to an understanding of the new meaning of "service." Help me to believe that the man prospers best and longest who is concerned as to the welfare of the people about him. Compel me to see that our organization is a huge experiment in cooperation and not a scramble for prizes.

Give me large portions of charity with which to regard the performances of my easy-going countrymen. Help me to judge every act by the intent back of it.

Increase my usefulness by giving me an X-ray vision, so that I may detect the goodness and deservedness of those who do not wear my kind of clothes, worship in my church, or live in my township. Make it open to me that integrity and patriotism cannot be monopolized.

Keep me from trouble, but make me dangerous if I am drawn into a fight. Convince me that every battle should be fought to a finish, so there will not be any argument later on.

Let me remain level headed when I am envied by the people of other lands, but do not take away the things which arouse their envy. Permit me to retain my heritage as long as I know how to take care of it.

At Purdue, the University opened the first phase of the Memorial Union building at State and Grant Streets. Jack Walters, a 1922 graduate, took office as manager. The secretary of the new Ross-Ade Foundation and a protégé of Dave Ross, Walters also had been president of the student body (Freehafer, 15).

Away but never far from Purdue affairs, Dave Ross remained the inventor, engineer, and man of industry. His spirit, if not his presence, had led both the Ross Gear and Tool Company and the Fairfield Manufacturing Company. Year after year, he had been getting patents for steering and power transmission gears and the advanced machines that could grind and polish them. American factories were turning out ever larger and heavier cars and trucks. These vehicles rolled on larger tires over smoother hard-surfaced roads and moved at faster speeds carrying heavier cargoes. So much progress demanded ever-more-reliable gearing.

In 1924, Ross obtained a patent for what became a runaway bestseller known as the "Ross Cam and Lever Gear." His cam and lever design allowed for what engineers called "variable ratios." The gear ratios were higher in the center where near straight-ahead driving occurs for precise control and kickback reduction, but lower in the ends for maneuverability. To go with that invention, Ross's colleagues designed an attachment for a milling machine that could cut and grind the odd-shaped cams. The cam-and-lever gear met with instant success. It offered efficiency, performance, and better traits for control of road shock. Its simplicity and safety created a wide demand. No competitor at the time could make variable ratio gears. Within two years, more than 300 Ross Gear factory men (and by 1924, a few women) were making and shipping 1,500 cam and lever gears a day. Dave Ross was storing up private wealth almost beyond measure.

On both the Ross Gear and Fairfield factory floors Dave Ross held to the common touch. He called nearly every employee by name. He liked being "Dave" instead of "Mr. Ross." By 1924, he alone controlled Ross Gear. Although he had been its vice president since 1920, he had kept shrugging off the presidency. When his uncle Will Ross retired as President, Dave let his uncle Linn

Ross take over. Why? Because Purdue affairs—not Ross Gear business—were paramount to him now.

∽

The finished Ross-Ade Stadium contained 13,000 seats with plans already drawn for 10,000 more when needed on the north curve. Built under the east and west grandstand seats were storage rooms and dressing rooms for the football players. Kemmer's men built restrooms for the spectators at the south ends of the east and west stands.

Away to the west and north stretched sloping tracts of farm fields and hardwood forests, red, yellow, orange, and brown in the fall. To the east the land gently sloped away. From the top row of the east bleachers one could see the trees lining the Wabash River on the horizon. To the south lay the streets, walks, paths, and buildings of the growing Purdue campus and that new red brick smokestack.

Fans eager to begin seeing games in Ross-Ade Stadium knew their math. They knew that since starting football in 1887, but before Stuart Field, Purdue teams had won five games and lost five. The teams had played five "home" games in those days at a YMCA field over in Lafayette. At their own Stuart Field (from 1892 until the last game there in November 1924) the teams won 126 and lost 111. Kellogg had hired Jimmy Phelan when Phelan was twenty-nine. Phelan had started coaching Purdue in 1922. In his first three full seasons, his talent-thin football teams had won eight games, lost ten, and tied two, but improvements were showing. Before the first Ross-Ade Stadium game in 1924, Purdue had won four and lost two.

∽

For several days before dedication, Henry Marshall's *Journal and Courier* devoted page after page to special stories about Ross-Ade Stadium:

The work that Mr. Ross has done for the university and his generous gifts place him in the top rank of Purdue's friends and supporters. He has been an indefatigable worker for the institution principally for the Memorial Union movement and now for the stadium. It was chiefly his initiative and efforts that led first to the stadium inception and then to its successful consummation. The stadium now stands as a monument to his efforts, together with those of Mr. Ade, for the university. (Lafayette *Journal and Courier,* November 20, 1924)

On November 20, one *Journal and Courier* story reported that T. B. "Monty" McGinley, a veteran Lafayette printer, received the first tickets drawn for a football game in Ross-Ade. McGinley had supported Purdue athletics for years and was familiar to many players. Purdue's ticket manager C. S. "Pop" Doan directed the Ross-Ade Stadium ticket takers to let McGinley keep his for souvenirs. McGinley intended to have the tickets framed together with a letter from Doan saying:

This is to certify that the enclosed two tickets, Sec. 9, Row C, Seats 13 and 14, are the first tickets ever drawn for the Ross-Ade Stadium.

Another story the week of dedication said modern stadiums had their inspiration in the Colosseum of ancient Rome and the Olympic Stadium in Greece.

Rome's ancient colosseum started in 72 AD and completed in 10 years was a large amphitheater four stories high. Marble and travertine stone were used in the construction along with cement. The seating capacity provided for 50,000 persons with standing room for 20,000 more comparing favorably with the largest stadiums of today.

And so came the idea for the modern stadiums and bowls— the stadiums with one end open in the shape of a U and those in the actual shape of a bowl.

Eight schools in the Big Ten Conference either have stadiums completed or under construction. The largest is the one at Ohio State where 63,000 can be accommodated. Next is the one at Illinois recently dedicated that has capacity for 60,000. Others include Minnesota 55,000; Michigan 42,500; Wisconsin 40,000. Indiana University's, torn up when nearly finished because of faulty construction, is again nearly finished. It will seat 25,000. Iowa has two large steel stands for its football crowds. Ross-Ade Stadium as at present completed will seat 13,200. Temporary bleachers will hold 1,000 more.

Grant Park Municipal Stadium in Chicago seats 100,000, Yale Bowl 80,000, Los Angeles Stadium 75,000, University of California 72,300, Princeton University 60,000, Harvard Stadium 40,000; Syracuse University 35,000.

Among the pre-game events on Friday night November 21 was a meeting in the new Memorial Union of members of the Ross-Ade Foundation. During that meeting, George Ade spoke:

> The stadium is now a reality instead of a dream...It was built to stay. I haven't a shadow of a doubt but that the stadium will be in use 500 years from now. I sat in the stadium of Athens 2,000 years after the first Olympian games were held there and it was still in a fair state of repair and it wasn't half as well built as the one that Kemmer has built for us...
>
> When Dave Ross and I acquired that tract two years ago we believed that some day there would be a stadium up in that hollow but we didn't dare to hope for one very soon, because everyone connected with Purdue had apparently gone the limit on the Memorial Union and it didn't seem safe or politic to ask Purdue men and women for more money just at a time when everybody was hard up.

And yet I am sure Dave and I kept repeating that advertisement you have seen in the paper so often—"Eventually—Why not now?" We had a talk one day about a year ago and confided to each other that we had an ardent longing to see that stadium before we died. We wanted it for ourselves and not for our grandchildren. As both of us are old bachelors the chances of our grandchildren using the stadium became more and more remote, and besides we didn't want to be involved in any scandal.

Well, the stadium is there, an accomplished fact and almost a miracle. I can hardly believe it myself. Last commencement it was simply a rolling hillside and now it is a magnificent work of art, a triumph of building skill and a gigantic monument which will endure forever.

It isn't all paid for, but we are assured that from now on the financial problems will solve themselves...Of course, we want to win that [Indiana] game, but whether we win or not we have come to a big and happy day in the history of Purdue.

On Saturday, three hours before the dedication game kickoff, J. B. Burris—the Purdue football captain from 1887—attended the Varsity "P" Men's Luncheon in the Memorial Union. There, he held up the leather football used in the first game at Purdue. The ball was round and somewhat smaller than the basketball being used in the 1920s. An "old dorm" to which Burris referred in a reminiscent letter he read to the "P" Men was still standing in 1924, but the building had not been used as a dorm for many years. Now it was Purdue Hall. In the 1880s, it was where Burris said the football pioneering "dorm devils" had resided.

Thirteen thousand football fans sat—and more than 5,000 stood—to watch Purdue upset Indiana twenty-six to seven in the first Ross-Ade Stadium game. Coach Phelan's team finished that season by winning its fifth of seven games. During brief dedication rites, the chilly fans heard the top-coated Dave Ross express his hope—echoing that of President Elliott—that "no professional player ever enters here. This place is for students. It is for our kids." It remained ironic that Ross's name would be so widely remembered because of Ross-Ade Stadium when, in truth, Ross ranked athletics a far lower priority. His labors with architect Scholer on the fifty-year Master Plan, for instance, rated higher. The *Journal and Courier* continued:

> The new structure is at once an acknowledgement of the university's growth and also recognition of the increasing popularity of football and the need for increased facilities not only for this sport but also for others. (Lafayette *Journal and Courier,* November 20, 1924)

On the Monday after the big football weekend at Purdue, the newspaper pronounced homecoming "a remarkable success in more ways than one":

> One of the most pleasing features was the skillful manner in which the traffic was handled. The problem, always a bugbear at large gatherings when thousands of visitors in motor cars assemble in a small area, was solved by the cooperation of Purdue traffic authorities, the West Lafayette and Lafayette police.

> It was the greatest jam of automobiles in the histories of the cities but there was no delay in getting to the parking places or away afterward. Parking management [at old Stuart Field] was ideal. No accident of any consequence occurred.

To climax it all the Purdue gridders administered one of the worst defeats ever received by an Indiana eleven at the hands of a Boilermaker team…The team's work was an augury of a promising future.

Good fellowship abounded. Purdue's big family was more firmly and strongly bound together than ever.

"Following the usual homecoming practice fraternities opened their doors to returning members" the newspaper said. Its report alphabetically mentioned more than thirty organizations from Acacia to Zeta Tau Alpha.

Sunday noon saw dinners at most of the chapter houses, with guests in some cases running from 50 to 150. There also were many dances in honor of the alumni. A general get-together was the alumni dinner-dance Saturday evening in the new Memorial Union attended by more than 500.

The paper listed a dozen hotels "filled to overflowing over the weekend. Townspeople opened up their homes to accommodate and entertain the many visitors. Restaurants did a record-breaking business. All business was suspended for three hours during the game, probably for the first time in the history of Purdue football. Streets and stores were alive with banners, flags and pennants."

A month after the game *The Purdue Alumnus* contained a rehash of the events by a writer named N. T. Crane, who regarded it as the Day of Days:

The boys and girls began to slosh in through the rain Friday afternoon.

As a starter the Tippecanoe County [Purdue Alumni] club got together in the Memorial Union building...at six o'clock Friday evening

We waited until ten o'clock for the meeting to adjourn so that we could have a meeting of the alumni advisory council and *Alumnus* editorial board...We managed to put in some time while waiting by attending the huge bonfire and yell-fest presided over by Major [athletic director] Kellogg on old Stuart Field...

The time from 8:30 to 10:00 Saturday morning was set aside to inspect the new buildings on the campus. Some of the old-timers would have sunburned roofs of their mouths in their wide-eyed astonishment had the sun been shining. To the old grads who had not been here for twenty years or more, the campus was indeed a revelation.

At ten o'clock the two freshman teams—the Reds and the Greens— lined up for their annual Homecoming hostilities on Stuart Field. Not more than three hundred spectators braved the chilly wind to watch.

Then came the class luncheons. That noon hour gave the Union its first real test "under fire." Besides the Varsity P Club luncheon and the class luncheons the cafeteria was taxed to its limit. Between 1,700 and 2,000 people passed through the lines at the steam tables in less than two hours. During the day about 4,000 were served in the building.

An event which really is a milestone in the annals of the Alumni Association was the Varsity P Club luncheon. It was the first assemblage of its kind and, like the alumni banquet, will be made a tradition as an annual function...

Then the impressive and epoch-making dedications of the Ross-Ade stadium. There were no superlatives, no frills...The cannon roared, the banners went up, the bands played and the magnificent structure was dedicated to the welfare of Purdue throughout the world.

But it required Sir Jimmie [football coach Phelan] and his valiant knights to give the field its glorious baptism. They made it the DAY OF DAYS which shall live as long as time in the records of achievement...

Before the record crowd of nearly 20,000 the stadium was dedicated...with the salute of twenty-one guns fired by the Purdue Order of Military Merit, the playing of The National Anthem by the Purdue band while the Stars and Stripes were raised. George Ade, David E. Ross, Prof. George Spitzer, President E. C. Elliott, [Indiana University President] W. L. Bryan and the great assemblage of "P" men formed a semicircle at the north end of the field. "Hail Purdue" and "Indiana" were played by the Purdue and Indiana bands and the president of the student council presented bold medallions in the name of the student body to Mr. Ade, Mr. Ross and Prof. Spitzer...

Four army aeroplanes from the flying field at Kokomo brought the huge crowd to its feet with nosedives and loops. One of the novel stunts was the dropping of the ball to be used in the game from one of the planes. The ball was decorated with the colors of the two schools.

"It was a jovial crowd of alumni that gathered around the board in the Memorial Union building for the first alumni banquet," Crane reported. "With the taste of victory still fresh on their lips, they were ready to celebrate...The most enjoyable number on the program was the paper read by Mr. Ade":

For several years we have had, at Purdue, an era of cheerful cooperation. The Memorial Union and the stadium are splendid proofs of the fact that all of the individuals and all of the minor organizations in the great Purdue colony now gladly acknowledge that their first obligation is to the university. Brothers may come and brothers may go, but mother still sits in the old armchair...

We have some comrades who are a little slow in paying what they owe, but I am not disposed to be too critical when I recall that it took me five years to pay for a pair of trousers purchased from a Lafayette tailor in the spring term of my senior year...

Purdue is just arriving. The sons and daughters are bringing in their gifts. We can feel, in the air, the radioactivity of a new and more intense loyalty. The old boys are stepping higher than ever before...

My good friends, this is one of the days for which we have waited. We know this evening that the Purdue spirit which made the Memorial Union and the stadium possible, which injected a fighting determination into our athletic teams, which has made Homecoming a jubilee—which spirit will abide with us. We are on the map...The stranger who spells Purdue with an E will now get the electric chair instead of a life sentence...

Hereafter, when we think of Purdue sitting in queenly splendor among these hills we will be a little proud and puffed up to know that this beautiful Memorial Union building, which she wears as a breastpin, and the stadium, which are the graceful sidecombs crowning a head now tinged with gray, are prized by her in remembrance of her wayward children. The boys and girls are scattered all over the world, but she has not forgotten them. Toward them her hands are always extended in greeting. Above the wide portals there is a modest inscription: *Be it ever so much better than any other school in Indiana, there is no place like home!*

Fred C. Kelly, an eventual biographer both of Dave Ross and George Ade, wrote more than twenty years later that Ross-Ade Stadium gave the University a lift in prestige as well as athletics: "All over the country people began to hear about Purdue" (Kelly, *Ross*, 77).

Not long after the inaugural game the Purdue Athletic Association awarded black letter sweaters to both Ross and Ade. A gold "P" like the ones given varsity football players had been sewn on each sweater.

"Mine must be a tribute to my athletic prowess," Ross joked. "I played baseball once when I was in high school."

"It makes me think of Eddie Allen," Ade quipped. "Allen made good in the business world and became president of the Mathieson Alkali Works. But when I knew him back in the 1890s he was a young student at Purdue. At a party one night a woman asked if he went in for athletics. 'Well, in a way,' he said. 'I'm the champion standing broad spitter!'" (Kelly, *Ross*, 77).

Part II

Ross-Ade: Their Stadium

A time for reflection

It was a time for reflection, celebration, progress, pride, and controversy. Lafayette turned 100 years old. Purdue started on its second fifty. West Lafayette ventured into its second year as a city instead of a town. Ross-Ade Stadium remained a topic of pride. So did Harry Leslie. On January 7, 1925, the Republicans in the Indiana Legislature elected State Representative Leslie as their presiding officer—Speaker of the House.

Then in a speech in early April, Edward Mahin, a professor of analytical chemistry at Purdue, stunned a conference audience in Ohio and the college football world. He said:

> Intercollegiate sport is now on a professional basis. The homecoming football game is the occasion for liquor drinking debauches. The present system of college football is a detriment to the health and physical soundness of many of its players and even to their lives.

> One of the principles of the Western [Big Ten] Conference is that *control of athletics shall be in the hands of the faculties.* I venture to say that if the principle was really enforced literally and in spirit the conference would no longer be known as the Big Ten. It would be the Big Zero.

> The only practicable solution for this momentous problem of higher education is to be found in the absolute divorcement of the

college from this enterprise of intercollegiate athletics. The few outstanding coaches demand and receive salaries that are absurdly out of proportion to those paid real teaching and research geniuses in the scientific and research fields. Under these circumstances it remains for the college that can obtain large athletic funds to get and to keep these coaches, and it is these schools that are, in the long run, able to win high places in the championship tables...

The championship business revolves itself into the matching of the wits and skill of the coaches and the wits and the purses of the alumni and the sporting public, each college against the other...

And we have the stadium with us. No college today is complete without it. When the decision is given by a certain college not to be outdone in the stadium race, a drive for funds must be organized. There is a commonly held notion that students are back of these athletics 100 percent. This is a fallacy. (Lafayette *Journal and Courier*, September 2, 1978)

Fourteen weeks after his tirade, Mahin left Purdue for another job he described as being "in the heart of an industrial district where training students in metals testing and in the investigation of research problems are of the highest importance. It affords a broader field for my research work." The name of the "industrial district"? South Bend, Indiana. The place? Notre Dame.

On August 9, Harry Leslie took over as General Secretary of the Purdue Alumni Association. By that time, the long-awaited Purdue history, *Fifty Years of Progress*, 203 pages written by Hepburn and Sears, hit the bookshelves. Part of the book read:

The character of alumni appointments to the [Purdue Board of Trustees] already has [in 1925] more than vindicated the [new state] law of 1921. Franklin F. Chandler, Lafayette, chief engineer of Ross Gear and Tool Co., Class of 1889, was joined by Perry

Part II: Ross-Ade: Their Stadium 187

Howard Crane, of Zionsville, Class of 1909, a dairy farmer and cattle breeder, and David Edward Ross of Lafayette, Class of 1893.

> Ross will be remembered in the gratitude of all succeeding generations at Purdue as the donor, with George Ade, of the Ross-Ade Field. He has been one of the heaviest contributors to the Purdue Memorial Union Building and as chairman of the building committee has rendered an invaluable service. Less spectacular, but of equal value, are his quiet contributions to the procedure of the Board. His sound judgment as a businessman is of the utmost usefulness to a body whose concerns in last analysis are chiefly those of business. (Hepburn and Sears, 138)

Certain of the book's comments pointedly countered Professor Mahin's anti-football diatribe:

> Toward athletics the alumni of Purdue as of other institutions feel a special patronage. In respect [to] football, for reasons not necessary to recount, this solicitude has become increasingly tender. A special jinx has seemed to take the team in charge and the utmost efforts of team members and their coaches, of students and alumni, and of friendly "boosters" have seemed unequal to dislodging him. Only with the coming of Coach James M. Phelan, formerly of Notre Dame and an exponent of that institution's technique, has a new day seemed to dawn. With new hope among the men there came material encouragement besides in the gift to Purdue of sixty-five acres of land lying west and north of Stuart Field.

> This tract of land...was strategic for university expansion Its acquisition releases Stuart Field [space] for eventual development on other lines, and makes the power plant the center of the future university. [The stadium] represented a most generous gift from two of the university's progressive and most loyal alumni, David

E. Ross of the class of '93 and George Ade of the Class of '87. (Hepburn and Sears, 127)

Throughout 1925, George Ade mostly wrote articles for *Hearst's International* magazine. Among them—rare for Ade—were autobiographical pieces like "For the First Time in My Life I'm Going to Talk about Myself," "George Ade Remembers the Good Old Days When One Might Have a Big Night for 45 Cents," and "To Get Along, Keep on Being a Country Boy." *Liberty* magazine printed Ade's story titled "The Persecuted Wife."

On the night of October 21, 1925, the noted entertainer Paul Whiteman and his orchestra played a concert for about 500 patrons in Purdue's Memorial Gymnasium. Less than two weeks after that, John Phillip Sousa's military band played two shows in the Purdue Armory.

On November 21, one year after the triumphant dedication game in Ross-Ade Stadium, Purdue visited Indiana University for football in Bloomington. At that point, the 1925 Purdue team under Coach Jimmy Phelan had won three games and lost four. On its new Ross-Ade Stadium field, the team had lost to Wabash thirteen to seven, then had beaten DePauw thirty-nine to nothing, Rose Polytechnic forty-four to nothing, and Franklin twenty to nothing, then lost to Northwestern thirteen to nine.

In Bloomington, George Ade, who had just written the screenplay and titles for the silent movie *Old Home Week*, stood for Purdue alumni in a halftime ceremony. Harry Kurrie, president of the Monon Railroad, represented IU alumni. The men shook hands, then unveiled an "old oaken bucket" trophy. About 25,000 fans saw the teams play to a scoreless tie for the first honor of possessing the bucket. The bucket was said to have come from a well on a farm near North Vernon, Indiana. Legend held that Confederate

John Hunt Morgan's thirsty forces from Kentucky drank well water from that bucket during their Civil War raid through southern Indiana and Ohio in July 1863.

A chain bolted to the rescued bucket would display shiny new metal "P" or "I" links to be added each fall. The links would show which team won each annual game. In the case of 1925, though, an "IP" would need to be crafted to reflect the tie game. In this situation, the schools each would display the bucket in their trophy cases for six months. The next "bucket game" would take place in Ross-Ade Stadium on November 20, 1926.

Out of the Joke Division

Purdue sports talk had been centering on football in Ross-Ade Stadium, and justifiably so. But since the winter of 1896-1897, Purdue basketball had gained respect, too. A coach named Homer Curtis had directed Purdue's first men's team to one win against a throw-together YMCA club from Lafayette and one loss to a team from Wabash College. By the time Ward L. "Piggy" Lambert became coach during 1916-1917, Purdue basketball teams had found success. The seasons for this new sport mainly ran from November to the following February.

Entering the 1925-1926 season, Lambert's eight previous teams had won one 102 times and lost forty-six. Lambert did not coach in 1917-1918 while serving in World War I. The team ended 1925 with five straight wins, one loss to Ohio State, and then three more wins. When the University of Chicago came to West Lafayette for a game in Memorial Gymnasium the night of February 17, 1926, a historical moment occurred. Purdue's WBAA radio announcer Harry Clark described the game action—play-by-play as it happened—from a microphone at courtside to listeners tuning in. Purdue lost that game twenty-one to nineteen but finished the season with thirteen victories, four defeats.

The U.S. Patent Office, in April 1926, granted Dave Ross protection for a reducing gear he had designed in the heat of competition. The rival Gemmer Company that year had begun making "worm and roller tooth" gears. These were the first to stop friction-causing contact by putting rollers between metal surfaces. The Gemmer design made cars and trucks easier to steer. Ross Gear Company engineers hurried to master the use of roller bearings, too.

In the mid-1920s, Dave Ross as a Purdue Trustee had begun to look into the need for a summer surveying camp for civil engineering freshmen. Purdue had conducted a camp since 1914 on state-owned land 150 miles away near Henryville in southern Indiana. Later, Purdue rented equally distant land near Pentwater in southern Michigan. Engineering Dean Potter complained to the Trustees from time to time that Purdue ought to have its own camp.

In May 1926, Ross bought 150 acres for such a camp. The rugged land twelve miles southwest of Purdue's campus contained wooded bluffs overlooking the Wabash River. Ross paid $8,940 for the campsite and deeded it to the Ross-Ade Foundation. President Elliott called this Foundation, incorporated on November 26, 1923, "a device to do things that the university as a branch of state government could not do." Through the years this "device" served Purdue well. It could receive gifts of land or money, or it could hold property Purdue might need later for its educational needs (Topping, 213).

Later, Ross bought and gave seventy more acres for the engineering camp. Freshman students (working for fifty cents an hour under faculty supervision while they learned surveying) improved the camp over the next several years. Ross and Josiah Kirby "J. K." Lilly paid the boys to install a water well and related pumps, pipes, and other equipment. The ultra-wealthy Lilly (1861-1948), son of the founder of the Eli Lilly pharmaceutical empire, joined the Purdue Trustees from Indianapolis in 1927 and served until 1938.

Within five months, Purdue dedicated Ross Engineering Camp on 112 of the donated acres, and soon after that Ross paid $2,700 for the materials so that students could learn even more by building a Ross Camp swimming pool. Ross pushed industrial research at Purdue. In April 1926, Ross and President Elliott organized a national conference of industrial leaders at the West Lafayette campus. On June 1, the conference attracted men from all over the nation. There President Elliott proposed that an advisory committee be formed to establish links between the several Purdue research labs and the problems of the various industries, especially in Indiana. With Dean Potter, Ross shortly visited research labs and dropped in on several other universities and industries to find out how Purdue might help. Ross later made an elaborate report to the trustees, advising them that Purdue needed to place greater emphasis on the ways the University could help industries solve problems.

Certain friends gently chided Dave Ross for not knowing what to do with all his money. "But they were wrong," Kelly wrote. "Dave had no intention of starting a racing stable or interesting himself in the silly things rich men sometimes do when they find themselves with money. Because he knew how to use wealth intelligently, the important part of his career was still ahead" (Kelly, *Ross*, 61).

That career involved Ross becoming one of Purdue University's best and most generous friends. For starters, Ross continued urging the Trustees to review industry-University cooperative ventures in research.

In late June 1926, standing in cap and gown beside two old Purdue friends also being feted—John T. McCutcheon and Clarence Hovey "Big Robbie" Robertson—George Ade received an honorary doctor of humane letters degree. Purdue called it "an appropriate recognition of [Ade's] unremitting service to the up-building of this university, of his achievements as a journalist, author and playwright, of his distinctive interpretation of American life and manners, and of the joy he has added to the world."

The honor came in mid-year of another busy period of magazine article writing for the sixty-year-old Ade. It also came at a time when, under contract with *Hearst's International*, he was telling his life story in installments. *Hearst's* published "How to Live in the Country" in January, "I Keep Myself Young by Doing Twice as Much Work as I Did 20 Years Ago" in February, "My Mother and Father" in March, "Log Cabin Days" in April, "The Dark Ages" in August, "The Mushy Seventies" in September, "When I Sowed My Wild Oats" in October, "The Busy, Boiling 90s" in November, and "I Knew Them When" in December.

These personal tales made up the only series of his articles that Ade *never* collected. In them, he wrote about himself only indirectly. He chose to project an image of a man who surrounded himself with luxury, reveled in mirth, enjoyed popularity, insisted on being amiable, and was sometimes lonely. The personal stories revealed no great loves, no tragedies, no passions, and neither convictions nor aspirations, but they were loaded with funny stories, quips, memories, comments, and mild confessions. All told, Ade published thirty magazine pieces of this sort in *Cosmopolitan* or *Hearst's International*. In them, Ade came across as a good-hearted man with a highly profitable gift. Reading the stories caused one critic to remark: "It is idle to speculate on what might have become of his rare talent had it been burnished at Princeton rather than Purdue, or had he aspired to the *Atlantic Monthly* rather than to the Chicago *Record*" (Coyle, 138).

In October 1926, during the second full football season that Purdue's teams played home games in Ross-Ade Stadium, Ade boasted in a letter to his syndicated sportswriter and author friend Grantland Rice (1880-1954):

> Purdue is out of the Joke Division. We played a close game with the Navy [losing seventeen to thirteen in the East] with hardly any practice and licked Chicago [six to nothing before forty thousand in Chicago.] I am afraid Northwestern is a little too husky for us...

Anyway we are out of the cellar and going strong. Jimmy Phelan is a good coach and we have a freshman team almost as good as varsity. We are beginning to get some results from years of patient battling. (Tobin, 114)

While Phelan and the Boilermaker football fortunes rose, so did the careers of three other noted Purdue men: the honorary doctors McCutcheon and Robertson and House Speaker Harry Leslie. Leslie had recovered slowly and painfully from the 1903 football train disaster. He had missed graduating with his class in 1904 but had been elected president of the Class of 1905. Gaining in popularity both before and during his recovery, Leslie, after finishing Purdue, had won elections as West Lafayette clerk-treasurer, then as Tippecanoe County treasurer, then as joint state representative from Tippecanoe and Warren counties.

Now on November 2, 1926, voters re-elected Leslie to the Indiana House. When the legislators met to organize in Indianapolis on January 5, 1927, they again chose Leslie as Speaker. It helped him politically, too, that he now was General Secretary of the steadily growing Purdue Alumni Association.

Jimmy Phelan's 1926 team won five football games, lost two, and tied one. In Ross-Ade Stadium, the team beat Wabash twenty-one to fourteen before 8,000 spectators; tied Wisconsin nothing to nothing with 11,000 attending; beat Indiana State thirty-eight to nothing; beat Franklin forty-four to nothing; and then won the Old Oaken Bucket by topping Indiana twenty-one to fourteen before an overflow throng of 14,000.

The University crowned the productive year on November 11 by dedicating a new Horticulture Building on Marstellar Street south of State Street.

Events of great importance

The year 1927 brought events of great importance at Purdue. One was that the Trustees elected Dave Ross as their President. He moved his office from the Ross Gear factory to the narrow three-story Ross Building on the courthouse square. On January 4, 1927, the Trustees at last, after nine months, named a committee to review questions Ross had raised about research. Ross hoped that this would help make research more of a teaching tool at Purdue (Kelly, *Ross*, 108-109).

On March 26, Dr. Arett C. Arnett, a forward-thinking physician who had founded a medical clinic in Lafayette, took office as Chamber of Commerce President. Dr. Arnett, like Dave Ross and a few others, had been intrigued by the fast growth and acceptance of aviation. Lafayette native Henry Boonstra, a World War I flight instructor, had become an important pioneer in the U.S. Air Mail Service in the American West. Another teacher of wartime pilots, Lawrence I. "Cap" Aretz, an Indiana National Guard captain, was gaining renown at the Guard airfield in Kokomo, Indiana. People also were following via radio and newspaper reports the flying exploits of Charles A. Lindbergh as he prepared for an attempt to fly across the Atlantic Ocean. Still another engaging personality in aviation was an intrepid woman from Kansas named Amelia Earhart.

Dave Ross now divided his efforts between Purdue, Ross Gear, and Fairfield affairs. On March 15, 1927, the close family of Ross Gear stockholders voted to raise the number of Directors from three to seven. Management changes soon followed. David Linn Ross resigned as President so as to function as Board Chairman. Edward A. Ross rose from Secretary to President. Dave Ross resigned both as Vice President and General Manager. He desired to spend more time at Purdue as President of the Board of Trustees. He also had in mind forming yet another private corporation

Supporting Ross's insistence on Purdue research for industry, some exciting work came to light in April. Henry Marshall's *Journal and Courier* on April 8 reported the role of Frank Gray (Purdue Class of 1911) in perfecting "television"—technology compared by some to "visual radio"—in New York City.

On Thursday, April 14, the humorist, entertainer, and syndicated newspaper columnist Will Rogers appeared in Lafayette. He was guest of the Lafayette Armory board and visitor to a friend's livestock farm a few miles away. At Lafayette's Jefferson High School, Rogers spoke at a student assembly. In a half hour, Rogers kept 900 boys and girls laughing until he turned serious:

> I never had the advantage of an education, but it's a great thing, especially for children, to go to high school and college.
>
> You know, you are just at the arguing age now, and in a year or two you will be more of an arguer. I know how you look at dad at home and imagine he doesn't know anything, then you go away to college and come back after four years and look at him again. And you wonder how he ever lived so long without knowing any more than he does.

Rogers said half the students in that audience should go on to college and half should go to work instead. That way those who finish college will have someone to work *for* when they complete their education. Later, Rogers visited Purdue, addressed a Lafayette Advertising Club banquet in the Lahr House, and then headed for the Purdue Armory. There, the *Journal and Courier* reported, he delighted about 1,200 people "with his wit and philosophy":

> Mr. Rogers talked about everything of interest and about everybody of international importance, and he kept on talking and talking, and his hearers seemed to enjoy it more and more, until, finally, Will began to grow sleepy and he called it a night.

> Politicians including President Coolidge…came in for their share of attention, as did Hollywood, China, Europe, England's national game, grouse shooting in Scotland, Indiana politics, Chicago, international relations, aviation, preparedness, education, the touring habit, the agricultural crisis and many other topics that have found their way to the first pages of the newspaper. In the exhibition with the lariat, Mr. Rogers proved himself a master of the lasso in all its intricacies. He made the rope dance and leap in the air and describe circles in all directions and finally he danced in two loops, both rotating at dizzy speed.

Several owners were turning their Tippecanoe County farm fields into makeshift aircraft landing strips as early as 1919. In 1927, another came into use on McCarty Lane near what is now County Road 500 East. This was level, wooded, and pastured farmland owned by Lafayette businessman Julius Berlovitz. Barnstorming pilots touring as the "Gates Flying Circus" performed on and in the sky over Berlovitz's land on May 7-9 in 1927. Excitement, pathos, tales of courage, and foolhardiness all played roles in the accumulating lore of American aviation.

Most American pilots, including the ones in the Gates show, had learned to fly in a Curtiss JN4D designed as a World War I primary pilot trainer. The Curtiss series of "JN"-lettered biplanes led fliers to call them "Jennies." These planes had a top wing forty-three feet long and a fuselage twenty-seven feet long. A Curtiss OX-5 engine developed ninety horsepower, enough to allow war surplus Jennies to cruise at about seventy miles per hour. The planes weighed a little more than 1,900 pounds.

Due to the popularity and quantity produced (about 6,000) the Jenny became the surplus machine of choice for pilots home from war. They bought Jennies from the military and flew them to earn a living.

Mississippi River floods had ravaged parts of Mississippi, Arkansas, and Louisiana early in 1927. This caused members of Lafayette's postwar American Legion Post 11 to decide to split proceeds from an "air meet" with a Red Cross flood relief fund. The Gates people offered a collection of aerial entertainers comparable to others crisscrossing the nation. They stunted at airports, less-sophisticated "landing fields," or on any safe and level stretch of land to which the public had reasonable access and places to park horses, wagons, buggies, or cars.

In this instance, the Legionnaires arranged to use Berlovitz's field a few miles east of Lafayette. The Gates Flying Circus at the time featured "Diavalo, Chief of the Dare-Devils." The Legionnaires charged no admission but levied a parking fee for those who rode or motored out from Lafayette and surrounding towns. In the course of the meet, pilots flew to 2,000 feet, purposely shut off the motor, and then glided to safety in front of the spectators. Parachute jumpers leaped from planes half a mile in the air and guided their 'chutes to landings near the crowd. The Gates pilots arranged to drop twenty small parachutes during the three days. Each carried a prize offered by a Lafayette merchant sponsoring part of a double-page advertisement in the *Journal and Courier*. The newspaper's news editor, Herb Heimlich, rode in one of the Gates planes from Frankfort, Indiana, to the Berlovitz farm. Heimlich's rhapsodic first-person account of the forty-mile morning round-trip appeared on the front page the afternoon the air show opened:

> The sight, on a bright May morning from a plane, is beautiful beyond description. Freshly plowed fields, with their graduated shades, beautifully blended, a contrast with nature which is breaking forth into a brilliant green, furnishing a vivid panorama.

Roads, stretching out for miles, afford another contrast as do winding creeks and streams. There is a sort of checkerboard effect, and everything appears in miniature, even the whole city of Lafayette, looking like a small spot, as seen from the clouds.

The Gates Flying Circus near their father's neighboring dairy farm, just up the dirt road from the Berlovitz field, provided enough wonders for three young brothers who caught the flying "bug" that day. They were Joseph, John, and Francis Halsmer—eventual founders of Halsmer Flying Service (1931-1988).

Then, during May 20 and 21, listeners in Lafayette, the state, the nation, and the world followed by radio news and read in their newspapers about the flight made across the Atlantic Ocean by Charles Lindbergh. The twenty-five-year-old native Detroiter flew alone in the single-engine airplane called *Spirit of St. Louis* from New York to Paris, France. The flight covered more than 3,600 miles and took about thirty-three and one-half hours. Lindbergh's plane left Roosevelt Field near New York City on May 20 and landed at Le Bourget Field outside Paris, France. "Lucky Lindy" became a household word and an aviation icon for the ages.

Lafayette and Indiana pride reached another level shortly after the Lindbergh epic when on May 30 twenty-seven-year-old George Souders won the 500-mile Memorial Day automobile race at Indianapolis. Souders—a Lafayette native—drove a Duesenberg racer built in Indianapolis, steered by a Ross gear made in Lafayette, at an average speed of ninety-seven and a half miles per hour.

In mid-June, after some brisk debate, Frank Cary gave Purdue $50,000 for a men's dormitory. The dorm would be named for Cary's son, Franklin Levering Cary. The boy had died of appendicitis at age eighteen in 1912. The Cary-Purdue debate had centered on a site for the dorm. Cary wished for the high-visibility southeast corner of State and Marstellar, a block or so west of the new Union Building. Purdue historian Robert W. Topping explained:

> One of [President] Elliott's highest priorities in 1927 was developing adequate student housing operated by Purdue. The 1927 Indiana General Assembly passed a law permitting state-supported colleges and universities to issue revenue bonds to build and furnish dorms. At the time it seemed rather an ordinary piece of legislation; actually it was a landmark statute that made possible many cultural and living improvements most state schools would not have seriously contemplated otherwise.
>
> Within a year Purdue was attempting to put together the finances for the first new dorms built since Ladies Hall and Purdue Hall between 1869 and 1874. The system Purdue [eventually built] began with a proposal by Frank C. Cary, a Lafayette industrialist and entrepreneur, to make a $50,000 gift to Purdue to honor the memory of his son. When Mrs. Cary died in 1927 Frank Cary pursued the idea of the gift to honor both his wife and son. Cary had retired from the presidency of Barbee Wire and Iron Works, and was sometimes credited with crafting padding and heavy wire into the sport of baseball's first catcher's mask.
>
> Cary first approached President Elliott and Trustee Henry Marshall about the possibilities and proposed purchase of the southeast corner of Marstellar and State Street for a dorm for forty men. But the Trustees had already adopted in their Master Plan a dorm for up to one hundred fifty men. The Trustees, Elliott and other staff members tried to divert Cary's attention to other possible dorm sites without success until R. B. Stewart...finally convinced him.

Cary was not impressed with the [idea of building a dorm] between Ross-Ade Stadium and Stadium Avenue. Stewart remembered that he probably drove Cary by that location "at least a hundred times" in his attempt to convince Cary that this was where Purdue had planned to build its men's dorms. The site was even in Scholer's 1922 Master Plan. "But you can't see it" Cary protested. "People will drive through the campus and no one will ever see it."

"Give us the $50,000," Stewart replied. "I'll use the university's [new] bonding power and give you a $150,000 building that will be the first thing that anyone going to football games on a Saturday afternoon will see."

After Scholer had shown Cary many sketches and blueprints, Cary became persuaded and gave Purdue the money for Franklin Levering Cary Hall, known also as Cary East. (Topping, 230-231)

George Ade, at age sixty-one, pocketed an honorary doctor of laws degree from Indiana University in June 1927. IU cited most of the same "life achievements" Purdue had mentioned when giving Ade his degree the year before. "But," Ade still quipped, "I'll bet no one ever calls me 'Doctor'" (Kelly, *Ade*, 241).

Ade continued to write and mail off magazine articles from Hazelden during 1927. The February *Hearst's* printed "When Good Fellows Got Together." In August, Ade's essay "The Perfect Play Is One Which Entertains the Audience Without Poisoning It" showed up in *The Theatre* Magazine. During 1927, cartoonist Art Helfant drew for the Bell Syndicate a short-lived cartoon strip titled "Fables In Slang by George Ade." Ade also wrote motion picture screenplays adapted from two of his stage plays for the 1927 silent movies, *The Fair Co-Ed* and *The College Widow*.

Dave Ross remained obsessed with the idea of "educational research." He told Engineering Dean Potter to "let our students know that if anyone here ever has an idea worth patenting, I'll gladly bear all the expense of getting the patent and give whatever help or advice I can." Ross was convinced that more scientific investigation should be used as a method of teaching and that there should be greater effort to uncover superior students and give them a chance to develop their talents. He cleared the top two floors of his Ross Building for work areas and informed another of his friends, Professor Harry C. Peffer, Head of the School of Chemical Engineering, to "look for gifted students, send them to me and I'll put them to work." The Ross Building soon became one of the most active research centers in the Midwest.

Peffer, whose daughter worked for Ross as a secretary, sent Ross a young chemical engineering graduate student, Richard Harrison. Harrison helped start Ross's third industry. Ross convinced Harrison to follow up certain phenomena that he and Peffer had noticed in nature, which might lead to making artificial stone from common earthen materials. Harrison discovered a definite, if somewhat unstable, reaction at relatively low temperatures, between the alumino-silicic acid found in slate or shale and hydrate of lime. Ross saw his chance to show the Purdue Trustees the value of research to education. He convinced Peffer and Harrison that the three of them should start a research company devoted to the development of a synthetic stone for building material.

They founded Rostone Incorporated on July 11, 1927, with Ross President, Peffer Vice President, and Harrison Secretary and Treasurer. The articles of incorporation stated:

> The object and purpose of the corporation shall be to carry on a general manufacturing business and to manufacture building material from mineral substances. The buying and mining of mineral substances to be used in the manufacturing of said materials

and to acquire by purchase, lease, grant, or otherwise real estate that is necessary to carry on the business of said company, and to sell, lease or otherwise dispose of real estate that can no longer be used in said business. Also, to acquire by purchase or otherwise letters patent covering any of said articles to be manufactured and to buy and sell merchandise to be manufactured, and for the sale of such merchandise when manufactured; and to do any and all acts that are necessary to carry on said business.

The company purchased 120 acres near the facing Wabash River towns of Independence and Riverside, in neighboring Warren and Fountain counties, for $9,863. The men deposited another $25,000 for buildings and materials. The capital stock of the corporation was $100,000 divided into 1,000 of $100 each. On July 20, Rostone hired recent Purdue graduates Paul Jones, a chemical engineer, and Floyd Wymer, mechanical engineer, to work with Harrison at a new pilot plant.

They chose the plant site at a large outcropping of shale. Harrison, Jones, and Wymer spent many days traveling between there and Lafayette before they moved into a garage that was to become their home for several years. Jones and Wymer wrote in a diary:

> July 23, 1927 (Saturday) was the biggest of all days. After a strenuous night of packing, we loaded the truck up with trunks, bags, tables, chairs, bushel baskets, etc. We hustled about town to every grocery store, hardware and other merchants of household necessities. The ground was broken for the factory today, and we all rejoiced over that.

Ross's goal was to market the cheap "imitation stone" by blending shale, lime, alkaline, and soil. It could be made into slabs for outside veneer walls that, even up close, looked and felt like solid stone. But it would take more than four years to reach the patent, manufacture, and marketing stage.

Purdue President Elliott, in 1927, proposed an all-University Department of Research Relations with Industry. The Trustees approved the idea in October, but the University then began to find that modern industries were much more interested in Purdue's ability to train *thinkers* capable of solving problems than to fix them. Like so many other little facts of life, this situation set Dave Ross to deeper thinking. He wondered why more Purdue students weren't inventing. "We don't give them enough incentive to be *thinkers*," he decided. "Too many who *could* think get caught by the distractions—by athletics, fraternities and social activity. Maybe only a few are naturally interested in new solutions to problems, but we [Purdue] ought to try to *find* them and *encourage* them" (Kelly, *Ross*, 100).

Ross believed that the United States owed any greatness it might claim to its roster of inventors. "What a [great] thing it would be," he said in one speech, "if universities could spur their alumni to [recruit] students with natural aptitudes for research, invention and creative thinking." He continued:

> It isn't necessary for the professor of football to order his graduate scouts to look for good material, but that is the only field in which most colleges have encouraged their graduates to scout for recruits. A professor of football points with pride to the number of all-Americans he has produced. I wonder if a technology teacher ever stops to ask if he is producing distinguished graduates? It may be that the professor of technology should take a hint from the professor of football. He could then point to the number of his students starred in *American Men of Science*. (Kelly, *Ross*, 101)

Ross time and again urged Purdue to acquire more research space, more teachers, and more research-inclined students, but he came to see this as being different from the work of industrial labs. "The university's main interest is in *human beings*" he concluded, "in developing human aptitudes and possibilities. Industrial research deals with *things*. University research should dig into new ideas that help to train the mind for objective thinking. Those who are trained may then go into the industrial labs that deal with *things* and apply their clear thinking to problems at hand" (Kelly, *Ross*, 101).

In late October 1927, the Indiana State Highway Commission, in its campaign to build more than 900 miles of hard-surface highways, opened new pavement between Lafayette and Indianapolis and designated it as "Road 52." This provided a new channel of thinking for Ross.

For Ross, a word of conversation or a look could spark an idea. The state highway people responsible for more and better roads (and higher speeds) were starting to worry about accidents. Someone suggested they ask Dave Ross what could be done to improve road lighting. One night as Ross drove out to The Hills he saw a few yards up the road the gleam of a stray cat's eyes. He thought, if there were enough cats' eyes along a road night driving would be safer.

At home, Ross sketched a small teardrop shaped piece of metal containing a bead of reflecting glass. A series of such teardrops fastened to pavement to reflect lights from vehicles could mark the edge or center of a road at night. Ross even designed a groove in the teardrop so rain could keep the glass beads clean. He tried a few of the markers along his familiar road and drove at them. He tried different distances and angles. He put the first markers he made to sell on a sharp curve at the edge of Lafayette. The idea proved effective but easy to copy. Rival designs came on the market. Ross disliked patent lawsuits, so he never made much money from this invention, but he did feel good about helping solve a safety problem (Kelly, *Ross*, 90-92).

Jimmy Phelan's 1927 football team won six games and lost two. In Ross-Ade Stadium the team beat DePauw fifteen to nothing; topped Montana State thirty-nine to seven before 7,000 fans; defeated Northwestern eighteen to six before 15,000; and drubbed Franklin forty-six to nothing. Borrowing George Ade's phrase, Purdue football had "left the Joke Division."

It was getting to be old business, but by November 1927, Dave Ross had obtained five more patents. Four dealt with his designs for compensating gearing, a steering post control lever assembly, and differential gearing. The fifth was for a sectional tunnel:

> [Ross] was walking across the Purdue campus with a student who expressed the opinion that the great number of inventions already made had reduced inventors' opportunities. Dave stopped. "There's scarcely a thing we do," he said, "that can't be done better."
>
> The words were hardly spoken when he saw a large tunnel being dug from the power plant. "Now look at that!" he exclaimed. "They dig a tunnel; then in a few days a gang of men comes along with brick to wall it up. There should be a sectional wall to go in as rapidly as the tunnel is dug."
>
> That night he worked on a plan for a sectional tunnel. His plan provided for sections of concrete of parabolic shape, the opposite sides to support each other by fitting together at the top. He obtained a patent for it. (Kelly, *Ross*, 94-95)

Each year for thirty-four years Ross received at least one patent and sometimes six or seven. All told, he received eighty-eight, including thirty-two for automobile steering gears and fifteen for Rostone and other building materials and structures such as the sectional tunnel.

Governor Leslie

Fire in the Purdue Armory on January 13 started 1928 in a troublesome way. The blaze destroyed vehicles, guns, military gear, and furnishings, but sunnier news came soon. *The Scrivener*, a new monthly literary magazine, debuted at Purdue. For this issue Ade composed "Welcoming the New Magazine":

> Some one long ago declared that Purdue University was to specialize on the teaching of Science, Agriculture and Engineering, and, because some one said that many students at Purdue have believed that it would be slightly improper for them to learn how to write for publication or to speak in public. It is true that Purdue never has been labeled a "literary" school and has not competed with the academic courses in other large institutions. But just the same every Purdue graduate should know how to write for the printer and should cultivate the usual knack of talking to various assemblages. It is too bad that the debating societies of long ago became overshadowed by other college organizations which went in for music and social affairs. I am glad to learn from Doctor Elliott that Purdue men and women are reorganizing societies which will meet for general discussion of current topics.
>
> The engineer, the scientist, the research worker and the modern farmer will be called upon to deal with the public through the printed page and at all sorts of conventions and conferences. Some may even be tempted to take a fling at fiction or the drama. Booth Tarkington, John McCutcheon and other men who were in Purdue about my time went out into the world and began to write

books. It is an interesting fact that Purdue, which is supposed to be a "technical" school, has produced just as many authors as Indiana, Wabash and DePauw, to the south of us, all of them striving to plant the literary germ in the undergraduate. There is no reason why *The Scrivener* should not be an interesting publication and prove that Boilermakers can do something besides make boilers. (*The Scrivener*, January 1928)

In early February 1928, House Speaker Harry Leslie revealed that he would run for the Republican nomination for Governor of Indiana. Leslie promised old-fashioned honesty in government. That was timely talk. George Ade's disgraced brother-law, former Governor Warren McCray, languished in prison in 1928 for mail fraud. McCray's successor Governor Ed Jackson, although indicted for bribing McCray, won acquittal and stayed in office.

Cashing in on the momentary Harry Leslie pride, the *Journal and Courier* printed his biography. In it Leslie said that he believed "there is something radically wrong with the primary [election] system in Indiana." He vowed to abide by the Republican Convention's choice for governor. He added: "I [also] am opposed to the furtherance of political ambitions from the pulpits of the church. I have too high a regard for the churches and will accept no invitation to speak in any church while a candidate." (Leslie, his wife Martha, and three sons attended First Methodist Church in West Lafayette.) The primary election that Leslie criticized, scheduled for May 8, would not be binding. The traditional Democrat and Republican nominating conventions would as usual take place in late May.

George Ade kept on writing. In February, J. H. Sears and Company published *Bang! Bang!* illustrated by McCutcheon. The promoters called this book "a collection of stories intended to recall memories of the nickel library days when boys were supermen and murder a fine art." The volume contained eight of Ade's works from the

Chicago *Record* in 1897-1898, stories that amounted to "a burlesque of blood -and-thunder dime novels and nickel libraries" (Russo, 100).

In July, *Hearst's International* and *Cosmopolitan* included Ade's "On His Uppers" in "Literary Treasures of 1928." *Country Gentleman* magazine published Ade's last one-act play, "The Willing Performer." Ade contributed four more of his "At Long Range" observations between February and December to *The Purdue Alumnus*. His essay on "Farming in Indiana—Then and Now" came out in the July 1928 *Purdue University Department of Agricultural Extension Bulletin*.

Steering gear competition stepped up in 1928. Saginaw Products became the Saginaw Steering Division of General Motors. The Gemmer Company improved its single roller-tooth gear by producing a two-tooth version for even easier steering. On April 2, Ross Gear directors approved up to $100,000 worth of additions to the plant's assembly and machine shop. This would raise production capacity from 2,200 units per day to 2,700. Within a month, the Directors further approved a five-for-one stock split.

It was probably in early 1928 that Dave Ross sat—in an upholstered armchair—for a formal portrait. The noted artist from Michigan City, Indiana, was Robert Grafton (1876-1936.) The occasion was Ross's elevation to the presidency of the Purdue Board of Trustees. In the portrait, Ross, wearing a light-colored business suit with stiff collar and bow tie, gazes with quiet tolerance toward the painter.

On Wednesday night, April 4, Will Rogers returned to wow a Purdue crowd jammed into the Memorial Gym. "It was at the close of [Rogers'] monologue," the *Journal and Courier* reported, "that Russell Gray of Chicago, president of the Purdue Alumni Association, gave Rogers a certificate of [honorary] membership. Rogers beamed gratefully, then turned to the large assemblage of students. 'Boys,' he said, 'I just got in five minutes something it takes you four years to earn.'"

> In the course of his rapid-fire utterance, he lauded Lindbergh, but made fun of the...Lone Eagle as "the first man who ever carried a ham sandwich to Paris." (Lafayette *Journal and Courier*, April 5, 1928)

On April 10, Lafayette's Buick automobile dealer Charles Shambaugh announced that he had leased an eighty-acre cornfield near the Tippecanoe County Fairgrounds at the southeast edge of Lafayette. On the field he would develop Lafayette's first airport. The Chamber of Commerce and the American Legion would help promote the venture. A mechanical tinkerer, Shambaugh had built and fixed carriages and wagons since the horse-and-buggy days. He had been building and racing primitive engine-powered cars, too, and had become a car dealer in the early 1900s. Now he told of planning to smooth the old cornfield furrows, seed the field with bluegrass, and build a sheet-metal hangar for office space and aircraft storage.

Money put up by Shambaugh and Dr. Arnett quickly put the field in shape. The first plane, piloted by a man from South Bend, landed on May 10. Shambaugh and Arnett enticed Indiana National Guard Captain Lawrence I. "Cap" Aretz to move over from Kokomo to run the Lafayette airport.

In Indiana politics a certain Fred Schortemeier led a statewide field of ten Republican primary election candidates for the Governor nomination. Harry Leslie, pledging to abide by the nominating convention coming May 24, trailed Schortemeier by 60,000 primary votes. But by law, the convention delegates had the final say. On convention day the delegates listened to all the speakers, weighed their "electability," whispered to conduct the usual "horse tradin'," and then chose Leslie on the seventh ballot.

The wonder of aviation remained new in the public mind after Shambaugh Field opened and each time *Journal and Courier* stories told of amazing feats of flights from all over the globe. Among them was the hometown story that involved Lena Stafford. Lena received a letter from a cousin mailed from Germany. The new 800-foot German airship *Graf Zeppelin* had carried the letter aboard one of its first trans-Atlantic flights before landing at Lakehurst, New Jersey.

As the local talk of Shambaugh Field gained volume and speed, followers of other flying news began to hear more about Amelia Earhart. In June 1928, Earhart became the first woman to cross the Atlantic Ocean by air (as a passenger and part-time pilot.) Reports also told about her buying an English Avro "Avian" biplane and starting to write a book, *20 Hrs. 49 Min.*, about the trans-ocean trip. G. P. Putnam's Sons, of which Earhart's friend George Palmer Putnam (son of one of the Sons) was treasurer, would publish the book. Then in September, Earhart made the first solo transcontinental flight by a woman. She was becoming rather a protégé of the promotion-minded, forty-one-year-old Putnam.

Putnam (1887-1950) in time became noted as an author, explorer, and publisher of scientific adventure books. A grandson of G. P. Putnam, founder of the publishing firm, George had led two expeditions to the Arctic—one in 1926 and one in 1927. One future biographer of Earhart would see fit to point out:

> It is a popular misconception George Palmer Putnam used Amelia and drove her too hard, with the implication that he did this for his own ends, and of course he was earning a management fee from Amelia's earnings...But in fact George was simply ensur-

ing that the maximum amount of benefit was gained from a unique opportunity. He realized that once Amelia's name dropped out of the newspapers she would be just another woman aviator. No one would pay to hear her speak once the next record breaker seized the daily headlines. Amelia would undoubtedly have recognized the sense of this, too.

> Amelia also saw the career George sketched out for her, and she wanted it. She was just as much committed to the property "Amelia Earhart" as George and, if anything, was probably self-driven. (Lovell, *The Sound of Wings*, 133-134)

On August 21, 1928, Shambaugh and Dr. Arnett disclosed that they would improve Shambaugh Field with lights and a beacon and get it placed on two airmail routes. Dedication of the field took place on August 26. Standard Oil of Indiana's "Stanolind" publicity plane—a loud, lumbering corrugated metal-covered Ford AT-5 Tri-motor—landed for an air show and to offer rides.

Under Aretz's management, Shambaugh Field gave Lafayette boosters a new selling point. The airport also inspired enough people—Dave Ross among them—to start thinking about a Purdue University Airport and to create more aviation courses.

From Shambaugh Field, the busy Aretz gave flying lessons and carried out charter service and emergency and goodwill "mercy mission" flights to rush sick or injured patients to distant hospitals or fly medicine to their bedsides. Among Aretz's students in those days was Michael C. "Mike" Murphy, a Lafayette boy who would earn the nation's highest award for "outstanding contributions to American aviation." Alberta Clark, a nervy twenty-one-year-old *Journal and Courier* reporter, wrote a series of stories about learning to fly with Aretz.

The wife of a Purdue purchasing agent made the first long-distance flight from Lafayette by a woman when Aretz flew her to Columbus, Ohio, for a conference. Federal inspectors who checked Shambaugh Field from time to time praised Aretz's management.

Shambaugh added safety features over the years, among them better lights, and two-way radios.

On the other hand, there were risks and dark days in aviation. On September 9, 1928, there occurred the first fatal aircraft accident in or near Lafayette. Two joyriding students from the high school in Otterbein, Indiana, died in a Sunday afternoon crash on John Lugar's farm half a mile west of the town. They were riding in a WACO piloted by Donald Burget, twenty-one, of Chalmers, Indiana. Burget survived serious injuries.

Coach Phelan's 1928 Purdue football team—still distant from the Joke Division—won five games, lost two, and tied one. In Ross-Ade Stadium, the players thumped DePauw thirty-one to nothing; tied Wisconsin nineteen to nineteen before 15,000 fans; beat Case nineteen to nothing; beat Wabash fourteen to nothing; and shut out Indiana fourteen to nothing before a new record attendance of 25,000. Cries began going up from the many standees to build more Ross-Ade Stadium seats.

In the general elections conducted on November 6, Harry Leslie defeated Democrat Frank Dailey for Governor. Leslie won by about 45,000 votes. His popularity helped Republican Herbert Hoover, Iowa mining engineer, war relief commissioner, and cabinet member, carry Indiana on the way to crushing Democrat Alfred E. Smith by more than six million nationally for U.S. President.

Darkest memories

Decades afterward, the year 1929 has remained linked with America's darkest memories. In late October, the first signs of the economic Great Depression began to show. But until then, the times still sported a certain Roarin' Twenties swagger.

On January 14 in 1929, Purdue-proud Harry Leslie took office as Indiana's thirty-third governor. He was the first to come from Purdue and the first from Tippecanoe County in twenty-four years.

A few nights later, Lafayette's eight-year-old Mars Theater showed Warner Brothers' *On Trial*. This was the city's first "talking" motion picture. Some patrons called them "soundies" because of the new sound-track technology. And at his desk up in Hazelden, George Ade was starting a story for a 1929 movie that would be called *Making the Grade*.

On April 26, the thirty-one-year-old aviator Amelia Earhart, darling of skillful publicists and marketers and steadily rising in national esteem, circled to land at Shambaugh Field. But it had been a soggy spring. The runway bluegrass lay drenched in brown water. Earhart feared that she could not safely land her loud, heavy, fourteen-seat Fokker monoplane at Shambaugh that day, so she dropped a note of regret and flew off.

Don Abbott would remember her anyway. He was nineteen then and majoring in aeronautics at Purdue. His dad, Professor

Raymond B. Abbott, was teaching physics. "I happened to be one of the group sent out to meet Amelia Earhart," Don Abbott recalled. "Lots of fliers came in there, some with the [national publicity] tours. There were six or seven of us [chosen] to meet her. It had rained all night, but the sun had come out bright. She flew over, made several low passes at the field, but then dropped the note. I saw the note, and always wondered who got to keep it. Maybe no one!" (Abbott to author, 1991)

George Ade was the natural choice to introduce the guest speaker the night of May 21 at Purdue's annual Literary Banquet. The guest was Elmer Davis, a bright young journalist and new author from Aurora, Indiana, with a hall-of-fame future in the field of radio news. He had attended Franklin College and had been a Rhodes Scholar at Oxford in 1920 when his father became ill and died. Davis came home, became editor of *Adventure* magazine, then a reporter and editorial writer for the *New York Times*. In 1928, Davis's novel *Giant Killer* retold the biblical story of David. Ade began by reciting the names of twenty-five Indiana authors:

> I have met and known twenty of them. It seems to me that I had my innings during a most fortunate period. No other state in the Middle West and probably no other state in the Union can check up a list of twenty-five writers to compare with those I have just named, all of whom have been alive and in evidence at some time since 1890, when I emerged from the tall grass and began to have ambitions that dealt with putting stuff down on paper and handing it to a printer.

> I treasure my recollections of General Lew Wallace and James Whitcomb Riley and Charles Major and George Barr McCutcheon. Even in the dark days when it seemed that Indiana had given up reading in the evening in order to put on the night-shirts of the Ku Klux Klan I found some consolation in the fact that Booth Tark-

ington and Meredith Nicholson and Kin Hubbard continued to reside in the state. I am not disposed to forget that I first met Tarkington and the two McCutcheon boys right here on the Purdue campus.

This evening it is a real pleasure to meet one whose books I read long before I knew he was coming here tonight—a comparative youngster for whom I have a genuine admiration, Elmer Davis. (*The Scrivener*, December 1929)

On Thursday morning, May 15, a touring airplane called the "Independence" landed at Shambaugh Field. Owned by the Reid Murdoch Company of Chicago, the craft promoted Monarch brand foods. Monarch had converted the three-motored, corrugated metal monoplane with its seventy-four-foot wingspan and cabin seats for eleven, into a "flying grocery." The "Independence" displayed on its shelves the Monarch line of food products the way any grocery store would. Visitors who entered the "food plane" viewed the grocery exhibit all that day. Big airplane arrivals still made newspaper columns. The *Journal and Courier* mentioned:

> Shortly after arrival a trip was made over the city, passengers including Mayor Myron H. Morgan, of West Lafayette, Capt. L. I. Aretz and two local newspaper representatives, Walter Nelson and Gene Kantz, with R. A. Patterson, local representative for the Reid Murdoch Company.

Four days passed. On Sunday afternoon, Freddie Lund, a stunt pilot of some fame, visited Shambaugh Field. Lund, on the factory staff, piloted a new, blue and silver WACO built in Western Aviation's Ohio plant. The free show brought out 5,000 people and hundreds of cars. Lund flew vertical rolls, Immelmann turns, and—new to stunt-flying—a "triple straight-up roll."

The *Journal and Courier* further reported that "Dick Arnett did some pretty flying in his plane, and advanced students of Capt. Aretz also showed skill in the handling of their ships." Arnett, son of the physician and Chamber of Commerce leader, was on his way to a career in flying cut short by accident.

Aviation made the news again on May 28-30 when Aretz flew Studebaker car dealer Charles Murdock and Purdue football coach Phelan from Shambaugh Field to Kansas City, Missouri. They used the airport's new Curtiss 50C "Robin" high-winged cabin monoplane equipped with three seats and a 150- horsepower engine. In the "Robin" Aretz could fly from Shambaugh Field to Indianapolis—sixty miles—in twenty-some minutes.

Early that summer of 1929, Purdue, heeding advice from Dave Ross and President Elliott, hired G. Stanley Meikle to head a new Department of Research Relations with Industry. Purdue called Meikle "widely experienced as a research and engineering executive and a consulting scientist" (Kelly, Ross, 111). This set in motion a rare visit on June 26. On that day the nation's premier car builder Henry Ford (1863-1947) came to review some of Purdue's research projects.

Ford, then in his mid-sixties, arrived with his private secretary, Frank Campsall, from Detroit by Wabash Railroad train on Tuesday night June 25. Top people at Purdue knew that Ford was coming, but the public did not. Ford and Campsall stayed unnoticed for a night in Lafayette's Fowler Hotel. The next morning, Meikle, Dave Ross, and Dean Potter led Ford and Campsall on a Purdue tour.

Marshall saw to it that a *Journal and Courier* man tagged along taking notes. The paper's story that evening publicized Purdue's rising reputation for research. On the tour, Ford "showed a ready smile, pleasant features, sparkling eyes and desire to talk to anyone he met." He also showed a firm grasp of "technical stuff" and asked "good questions." Ford accepted a souvenir kewpie doll forged from iron in the Purdue foundry. When Dean Potter handed Ford a brass PU monogram watch fob for another memento, Ford mentioned that his four grandchildren sure would like those. Potter gave him six.

Ford studied mechanical, physics, and electrical research with the comment that "they all go together." Ford liked the "practical way" Purdue was helping industries solve problems. He rated this type of work "of inestimable value to training young men to take important places in industry."

Ford spoke of a museum and village he was building at his home city of Dearborn, Michigan. It would be the Edison Institute of Technology (later Greenfield Village.) The museum front would resemble Independence Hall in Philadelphia. The Village would reflect pioneer times and occupy 150 acres. It would contain Edison's first laboratory. Antiquated equipment from that lab in New Jersey was being moved to Dearborn for display. Ford said the Edison Institute would be an educational project open to students of the world and that his visit to Purdue gave him many ideas for it. "We can't know much of the future unless we know the past," he said (*Journal and Courier,* June 26, 1929, 13).

In his walk through mechanical engineering projects Ford saw a Lincoln automobile engine he had given Purdue for study some years before. Ford said he had known one Purdue man since 1891. The man was the tall, lanky YMCA teacher and missionary to China, "Big Robbie" Robertson. Back in 1891, Ford had been a foreman in the Detroit Edison plant and Robertson had been a Purdue mechanical engineering student. Ford said he had followed Robertson's religious, instructional, and scientific lecture work in China with great interest ever since.

Ford also discussed auto lubricants. Oil derived from castor beans then was being tested to replace motor oil. "We have been taking our oil from the ground," Ford said, "but some day that will be exhausted and then we'll have to get our oil from the *top* of the ground" (*Journal and Courier,* June 26, 1929, 13).

Ever the newsmaker, Amelia Earhart acquired a modified 1927 Lockheed "Vega," a seven-seat cabin monoplane with a 300-horsepower engine. With it she finished third in the first Women's Air Derby from Santa Monica, California, to Cleveland, Ohio.

When the September semester began in 1929, Purdue prevailed upon Captain Aretz to teach at Shambaugh Field so as to add eleven aviation courses. On a promotional air tour of Indiana that fall, Aretz again flew a Curtiss "Robin." Lafayette firms that sponsored him arranged to have their names painted on one side of the "Robin." Lettering on the other side advertised the eight 1929 Purdue football games that would start October 5 against Kansas State in Ross-Ade Stadium.

On November 1, 1929, the Indiana Supreme Court settled a seven-year-old case vital to Purdue. The court ruled that Purdue and the other state universities could *condemn* land for dormitories or military projects. This thorny and contentious eminent domain issue had arisen back in 1922 when Purdue, namely Dave Ross, wished to acquire for a dormitory some of the Dick Russell land in rural Wabash Township north and west of the existing campus. Tippecanoe Circuit Court Judge Homer W. Hennegar had ruled in December 1927 that Purdue could condemn under the terms of state laws enacted in 1911 and 1927, but legal counsel persuaded Russell to appeal. Russell argued that the 1911 and 1927 laws gave Purdue privileges *not enjoyed by all citizens* and was thus unconstitutional. Now the Supreme Court viewed the state colleges as a class by themselves that *could* be helped by special laws.

Since 1921, Dave Ross had been bringing to the Purdue Trustees the confidence of a self-made man of industry and wealth. His vision had led to and inspired the court battle with Russell. Ross also voiced practical, down-to-earth views about farming. To fellow Trustee Joseph Day Oliver, President of the Oliver Chilled Plow Works in South Bend, Ross once remarked: "If I were in the plow business I'd have one that not only turned over the soil but disintegrated it ready for planting."

"That might be hard to do," said Oliver.

Touché! Professor William Aitkenhead in Purdue's School of Agriculture helped Ross design a plow with a rotating part beside the moldboard that could break up soil. Ross received a patent for the plow in the fall of 1929 with three other patents for steering gear control assemblies he had designed.

While enmeshed in progressive work at Purdue, Ross in no way neglected his Ross Gear Company. Ross gears equipped seventeen of the twenty-six car models in the 1929 New York Automobile Show. The Lafayette plant produced its first roller-bearing-mounted cam followers. They improved by fifty percent Ross cam and lever gear efficiency.

Even before the stock market crash of 1929, the number of American car companies had been declining. Only a few large ones still made cars, trucks, and buses. So Ross Gear engineers worked at ways to steer farm tractors, combines, road graders, and other "off-highway" machines while retaining the lead among independent commercial steering gear makers.

The company had enjoyed good Roaring Twenties business. On February 14, 1929, Ross Gear directors had reported assets and liabilities of $2,657,567 with outstanding capital stock of 150,000 shares and a treasury surplus of $950,809 at the end of 1928. In the first quarter of 1929, the company showed a profit before taxes of $279,612—up more than $100,000 over the same quarter in 1928. All told, Ross Gear reported $565,581 in profit for 1929. This compared with $452,830 for 1926, $403,500 for 1927, and $751,351 for 1928 (*The Gear,* 11-12).

Business was going so well, in fact, that on December 16, 1929, Ross Gear directors raised the threshold of company earnings for executive payroll bonuses from $400,000 to $500,000. Just six years earlier the bonus threshold had been $60,000.

Coach Jimmy Phelan's 1929 football team, one of Purdue's best ever, won all of its games. It outscored eight foes 187 points to forty-four. In Ross-Ade Stadium the team beat Kansas State twenty-six to fourteen before 9,000 fans; Michigan twenty-to sixteen before standing-room-only 25,000; DePauw twenty-six to seven; Mississippi twenty-seven to seven; and Iowa seven to nothing before a stadium record 26,000. Football fans kept howling for more seats.

The Purdue Alumnus in the glow of victory—and pride—published a four-page Football Supplement on November 22. "Purdue Big Ten Champion" screamed an inch-tall front-page headline. A small, boxed item on the back page contained a comment titled "Wonderful:"

> The students are happy, the townspeople are jubilant, sport lovers all over the country are forwarding congratulations, prominent sport writers everywhere are using unreservedly high-powered adjectives about our team, and the old grads who have been rooting for Purdue all thru these many years of heartbreaks and disappointments are simply gurgling and incoherent. - GEO. ADE

Yet for Purdue fans, the football news turned dark. Coach Phelan had led Purdue to its first undefeated, untied season since 1892. This team had finished with a thirty-two to nothing route of rival Indiana at Bloomington for possession of the Old Oaken Bucket. Among this team's stars were halfbacks Glen Harmeson, Harry "Monk" Kissell, Ralph "Pest" Welch, Duane Purvis, and fullback Alex Yunevich, but then Phelan resigned to take the football job at the University of Washington. On December 24, Kellogg signed Noble E. Kizer for three years to succeed Phelan. Kizer, one of Phelan's assistant coaches at Purdue, had been another Notre Dame product but with a less fiery approach. Two other coaches who had helped Phelan, A. K. "Mal" Elward and Earl Martineau, stayed at Purdue.

In the last days of 1929 the *Journal and Courier* found it necessary to print upsetting headlines almost every day about the nation's economy. One read, "Tension Lifted in Wild Stock Market Flurry." Others followed like one about a St. Louis stockbroker who swallowed poison, "Ends Life After Losing $400,000."

The financial news would only get worse. There soon appeared full-page ads in American papers from the Ford Motor Company about this tense time. An economic panic slowly was setting in. Nervous investors were selling their stocks at sinking prices to avoid deeper losses. Plants were closing. Workers were being laid off.

Ford announced price cuts on twenty models of coupes, sedans, town cars, station wagons, taxicabs, pickup trucks, delivery trucks, and panel trucks. The price of a Standard Coupe—formerly $550—would drop to $500. Ford lowered its Roadster price from $450 to $435. A Phaeton that sold for $460 would drop to $440. The cost of the company's most expensive Town Car sank from $1,400 to $1,200.

Ford told those who read the ads that the company "believes that basically the industry and business of the country are sound":

> Every indication is that general business conditions will remain prosperous. We are reducing prices now because we feel that such a step is the best contribution that could be made to assure a continuation of good business throughout the country. It has always been our policy to pass on to the public as rapidly as possible the advantages of quantity production and newly developed manufacturing efficiencies. (Lafayette *Journal and Courier*, November 1, 1929)

Well and good, but on December 18 and 19, a shrieking Midwest blizzard dropped eighteen inches of snow on Lafayette, and the howling wind whipped it into six-foot drifts.

The Roaring Twenties still had roar, but had run out of days.

Maybe sports?

Maybe sports news could calm the growing Depression jitters. In Lafayette, the American Legion and other sponsors in January 1930 launched the first annual Golden Gloves boxing tournament. Amateurs from thirty-five miles away could enter. Their nightly bouts ran until February in the National Guard Armory. The first-year champions included four students from Purdue. They were flyweight Bernard Silverman, middleweight J. E. Campbell, light heavyweight Lin Harvey, and heavyweight Sig Grecius.

Purdue's basketball team won the Big Ten crown in March mere months after Coach Phelan's team had claimed the 1929 conference football title. On April 10, 1930, the Purdue Trustees, hearing from so many hopeful fans, voted to add 10,000 bleacher seats to the bowl-shaped but empty north end of Ross-Ade Stadium, install a radio broadcasting booth, and move the press box from the west to the east grandstands.

Workmen poured concrete and bolted in seats where, since 1924, only the terraced earth had held football end zone standees. The men moved the playing field fifteen yards further north. The new seats raised stadium capacity to 23,074, and there was space left at the upper rim of the bowl for more standing room or extra seats or both.

That summer the Purdue Trustees voted to give a name to the old mechanical engineering building. It had been built, had been burned in a natural gas explosion, and was then rebuilt in the 1890s. Now "Heavilon Hall" would honor the structure's chief donor, Amos Heavilon. He was a benevolent Purdue man who farmed in Clinton County, Indiana.

On May 9, 1930, federal census takers totaled up 57,535 residents in steadily growing Tippecanoe County. Blue-collar Lafayette with its factory chimneys now contained 26,240, and prosperous West Lafayette 5,095. By the time Purdue's classes began in September, the red brick campus enrollment reached a record 5,750.

The Federal Radio Commission authorized a Purdue experimental television station in the School of Electrical Engineering. A week after that Purdue dedicated a new Pharmacy Building. An eighteen-hole public golf course opened north of Lindbergh Road outside West Lafayette. Twenty-year-old Joe Pottlitzer assumed duties as the course professional. In Washington, D. C., the venerable Dr. Harvey W. Wiley died at eighty-six. A member of the first Purdue faculty in 1874, Wiley had left Purdue for Washington and risen to fame as a leader in federal pure food and drug tests and laws. A commemorative postage stamp in Wiley's honor already was being planned.

During the summer of 1930, Purdue—again with the help of Captain Aretz and his Shambaugh Field equipment—became the first American University to offer flight training for college credit. The aviator Amelia Earhart took office as the first president of the Ninety-Nines, a women pilots' group, and joined the new Ludington Airlines in Philadelphia as a vice president. She set a women's speed record of more than 181 miles per hour over a three-kilometer course in July and acquired a transport pilot license in October.

In Hazelden at age sixty-four, George Ade touched up one of his old campus-football plays—*The College Widow*. Ade's new script served as the blueprint for a motion picture. The film played in theaters both as *Maybe It's Love* and *Eleven Men and a Girl*.

Part II: Ross-Ade: Their Stadium 229

Because he had invested in land, the economic hard times never quite reached Ade. He did experience difficulty in selling his writing. He did keep a hand in his craft by writing piles of letters. He reminisced in print and with cronies about happier days. There were winter sojourns to Miami Beach, Rotary luncheons, fellowship dinners, and occasional attacks on Democrats. The liberal, old newspaperman became increasingly conservative as he watched the changes of the century, but he also stoically followed his established routines (Tobin, 145).

Ade also wrote revealing answers to an inquiry from a Lafayette salesman friend and one-time Indiana Governor candidate, James Kirby Risk:

> I can hardly find time to tell you all of the things I have done around Purdue. When the Memorial Gym was planned and Purdue had to raise a certain sum to meet an appropriation by the state, the university fund was still short $2,500 on the last day. I chipped in with the amount required. I helped out on the Harlequin shows for a number of years and bought the boys about $2,000 worth of scenery, including the plush drop curtain still in use. I directed the building of the Sigma Chi house and spent about $25,000. Also I handled the alumni magazine for a number of years.

> Dave Ross discovered the site for the stadium and showed me the layout. We bought sixty-five acres of land and later matched up contributions made by alumni so that our total contribution to the project was somewhere between $60,000 and $70,000. I have no accurate record of the amount we spent.

> It is not my desire to blow about the things I have done for Purdue because I derived a real pleasure from getting in on such large and worthy enterprises. You must remember that Dave Ross and I are old bachelors. Every person who begins to grow old must adopt something. Old maids adopt cats and canaries. Dave Ross and I adopted Purdue.

It is only fair to add that Dave has done much more for the University than I have done. The amount of work he has given to the school and the amount of money he has given, without many people knowing about it, entitle him to first place among the alumni and I want it distinctly understood that I am not presuming to put myself in his class as a Purdue benefactor. (Tobin, 147-148)

Ade contributed an essay titled "Purdue" for the April 1930 issue of *College Humor* magazine. He wrote four "At Long Range" commentaries in *The Purdue Alumnus* for January, April, May, and June 1930. For *The Purdue Engineer* of October 1930, he penned "Trying to Get Along without Juice."

The economic tough times persisted. With an eye on their sinking profits, in September 1930 the Ross Gear and Tool Company directors reduced quarterly stock dividends from seventy-five to fifty cents per share.

Coach Noble Kizer's first Purdue football team won six games and lost two in the fall of 1930. In the expanded Ross-Ade Stadium this team topped Baylor twenty to seven before 11,000 fans, beat Wisconsin seven to six in front of 25,000, and drubbed Butler thirty-three to nothing. Another standing room only crowd saw Indiana win the Old Oaken Bucket seven to six in Ross-Ade on November 22.

However, a week later a certain gloom tried to set in. Football season revenue at Purdue showed a deficit of $97,000. President Elliott, Ross, and R. B. Stewart set forth to control and oversee Purdue's athletic finances for a while. The three decided to suspend baseball, track, and other minor sports and keep only the moneymaking football and basketball teams (Freehafer, 39). But they rescinded those decisions after deciding that the Ross-Ade

Foundation could help. For seven years, the concept of the Ross-Ade Foundation had, in fact, spurred high-level thinking about financing for, and cooperation with, Indiana industry, too. Ross, who some friends swore "had a new idea every morning," (Freehafer, 35) led that thinking.

Ross liked the way Hoosier farmers could come to Purdue for advice about seeds, plant varieties, fertilizer, insecticides, planting, cultivating, machinery, harvesting, or crop storage, or to learn about any other new research. Ross thought the same should be true of industry. To that end, he and Elliott had hosted the one conference of industrial leaders in 1926. Ross and Dean Potter had visited research labs and paid special attention to the Mellon Institute in Pittsburgh and the Wisconsin Alumni Foundation. In 1928, Elliott and Ross had created that Purdue Department of Research Relations with Industry. Henry Ford had come to look things over and to praise. However, it became obvious—at least to Ross—that the University could not readily manage the protecting and assigning of patents, the shielding of students and staff from exploitation, or the handling of money received from grants and trusts. So the team of astute minds embodied in Elliott, Stewart, Ross, and the other Trustees replaced the Department of Research Relations. The bill for legal counsel in setting up a new structure—nearly a three-year effort—came from Lafayette attorney Alison Stuart marked "no charge." Then announcement was made on December 30, 1930 of the incorporation of a Purdue Research Foundation or PRF.

Modeled after the Ross-Ade Foundation, the founders said that PRF's purpose would be "to assist in financing of research, and to handle matters pertaining to patenting inventions for the benefit of the university, the State of Indiana, and U.S. industry." Elliott supplied presidential clout, Stewart the financial acumen, Stuart the legal mind, yet Ross quietly received honors by common consent for having "invented" PRF.

Fast growing seeds

The top people drew up the Purdue Research Foundation to include several classes of members. The members were variously known as Founders, National Counselors, Purdue Trustees, Researchers, Alumni Research Counselors, and so on. At the first meeting on January 24, 1931, for "seed money" Ross gave PRF $25,000 worth of Ross Gear stock, but stock values slid rapidly owing to the Depression. To make up for the shortfall, Ross also gave PRF a 420-acre farm in Wea Township south of Lafayette.

Ross, in those days, used to chide Purdue's Agriculture staff because it so often begged the Trustees for extra budget money for operations. Ross thought that if *he* could make money by farming, then Purdue should, too. When Ross turned the Wea Township acreage over to Stewart to manage he said, "We'll show those boys in Agriculture how to make money on a farm." However, Stewart found the farm nearly stripped bare. A tenant had made off with so much, Ross said no more about farm profits for a while (Freehafer, 55-58).

Purdue Trustee J. K. Lilly also gave PRF $25,000 in start-up money, but PRF caught on so fast that it never needed to use even the interest on the Ross or Lilly "seed money" in order to grow. Early on a client company asked PRF to study chlorination. With this customer's grant of $5,000 per year for three years, a Purdue graduate student and his mentoring professor developed *12 Rules for Chlorination*.

More than half a century later, a Purdue history would state:

Ross's involvement in the establishment of the Research Foundation may be his most significant contribution to the university... His interest and contributions...and his relationship with Elliott were legendary...

Not many needs large or small escaped Ross' attention. Once when he learned of a student who needed surgery but had no money for it (there was no emergency university fund to meet such needs) Ross gave Purdue $7,500 worth of shares of his Ross Gear company to establish a fund to meet exceptional student needs...

Some promises of big-time giving [to PRF] fell through, in part because of the national Depression. But Ross was optimistic. "With [a lot of easy money] we'd have been busy planning great laboratories and not giving enough thought to picking the right men to do research," he said. "Besides, starting in a modest way gives us a better chance for sane, healthy growth." (Topping, 214)

PRF retained the services of Stanley Meikle when it organized. For rather a test case of PRF's effectiveness in handling patents, Ross in late January applied for one. Meikle has recorded that "several years ago Ross was requested by the Indiana State Highway Commission to interest himself in the problem of lighting the Indiana highway system." He continued:

A preliminary survey conducted with the Electrical Engineering School at Purdue made him realize that the cost [would be] prohibitive. Further study led Ross to conclude that the public was most interested in some means of positive indication of the lanes of traffic under all conditions of weather and during all hours of the day.

[A cat's eyes] gave him the idea for a way to mark the traffic lanes. If these perfect reflectors could be placed at frequent intervals along the centerline of paved highways the problem would be solved. This was the basis for the David E. Ross Traffic Marker of the Purdue Research Foundation and the many patent applications which have grown out of this concept. (Meikle)

During this period Ross found even more channels for giving to Purdue. He bought land and offered lots for sale to Purdue staff members for building summer homes. R. B. Stewart bought one of the first lots. He and Ross, working on weekends, built a cabin on the land. If the bachelor Ross at times became lonely he would find out when Stewart was going out and would show up ready for work, too. Although nearing age sixty, Ross still seemed to enjoy driving nails and sawing boards while he visited

During the 1920s, Fairfield's business grew steadily under George Kumming's leadership, but the onset of the Depression spelled his downfall. Just after the crash of 1929 Kumming had taken all of the company's capital and purchased gear castings from recently liquidated manufacturers. Before he realized it his financial commitment to the procurement of gear castings had left the company without the capital to meet payroll and pay debts. Dave Ross was forced to reorganize Fairfield. He set up his cousin, Edward Ross, and himself as executive vice presidents, but then he astonished his associates by appointing A. J. McAllister, a recent Purdue graduate, as the general manager. Ross's reason for placing such a young man in such a high position was "his mind won't be all set. He'll still be open to new ideas, to seeing new ways of doing things" (Kelly, *Ross*, 57). McAllister proved to be a huge success.

The depressed economy aside, the Ross Gear and Tool Company managed to record one-third-of-a-million-dollar profit for 1930, and Ross received patents on a steering gear and a steering gear control lever assembly.

Next, Ross gave PRF more than 4,400 shares of Ross Gear stock. PRF sold this stock for $380,000 and invested the proceeds in a four percent certificate of deposit. Ross had taken the action after finding that Purdue could not supplement retirement funds for any of its faculty. Now there could be money to benefit the president, deans of the schools, and heads of departments when they had been with Purdue ten years and turned seventy or were disabled earlier. Ross insisted he get no publicity about the donation. So, Elliott named this hush-hush gift the "XR Fund"(Freehafer, 17).

⁓ ⁓

Ross had concluded that aviation was going to be important in American life and world affairs, so he felt that Purdue needed to be a leader in aeronautical education. "And it should go farther than teaching theory from textbooks," he said. "Purdue should have an airport" (Kelly, *Ross,* 129).

Thus, in late January 1931, for yet another gift Ross paid $37,000 for 157 level acres southwest of the campus along the south side of New York Central Railroad tracks. The tract was nearly triple the size of Shambaugh Field in Lafayette. Ross meant for the purchase to be at least the start of a University-owned airport and be a basis for more aviation courses. The seller of the land was Maurice Neville, president of Western Indiana Gravel, a company like many others struggling in the Depression. Neville's men had been extracting, screening, and washing good quality sand and gravel from pits just east of the airport site. By trucks and railroad cars they had shipped the gravel off to buyers. The deal with Ross kept Western Indiana Gravel in business, and as a result the federal government soon chose Purdue and five other U.S. colleges for aeronautical instruction and research.

Speaking of aviation, Amelia Earhart left Ludington Airlines over some sort of policy dispute, and on February 7, 1931, she married George Palmer Putnam. With his help she acquired a Pitcairn autogiro made by a company in Pennsylvania. An autogiro was a type of heavier-than-air craft supported aloft by a whirling rotor instead of fixed wings. A nose propeller pulled it through the air like an airplane, and like a helicopter it had a rotor instead of wings, but air pressure drove the rotor instead of an engine. "With virtually every prestigious flying record already captured or broken by one of the dozen or so top women pilots," one of Earhart's biographers later wrote, "Amelia and George were looking for something that would keep her name a headliner, and the autogiro, they hoped, was just the vehicle" (Lovell, 169).

In April 1931, with her Pitcairn, Earhart achieved an autogiro record altitude of more than 8,000 feet. On May 22 she bought an improved Pitcairn PCA-2, saying she wanted to be the first person to fly an autogiro from coast to coast. Putnam, the adept promoter, sold the autogiro to the Beech-Nut chewing gum makers. Beech-Nut then leased the machine back to Amelia and retained her to be a flying ambassador. Starting in late May Earhart became the first woman to make a transcontinental flight in an autogiro. Some newspapers nicknamed the Pitcairn "the flying windmill" in their accounts of her much-publicized feat.

Early in 1931, Ross Gear Directors heard the numbers they had feared but expected. Company profit for 1930 after taxes had fallen to $336,000—down from $565,000 in 1929. But it *was* profit, and the company assets and liabilities still balanced at more than $2.5 million.

The Ross-Aitkenhead team that worked to design a better plow met with success in March 1931. The government patent office issued in Ross's name "U.S. No. 1795182" for a "Cornstalk and Clodcutter Attachment for Tractors." And more ideas kept on flowing Ross's way. The first time he saw a 1930s engine-powered airship, commonly called a "dirigible," he considered, then designed, one that contained a light, rigid, hollow cylinder from front to rear. This made an airship stronger and let air flow through it to relieve pressure on the front end when it was flying. This spur-of-the-moment idea for a hollow or tubular dirigible frame brought Ross a patent on June 13, 1931.

On June 15, because of business uncertainty, Ross Gear cut weekly and monthly salaries by ten percent. David Linn Ross remained chairman of the board and Edward A. Ross presided. However, when Edward died on July 9 Dave Ross agreed to assume the presidency without pay until the term expired in March 1932. Running the wobbling company in the Depression might have absorbed all his time. He did preside for the next six years, but Purdue affairs remained a high priority for him.

By comparison, George Ade was less active and less visible. By the time he had finished with Broadway in 1910 he had become wealthy. The book value of his investments in Indiana farmland had gained until he was offered nearly a million dollars for them. Now in the 1930s, with farm prices and property values falling, he was still syndicating fables and drifting into the good-money world of slick magazines. However, he did make one more literary effort. This was when New York City publishers Ray Long and Richard Smith brought out *The Old-Time Saloon* in November. Based on an idea from a former *Cosmopolitan* magazine editor, the nonfiction volume contained amusing chapters with titles such as "What Was a Saloon—and Why," "The Free Lunch," "What They Drank," "Why People Behave So," "The Bar-Keep," "Song and Story," and "The Talk." *The Old-time Saloon* bore the subtitle *Not Wet—Not Dry—Just History*. In the book, Ade told of a vaudevillean being chased out of an Irish saloon on St. Patrick's Day. The Son of Erin had eaten shamrock bar decorations thinking they were watercress.

Although he did still oppose Prohibition, in the book Ade did not lament the passing of saloons. His chapters about barkeepers, barroom talk, songs and stories, the art of bouncing, favorite drinks, and free lunches hit home with his older readers. Ade's biographer

Fred Kelly later speculated, "not long after publication of *The Old-Time Saloon* national Prohibition was on its way out. Perhaps the book played its part" (Kelly, *Ade,* 249).

Hard put to focus on anything much else that really interested him, Ade began taking orders for writing jobs. *Cosmopolitan* inspired him to compose a new series of "Fables" with drawings by McCutcheon. Hollywood still called, too. One 1931 movie, *Young as You Feel*, came from Ade's 1908 play *Father and the Boys*.

After 1931 Ade finished only eleven more contributions to *The Purdue Alumnus*. One in June 1934 was the transcript of a radio program he had broadcast over WBAA. The last article appeared in February 1941.

Coach Kizer's 1931 football team won nine games and lost one. In Ross-Ade Stadium, however, crowds and income fell short of hopes, probably owing to the Depression times. On October 3, Boilermaker fans could buy one ticket and watch two games in the stadium on the same afternoon. In the games Purdue beat Western Reserve twenty-eight to nothing and Coe College nineteen to nothing. But the 10,000 fans who paid stared at more than 13,000 empty seats. Purdue beat Centenary that season forty-nine to six and topped Iowa twenty-two to nothing before the highest Ross-Ade Stadium attendance of the year, 18,000. The '31 Boilers won the Old Oaken Bucket nineteen to nothing in front of 22,000 at Bloomington. The lone 1931 loss, twenty-one to fourteen to Wisconsin, took place before 30,000 in Madison, Wisconsin.

Promising news, growing Depression

The Purdue community felt both discouraged and proud during Depression-dreary 1932. Banks closed. Businesses failed. Unemployment soared. Values dropped. On February 25, as gloom of this sort grew thicker, the hourly workers in the Lafayette Building Trades Council accepted a ten percent wage cut and a five-day, forty-hour work week. The aim was to relieve unemployment and stimulate the building industry for one year starting April 1.

In early May, amid more factory and business closings and lost jobs, record numbers of candidates sought nominations for public offices. In Tippecanoe County's primary elections, for instance, twelve men ran for the Republican nomination for sheriff.

As part of Depression relief, a federal government-financed Civilian Conservation Corps (CCC) camp opened at the old Tecumseh Trail Park site on North River Road north of West Lafayette. The intent of the CCC was to provide work for jobless men. CCC projects in public places involved building roads, installing drain tiles and sewers, pouring concrete sidewalks, sprucing up places like the Indiana Soldiers Home cemetery, and the construction of a chapel nearby.

On May 26, the Chamber of Commerce organized a thirty-five-acre "community vegetable garden" in northeast Lafayette. There were spaces in the community garden for eighty-five private family plots plus crops-for-share of potatoes, carrots, tomatoes, and cabbage. Purdue's Agriculture faculty, the Tippecanoe County

Commissioners, and the International Harvester Company provided various forms of advice, tools, and help. On June 23, Purdue cut the price of a football game ticket by fifty cents—from three dollars to two-fifty—to encourage attendance.

⁓ ⁓

It was left for people like Dave Ross, George Ade, and a new face named Bruce Rogers to brighten the local gloom, and to Amelia Earhart to cheer the nation as a whole. A story in the *Journal and Courier* told about sixty-two-year-old Rogers, he being another in the lengthening list of accomplished Sons of Purdue. Working in England for nearly twenty years, the Lafayette native Rogers had at last earned acclaim as a designer of books and type fonts used in rare and valuable printing. Rogers had just finished a *Lectern Bible*. Rogers also had created a popular new book type he called Centaur that was beginning only then to be widely used. Rogers had finished Purdue with a degree in science in 1890, then joined the art staff of the *Indianapolis News*. Later, he branched out as a designer, moved to Boston and beyond in the elite field of fine arts, printing, and limited editions in the U.S. and Europe.

⁓ ⁓

Dave Ross gained momentum, Depression or not. He received four patents in 1932 for his composite, stone-like structural material Rostone; a method of making Rostone; an improved cam and lever steering gear; and a better clutch mechanism for cars and trucks.

David Linn Ross, co-founder and venerable board chairman of Ross Gear and Tool Company, a donor toward William Ross Sanatorium, and an 1890s developer of Highland Park homesites, died on June 10, 1932 at the age of eighty. Nephew David Edward, the lone surviving company founder, felt obliged to return to factory management. Uncle Linn's position as chairman of the Ross Gear board remained vacant. During Dave Ross's fill-in presidency Ross

Gear soon began licensing. The first went to Zahnradfabrik in Friedrichshafen, Germany (known as "ZF" in the Lafayette plant front office) to make and sell patented Ross cam and lever gears in Europe.

However, Purdue affairs remained a high priority. Ross continued buying land around Ross-Ade Stadium and giving it to Purdue for future use, and in the summer of 1932, Ross announced plans to make and sell Rostone for construction, even to show it at the Century of Progress World's Fair in Chicago.

The Rostone idea had remained a work in progress since 1927. It cost less than the same amount of brick or concrete to build with Rostone, but unlike cement-based products that needed days to dry and "set," Rostone could be ready in four hours. It could be hardened in 300-degree heat. That was much less than brick making required. Ross had applied for a patent for Rostone in February 1929. In the application, he wrote:

> Our invention relates to a new material, possessing chemical and physical properties that specially adapt it for use in decorative and ornamental arts and also for structural and other purposes, and includes the material and process for producing the same. The invention is based upon our discovery that, contrary to common belief, reaction will readily take place under proper conditions to be hereinafter set forth, between an alkaline earth base and the aluminosilicic acids comprising the so-called "clay matter" of clay materials, (slates, shales and certain clays) resulting in a new material, or new materials having new and useful properties.

Successful hardening of the material by use of heat, Ross explained, depended on maintaining just the right amount of water in the mixture. His employees' tests had confirmed that too much water caused boiling and crumbling, too little caused weak chalkiness. The U.S. Patent Office issued the patent, Number 1,852,672, to Ross on April 5, 1932. Rostone next began the task of informing the public of the work that had been under way for five years. It was felt that the best way was to build a public house—a "show home"—using the synthetic stone. Rostone made an agreement with the Indiana Bridge Company to furnish a skeletal steel structure to meet specifications from Rostone, and Rostone would supply the fabricated stone. A house was built on Lot 15 in West Lafayette's Hills and Dales addition and plans begun for a home to go up at the Century of Progress in Chicago.

Lafayette business directories thereafter began listing Ross as President and young Richard Harrison Secretary-Treasurer and General Manager of an otherwise unadvertised "Rostone Research Corporation" in the Ross Building.

As an experiment the Rostone men tried using the artificial stone as a base for electrical switches. It proved to be more resistant to current, with less deterioration than plastic and other materials. Ross named it Rosite, wishing people to pronounce it "Ross-ite." This part of the business in Depression times saved Rostone from operating at a loss. More work remained, however, to persuade architects and builders to use Rostone instead of real stone.

In 1932, appendicitis struck young Edward Ross while he was sailing to Europe. He would not allow his ship doctors to operate, and by the time they reached Southampton, England, he had died. This loss forced Dave Ross to make a serious new decision about Fairfield. It seemed to Dave that A. J. McAllister had proven himself to be a worthy general manager. It would be another matter to put McAllister in charge of the entire company. However, he named McAllister General Manager and Treasurer of Fairfield, and the ensuing years proved that Ross had made a wise choice.

The year 1932 marked the start of a short-lived housing research program that Ross promoted at Purdue. R. B. Stewart was looking for land where he could build a home. He wanted five acres on a hill north of Stadium Avenue west of the campus. He learned about seventy-six acres going up for sale. Because he couldn't finance that much, he approached Ross. The tract was the Marstellar dairy farm that the widow Marstellar was trying to run, although she had no money to replace a barn that had burned. The farm was appraised at $13,000. Dave Ross told her that "if you want to sell it, put a price on it and then I'll give you Federal Land Bank bonds or Purdue bonds equal to the price." She accepted the federal bonds, then selling at a discount. Ross deeded the land to PRF and suggested to Stewart that houses be built there for faculty with the septic systems under the front lawns because, he wrongly speculated, no one ever would have to water or fertilize the grass. Through PRF Ross then helped start and backed the Purdue Housing Project. It planned and built six houses on the Marstellar land. They were of various types of construction. Each offered three bedrooms and cost $5,000. The project did not last, and President Elliott agreed to transfer the New York based Better Homes in America to Purdue to take it over.

Asked to play a part in Purdue's first convocation in the September semester of 1932, Ade dusted off and recited a poem he had written in 1907 and titled "The Fountain of Youth."

Amelia Earhart, meanwhile, summarized her many exploits up to 1932 when she wrote (and George Putnam published) *The Fun of It*. She afterward became the first woman and only the second pilot (after Lindbergh) to fly the Atlantic Ocean solo. She achieved this during May 20-21 on the fifth anniversary of Lindbergh's historic trip.

In August 1932, Earhart set a women's record for the fastest non-stop transcontinental flight (Los Angeles to Newark, New Jersey) in nineteen hours and five minutes. Congress awarded her a Distinguished Flying Cross. France presented her a Cross of Knight of the Legion of Honor. U.S. President Herbert Hoover gave the Gold Medal of the National Geographic Society. The National Aeronautics Association bestowed upon her an honorary membership. She won the Harmon Trophy for America's Outstanding Airwoman.

Noble Kizer's strong 1932 Purdue team won seven games, tied one, and lost none. In Ross-Ade Stadium the team beat Kansas State twenty-nine to thirteen, edged past Wisconsin seven to six, then thrashed Indiana twenty-three to seven before a near-capacity throng that numbered 22,000.

To Dave Ross, intercampus cooperation over the years had become yet another issue of importance. A Purdue physics professor needed a magnet costing $1,500 for his experiments. After that the magnet would be of no further use. Ross told the professor: "I'll give you the money to build the magnet. And when it has been used I suggest that it be lent to other universities." Such thinking inspired Ross to join an Association of Governing Boards of State Universities. In 1932, in a speech to Association members, Ross addressed what he considered another growing evil, the practice of pushing young athletes to win games to increase gate receipts and of arranging football schedules so as to make money:

> When you place an athletic coach in a position where his success depends on what his team can earn, that is wrong. No college debt should be based on expected athletic earnings. If a coach is successful in bringing big earnings then he may tell his governing board that he is worth more than the president of the university. If you like wholesome sport for kids, keep it pure. Don't put it on an earning basis.

If Purdue teams lost in a football game Ross might say, "What of it? They tried hard didn't they? It doesn't matter if we lose so long as it wasn't from not trying." He sometimes recalled leaving one Purdue football game unaware of which team had won. He explained that while the game was ending he was trying to figure out better plans for streets and highways to disperse Ross-Ade Stadium traffic.

By the end of 1932, President Elliott reported to the Board of Trustees that in its first two years the Purdue Research Foundation had started more than fifty projects. They involved almost an equal number of professors and graduate students. PRF still enabled Purdue to make contracts for industrial research—even research of a proprietary nature, but which had clear educational objectives. PRF kept on assuming legal and financial obligations the University could not take on because of restrictive laws.

Ross, Elliott, and R. B. Stewart (now elevated to the job of Purdue Controller) remained careful to structure PRF's membership to avoid any chance that it could become a political power base. One important membership category since the start had been that of *Founder*—those who gave $15,000 or more. Other categories still included *Board of Trustees* members and the *University President*; ten men selected for their *Scientific and Professional Achievements*; twenty-five to fifty eminent *Purdue Alumni*; and a group of *Research* members who had contributed through some PRF project.

Meanwhile, by the end of 1932, the PRF prototype Ross-Ade Foundation had received more than $109,000 worth of land gifts from both alumni and friends.

All this promising news amid the worsening Depression.

A time of change

It was by any means of measurement a time of change. On January 9, 1933 the Democrat Paul McNutt took office as Governor of Indiana. This ended the statehouse life of Harry Leslie. Leslie then chose to cut most ties with West Lafayette and Purdue. He stayed in Indianapolis to help start and take a vice presidency in Standard Life Insurance Company.

Democrat Franklin D. Roosevelt, touting a series of Depression-relief ideas, took office as U.S. President.

The Purdue Research Foundation already was paying dividends. The *Journal and Courier* reported on January 31, 1933 that PRF research for Radio Corporation of America had produced a "television set." A Purdue electrical engineer team plugged the receiving set into an ordinary electrical outlet in a West Lafayette home at 503 University Street. Professor Francis Harding, Head of the Department of Electrical Engineering, lived there. PRF had contracted for grant money for the work from the Grigsby-Grunow Company in Chicago. Harding directed the work of researchers Ray Abbott, Roscoe George, and Howard Heim. The Federal Radio Commission had permitted Purdue, in the spring of 1930, to try to build a television transmitting station. That done, the challenge now was to make an affordable receiving set that consumers could buy and use to "see" the station's TV signals.

The 1933 tests involved a portable (albeit big and heavy) receiving set. The men conducted the first preview of it at Harding's home on the night of January 31, 1933. The first test involved tuning into pictures transmitted from the station's tower on high ground outside Ross-Ade Stadium at 9 p.m. Purdue's station had been assigned the call letters W9XG.

Pictures materialized seemingly out of the thin air in an almost eerie fashion as the receiver was tuned in on the Purdue station, but the momentary "ghost-like" effect was removed almost instantly by the sharpness and contrast of the pictures that moved across the "window" of the receiving set.

The receiving set has reached the state where it is ready for commercial production at a price that will be within the range of the ordinary radio fan. (*Journal and Courier,* February 1, 1933)

W9XG had been sending experimental programs since March 29, 1932. The Grigsby-Grunow Company had invested about $120,000 in the project. George and Heim achieved success with a smaller, lighter, and therefore portable receiver. George had earned Purdue engineering degrees in 1922 and 1927, the second one after he developed cathode ray oscillography crucial to TV success.

A depressing report heard by the Ross Gear stockholders in March showed that in 1932 the company's assets had fallen by about $200,000 to a value of 2.4 million. At Dave Ross's struggling Rostone Corporation the top people felt that demand for homes made of its synthetic stone could be created, advertised, and accomplished, and good will created more rapidly and at less cost, at the Century of Progress World's Fair in Chicago. However, before such a house could go up the nearly bankrupt Indiana Bridge Company withdrew from its agreement to build a steel skeleton, and Rostone had to build its own.

Rostone officers Paul Jones and Floyd Wymer gave a talk about producing synthetic stone out of quarry waste and a shale binder to the American Chemical Society at a meeting in Washington, D.

C., in early 1933. The July issue of *Industrial and Engineering Chemistry* contained the text of their remarks.

In late March 1933, George Ade finished writing "Autobiography of George Ade." Calling it "the hardest writing job I ever tackled," Ade mailed it off in response to a request from an editor and author named Stanley J. Kunitz. Kunitz put Ade's work in abridged form in a book he co-edited titled *Authors Today and Yesterday*. That book came out in 1933. Ade's piece showed up again in *Twentieth Century Authors* in 1942. Among its highlights:

• After high school I attended Purdue University, taking the scientific course because I had no ambition to be an engineer or an agriculturist. [I was] a star student as a freshman but wobbly later on and a total loss in mathematics. In 1887 I received my B. S. from Purdue.

• In 1905 I took up a permanent residence at Hazelden Farm near Brook Indiana, within fifteen miles of my birthplace. I have been away from this place very few summers since that time but the wanderlust was upon me every autumn. On checking up I learn that I have been to Europe ten times, cruised through the West Indies eleven times, visited China and Japan four times and have looped the globe twice.

• From 1913 to the present time I have promoted the Hazelden Country Club which has attractive buildings and a good golf course adjoining my home.

• Ten years ago David Ross, a worthy graduate of Purdue and now President of the Board of Trustees, invited me to go with him on an enterprise which involved the purchase of sixty-five acres of land [and] the incorporating of the Ross-Ade stadium high up on a majestic hill overlooking the campus and the Wabash Valley. It was not a million-dollar extravagance. A glacial drift some time ago did most of the excavating. It seats 25,000 people and is almost a replica of the stadium at Athens. Purdue began to climb toward Big Ten ascendancy on the day we dedicated the stadium. For quite a number of years I paid more attention to Purdue and various activities in my home state than I did to writing for the magazines.

- I am a bachelor but I prefer to live in my own home. My enthusiasms include golf, travel, horseracing and the spoken drama. My antipathies are social show-offs, bigots on religion, fanatics on total abstinence and all persons who take themselves seriously. I read all the periodicals, sober and frivolous, sacred and profane, and try to know what is going on in the world. I have a card-index memory for the words and music of old hymns, old popular songs and old 'numbers' from the light operas of day before yesterday. I love to put on big parties and see a throng of people having a good time.

- [My] books number twenty, not counting eight or ten plays.

- I nearly forgot to say that I am a member of the National Institute of Arts and Letters, and on the Executive Committee of the Authors Guild. Under an alphabetical arrangement my name was first on the list of those selected to direct the efforts of the Association for the Repeal of the Eighteenth Amendment. I belong to no secret orders, and I do not choose to make or listen to speeches. (Tobin, 14-17)

During 1933, Arrow Editions, New York City, also republished a collection of Ade's old articles titled *Thirty Fables in Slang*.

Meanwhile, the March 1933 issue of *The Purdue Engineer* contained Stanley Meikle's informative article, "The Ross Marker." The piece told about the cat's eyes reflections and so on. It also revealed that the Corning Works produced the mirrored reflector from Pyrex glass nearly the equal of perfect ground lens.

In 1932, the Indiana Highway Commission agreed to install several hundred of these markers if PRF would supply them. Ross Gear and Tool Company made 500 markers. The State installed most of the markers during the early summer on state highways within a radius of seventy-five miles of Purdue.

"At no other time do the reflectors show as brilliantly as while being washed by rain," Meikle wrote. "The first installation was made on Northwestern Avenue north of the university and extending from the West Lafayette city limits for one mile, including a compound curve and a straight stretch...Studies have resulted in minor changes and the marker is now [early 1933] being put into final form and arrangements are being made to offer the device to the general public." On April 6, a company in Marion, Indiana, began making the Ross highway markers.

Rostone operated its show home during 1933 and 1934 at the Century of Progress. This venture had cost Dave Ross hundreds of thousands of dollars. "But," he said "we have demonstrated that it is possible to build beautiful houses inexpensively from raw material available in many parts of the country. It isn't necessary to cut down trees in Oregon for a house in Indiana. I don't know how long it will take to convince the public, but this Rostone experiment will finally prove to be the most important thing I have done" (Kelly, *Ross,* 126-127). This, to be blunt, was Dave Ross's worst forecast, as time would tell.

On the first of August in 1933, the National Recovery Act or "NRA" took effect. In Lafayette, several cooperative unemployment relief programs involved industries and businesses. A shorter workweek cut down on the rampant unemployment by giving more workers jobs. The federal government urged American consumers to patronize stores displaying "blue eagle" NRA logos. A national goal was five million new jobs by Labor Day.

Noble Kizer's 1933 Purdue football team won six games, lost one, and tied one. In Ross-Ade Stadium, the team beat Ohio University thirteen to six before 10,000 fans, beat Carnegie Tech seventeen to seven before 18,000, and lost to Iowa fourteen to six as 16,000 people watched. In all three home games, there were thousands of unoccupied seats in the enlarged stadium.

The longer Dave Ross functioned at the highest levels of Purdue—as President of the Board of Trustees and as a morning-coffee pal of President Elliott—the further his vision extended. He came to believe that Purdue should have the land it might need for at least half a century. That explains why, in the early 1930s, he bought so many acres west of Ross-Ade Stadium and gave it to the Purdue Research Foundation. Ross shortly persuaded PRF to put part of the land to use for experimental housing projects and research. Eventually, part of the land became PRF's "campus."

The subject of housing still intrigued Ross and presented numerous problems to be solved. Rostone had been only a beginning. Ross patented a furnace so compact it could be carried through a household door. Then he designed a window-and-frame unit with glass on the outside. This allowed more daylight to come into a house. He influenced PRF to carry out studies of even more housing challenges. PRF became the agency through which a Purdue Housing Research Program took form in the mid-1930s. Ross encouraged several University departments to help in the research. If better paint was needed, Purdue's Department of Chemical Engineering worked on the task. Civil Engineering assigned students to find new ways to frame a house. Aspiring mechanical engineers dealt with home heating and cooling methods. Electrical Engineering and Home Economics added expertise to kitchens, lighting, and wiring. Lowering the overall cost of homes was another goal

Ideas for inventions—better ways of doing things—still came to Ross almost any time or anywhere. In his spare time, Ross invented a ventilating system for school classrooms, a diesel internal combustion engine, and an earthenware home humidifier. While waiting at a railway junction he studied the brakes on a freight car. That night he worked on a new type of brake drum. After a ride in a streetcar in Washington, D. C., he took a pen and envelope from his pocket and designed a new type.

Ross invented a baseboard for homes with electrical outlets every few inches apart. And one summer night while guests at The Hills were swatting mosquitoes, Ross decided to "rig up a bugcatcher." In his basement workshop he found a big can and glass funnel that would fit over the opening. He knocked the spout off the funnel and wired a light socket and bulb into the can. He then rejoined his guests, put out all other lights, set up, and plugged in his new device. Insects drawn to the light in the can crawled down through the opening in the funnel and were roasted by the heat of the lamp.

One time the Trustees heard an urgent appeal for funds for a new barn on a Purdue dairy farm. Ross reviewed the plans, then began firing questions. "Have you asked the cows what kind of barn they want? How many cubic feet of fresh air per hour does a thousand-pound dairy cow need? How many heat units does she produce? How much moisture does she exhale every day? We ought to use our need for a new barn to learn how to build a *good* one, better than most, and cheaper" (Kelly, *Ross*, 161-162). Ross once drew up a new kind of milk can with a hollow tube in the middle to hold dry ice and keep the milk cold. A friend kidded: "Why don't you apply the same idea to a cocktail shaker?" "I doubt if cocktail making *should* be any more efficient than it is," Ross responded (Kelly, *Ross*, 97).

Ross applied his "let's-do-it-better" philosophy to such things as buying postage stamps, bread, oranges, potatoes, apples, and canned goods from vending machines. When someone told him they were already doing that in Sweden, he simply smiled: "Does that show that I was stupid not to think of it first, or prove that those Swedes are smart?" (Kelly, *Ross*, 98).

Besides the Dick Russell land acquired by eminent domain and the Neville land bought by Ross for the airport, Purdue added other land during the 1930s. During the Depression, many farm properties were losing money. Ross, who knew the local situation, would study a Wabash Township map trying to plot a periphery around the campus that the University could control. If he thought certain parcels would benefit Purdue and could be bought, he would send R. B. Stewart to negotiate with the owners. Stewart's theory was to buy when the other fellow wasn't interested in the land and wanted to sell (Freehafer, 72).

In most cases, Ross's gifts of money, land, and other goods or services remained a secret. Purdue insiders who knew about them expressed wonder over his generosity. "Well," the bachelor Ross would say, "some men keep race horses or women. I'd rather help support a university" (Kelly, *Ross*, 132).

Purdue Airport

Depression news turned a little more promising early in 1934. On January 2 the federal Civil Works Administration (CWA) said it would take on Tippecanoe County projects that would create jobs for more than 1,500 men by April. The CWA would help develop more than 200 acres that Dave Ross had given or helped Purdue acquire for its airport. The work would include grading, putting in water lines and lights, and building a hard runway. Six-year-old Shambaugh Field, on its eighty acres in southeast Lafayette, would by agreement close. Purdue was getting ready to hire the Shambaugh manager and aviation instructor "Cap" Aretz to take charge at Purdue's airport.

The 1934 news turned unbelievable, too, on the night of February 24. It happened during a bridge game in the Delta Sigma Lambda fraternity house at 359 Vine Street in West Lafayette. Against odds said to have been 52 million to one, the dealer distributed thirteen hearts to Purdue junior George Wilcox, a "Delt" from Bradford, Pennsylvania. Wilcox bid seven hearts; his opponents doubled; Wilcox redoubled, laid down his hand, and scored 643 points.

The men running Rostone Corporation had no such luck. They tried to line up licensees to build homes using their synthetic stone. Their Century of Progress house had attracted architects, builders, retailers, and the general public. Sears, Roebuck and Company arranged to distribute and sell Rostone's stone-like material, as well as a company-designed steel frame for the homes. The Martin-Perry Corporation of York, Pennsylvania, agreed to make the frames for Sears. Sears also built and agreed to maintain a model home at the Century of Progress using Rostone. Sears further arranged to let a Rostone man meet visitors at the model home and demonstrate and promote the products Sears hoped to sell. Rostone hired Purdue mechanical engineering graduates Maurice Knoy and David W. Slipher to be the Rostone reps in the show home.

Rostone meanwhile had been quietly working since 1931 on a project to make building bricks out of flue dust also known as "fly ash." At one point during 1931, Rostone and a Chicago area partner had almost agreed to create a holding company to make the bricks. To improve the quality and size of its stone slabs, Rostone bought the old J. Horat Machinery Company building on South Earl Avenue in Lafayette and moved manufacturing to it from Riverside. Rostone bought a bigger hydraulic press, too, and a larger steam autoclave.

To avoid any legal problems with licensee holding companies Dave Ross convinced Harrison and a local contractor, Karl Kettelhut, to form the R-H-K (Ross-Harrison-Kettelhut) Corporation. Founded on April 21, 1934, R-H-K was Ross's fourth business venture (after Ross Gear in 1906, Fairfield in 1919, and Rostone in 1927). R-H-K's purpose was to make and sell the Rostone imitation stone. This allowed Rostone, the company, to return to its primary function, the research of building materials.

For Dave Ross, the affairs at Ross Gear gave him fewer headaches. In 1934, the company introduced a twin-lever gear, the invention of employee Percy "Alex" Newman. By the end of 1934, Ross Gear still retained a treasury surplus of nearly $337,000 (*The Gear*, 13).

Federal remedies aside, joblessness was so rampant that in the primary elections on May 8, 1934, a staggering 485 people, mostly out-of-work men, filed as candidates for nominations for public offices.

At the Founder's Day program at Purdue in May, George Ade responded to a request to be one of its speakers. He chose to accentuate the positive:

> All sorts of universities turn out all sorts of unexpected graduates. Purdue is a school of technology. Yet it has produced the dean of American letters [Booth Tarkington], the world's foremost authority on the printing and binding of beautiful books [Bruce Rogers], and John McCutcheon, who is America's greatest combination of world traveler, cartoonist and war correspondent. (McCutcheon, Jr., John T., 5-6)

On June 24, Ade composed an interesting political letter to Will Hays (1879-1954.) A native of Sullivan, Indiana, Hays led Republican Warren G. Harding's campaign for U.S. President in 1920 and served as Harding's Postmaster General. Hollywood movie studios hired Hays in 1922 as first president of the Motion Picture Producers and Distributors of America until he retired in 1945. In his letter to Hays Ade mentioned, among other things:

> We are between the devil and the deep blue sea out here in Indiana. The Republicans have nominated for Senator, to succeed himself, that oleaginous and unspeakable tadpole, Arthur Robinson. It will be a crime against the state if we return to the Senate a chattering demigogue [sic] who has earned the contempt of all the other senators. The Democrats have put every independent voter on the spot by nominating [Sherman] Minton at the dictation of Paul McNutt. Unless you have been in the state during the past year you cannot understand how general and deep-seated is the resentment against McNutt. He has turned the appointive power over to a lot of second-story men and door mat thieves and the result has been a slaughter reminding one of the Custer massacre or the Spanish Inquisition. We find an army of Republicans in angry revolt against Robinson. We find an army of Democrats...in

open mutiny against McNutt. Party lines will be shot all to pieces. (Tobin, 184-185)

Three days later, Ade wrote about the movies in a letter to his actor friend Charles J. Winninger:

> You have been my favorite actor ever since Edwin Booth died and I caught you in the parade at Eau Claire.
>
> The sad facts in regard to *The County Chairman* are that M.G.M. bought the talking rights and recently sold them to Fox. I understand that Fox had [Will] Rogers in mind for the title role but I do not believe that they have any definite plans regarding the piece. This is all too bad as the part would fit you and you could play it as well as you do your trombone...
>
> I have so many dates with women, being booked weeks ahead, that I find it almost impossible to escape them...Not long ago a tormenting old lady asked me, "Why did you never get married?" I don't know whether [the line] is mine, or whether I remembered it, but I said, "Because her father didn't own a shot gun." Go ahead and put that into the Maxwell House Coffee release for the family trade. We get you on the air every week and we long for television so that we can get a peek at your smiling mug. (Tobin, 186)

Meanwhile, in his screen writing labors, Ade tailored the lead in *The Hero of Eagle Creek* for Will Rogers. However, the entire project had to be shelved because Rogers died in an airplane crash on August 15, 1935.

Maybe the all-out push for research at Purdue—spurred by hard drivers like Dave Ross and the prompt success of PRF—did at times go a little too far. In the summer heat of July 2, 1934, the *Journal and Courier* told of a Purdue man making a "wrist air conditioner." It could cool one's blood with a dry-ice pellet, but that little idea went nowhere.

That summer, between July 20 and August 10, record-setting heat battered the Midwest. At Purdue, temperatures reached 108 on July 20, the highest in fifty-four years of record keeping. The heat inched on up to 110 on July 23 and July 25. Out in the open sun, some said a thermometer would measure 146.

On Tuesday afternoon, September 4, the U.S. Bureau of Air Commerce telegraphed all American airports and airlines that Shambaugh Airport had closed and Purdue University Airport had opened. Purdue featured twenty-four-hour service, boundary and obstruction lights, and a seventy-five-foot beacon, its rotating yellow ray swinging around and lighting the night skies. It was the tallest beacon between Chicago and Indianapolis. Aretz and student pilot Charles Daudt flew five privately owned airplanes housed in the Shambaugh Airport shanties over to Purdue. There a fireproof hangar and modern brick offices with classrooms awaited.

The *Journal and Courier* reported:

> The new Purdue field which is to be operated by the university in cooperation with the Purdue Research Foundation has been approved as an emergency landing field on the Chicago-Cincinnati route by the Bureau of Air Commerce. It covers 224 acres a short distance west of West Lafayette and is capable of handling any modern aircraft, either heavier or lighter than air, now in operation. It is equipped with the latest type of approved markers. Landing floodlights are to be installed soon.

Complete service for transient planes is available, according to Captain Aretz, and men are to be on duty at the port 24 hours a day.

Now Tippecanoe County could boast of three airfields. Frank Reimers operated a private one just south of Lafayette. Another was gaining use to the east. There the brothers Joe, Francis, and John Halsmer had, in 1931, bought a dismantled "Jenny" stored in a farmer's barn in Illinois. They had swapped forty bushels of their dad's corn for it, and they had driven the Jenny in pieces home in a truck. By 1934, the Halsmers operated their own private airfield on forty acres across from the family dairy farm in Perry Township. Their efforts evolved into the public Halsmer Flying Service that operated until 1988.

During 1934, Amelia Earhart won the Harmon Trophy for the third straight year. But more importantly, she met President Elliott at a luncheon. The event that brought them together was the fourth annual Women's Conference on Current Problems sponsored by the New York *Herald Tribune*. Both were speakers, her subject being the future of aviation and the roles of women in that future. She so impressed Elliott with her talk and positive attitude toward careers for women that he asked her to visit Purdue and lecture women students (Lovell, 220).

Within an hour after hearing the proposal from Elliott, Earhart re-arranged her schedule to make the visit. In less than a month she came to the campus to speak about "Opportunities for Women in Aviation." She returned to Purdue in 1935 to discuss with Elliott just what faculty status she was to have (Topping, 234).

At about the same time, Elliott was selling Dr. Lillian M. Gilbreth, a noted industrial engineer, author, and widowed mother of twelve, on coming to Purdue as well. The author of *Cheaper by the Dozen* and wife of an industrial engineer, the late Frank Gilbreth, she continued his work on time-and-motion studies and job efficiency. Her deal at Purdue was like Earhart's. Under her agreement Dr. Gilbreth was to be a "visiting professor" of industrial engineering. She would spend four or five two-week periods on campus to lecture and consult with engineering students. Dr. Gilbreth remained on this schedule until retirement in 1948, but she visited on occasion through the 1960s (Topping, 235-236).

Noble Kizer's 1934 football team won five, lost three. In Ross-Ade Stadium the players lost fourteen to nothing to Rice Institute; they beat Wisconsin fourteen to nothing before 18,000; then they lost the Old Oaken Bucket to Indiana seventeen to six with a near capacity crowd of 24,000 watching.

By mid-December 1934, Dave Ross had collected five more patents. They showed his increased interest in housing and traffic management. They covered his designs for a window sash, window and home construction, weatherstripping, and an improved type of road marker.

Ross also became active in the Farm Chemurgic Council as a Vice President and member of its first Board of Governors representing Indiana industry. In a general way, this Council tried, by using chemistry, to create new markets for farm products or by-products such as cornstalks or manure. The advent of soybeans as a viable cash crop is another example of its progress. There were, of course, detractors. Certain farmers irritated Ross when they remained set in their ways, causing him to complain: "There's nothing wrong with modern farming, but plenty wrong with farmers" (Kelly, *Ross*, 168).

Earhart at Purdue

On April 14, 1935, the noted aviator Wiley Post, trying to fly coast-to-coast in a high-altitude (36,000 feet) experimental plane, had to land his "Winnie Mae," a Lockheed "Vega," at Purdue because of oxygen-mask trouble. Post stayed three days awaiting repairs.

Dave Ross's R-H-K Corporation turned sour. Karl Kettelhut (the "K" in R-H-K) quit on June 1. "Karl left because we just couldn't give him enough business. He could do much better as a private contractor," Rostone's Paul Jones explained. R-H-K had, by 1935, taken over the Rostone factory space on Earl Avenue and had employed most of the Rostone production men. But R-H-K still counted on Rostone engineers to help sell homes and building materials.

R-H-K without the K kept trying to expand its markets, but it was largely unable to persuade architects, contractors, and home-buyers of the value of Rostone synthetic stone. The company did build a few homes and commercial buildings around Lafayette and Chicago. The Kappa Kappa Gamma Sorority House at 325 Waldron Street in West Lafayette was one example, but the company's struggles continued.

On June 3, 1935, Amelia Earhart accepted President Elliott's request to visit Purdue as a consultant. Her lectures would start in the fall. She and Elliott both understood that her visits would be limited to a few weeks each semester, yet the task enthused her. It was agreed that she be a "visiting faculty member" at a salary of $2,000 per year. In addition to its Women's Careers Department,

Purdue conducted its Aeronautics Department at the new airport. Earhart saw chances at Purdue to encourage women to plan careers *and* learn to fly—two subjects close to her heart (Lovell, 220).

⁂

Rostone remained focused on research instead of production or sales. The theory of creating building materials out of waste products such as fly ash, limestone, shale, and other substances dominated company efforts, but Rostone also veered into the field of electrical insulators. A convention of chemical engineers at Purdue introduced Paul Jones to a Purdue chem-engineering graduate named Powers. Powers worked for a rising new electrical control company, Allen-Bradley, of Milwaukee, Wisconsin. Powers saw and liked Rostone's research labs and results. He telephoned Jones about a problem he was having. As Jones put it:

> The beginning of the machine tool business started when they put separate motor control units on individual machines. Before that, there was no concept of separate motor control units; only belt or clutch drives off a central shaft that ran all the machines. No one knew how to run a machine with a separate control and the material in the control unit would begin to immediately carbonize, thus shorting out the motor control. Allen-Bradley wanted a non-carbonizing non-organic material and didn't know where to start.

Jones convinced Powers that Rostone could help if Allen-Bradley would provide a die and let Rostone use it to mold parts for electrical tests. This research led to a reinforced version of Rostone's original shale-lime creation. It offered high resistance to carbonizing. They called the new material "inorganic" plastic. At very high pressure it could be molded into good insulators in intricate shapes. The material became known by the trade name Rosite, pronounced "Ross-ite."

During a visit to Hazelden on June 26, 1935, John T. McCutcheon drew, signed, and dated an informal walking sketch of George Ade. In the sketch Ade wears long trousers, a suit coat, open-collared shirt, horn-rimmed eyeglasses, a straw hat, and carries a walking stick. His dog "Spry" trots a step behind him. Ade's face is grim but determined. Ade at the time was reworking his old play *The County Chairman* so that it could be made into a movie.

Dave Ross took on a new public service task that year. It was with the Committee on Education of a new State Commission on Governmental Economy. Ross's group studied education in order to make recommendations to the Commission. In the process Ross saw that township schools could be and, he thought, *should* be merged were wasting public money. He came to believe, too, that townships had become obsolete government entities and should be abolished. However, Ross found township officers strong, organized, and intent on keeping their jobs. He could not eliminate townships, but he did raise the issue and probably advanced the time when it was done regarding township schools (Kelly, *Ross*, 166-167). Indiana began that reform seriously in 1943, and by the mid-1960s, the state had done away with most township schools through school reorganization.

Among the many failures in Depression-era 1935 was the Purdue Housing Research Program, which Dave Ross had inspired in 1932. However, by 1935, it was clear that the plan to build homes for Purdue faculty was going nowhere. The project simply did not do what Ross and PRF had hoped. A New York-based corporation known as Better Homes in America moved in to continue the work.

The mission of Better Homes, started in the East back in 1922, had been to help American families make their homes more convenient and attractive. As more and more communities participated in local Better Homes campaigns, activities were concentrated in home and community improvement, urban-rural relationships, and spreading facts about housing and homemaking. The University of Chicago Press, in 1931, had printed a *Better Homes Manual*. By 1935, the number of communities participating in the Better Homes Week campaigns had reached 10,000.

But due to lack of funds—the familiar Great Depression story—the corporation had to be liquidated. It transferred its research and publications work to the Housing Research Foundation, part of PRF at Purdue.

Contributions came slowly and Dave Ross eventually hired researcher and architect Carl Boester to take over and test housing ideas. Ross had believed that too little attention had been paid to finding better ways of building homes and that Purdue's schools of engineering would be good places to test materials and types of construction.

When Better Homes in America first moved to Purdue, Ross hosted several Purdue housing conferences. However, Purdue opted to shelve the entire program in 1940 because of the growing needs of "national defense research" and scrapped housing studies altogether in 1943.

According to independent accounts by George Putnam, Amelia Earhart, and President Elliott, Putnam planted the idea of a Purdue Flying Laboratory in Elliott's mind. There it stayed until September 1935 at a party in the Elliotts' Lafayette home. During dinner talk Earhart told of her ambitions for women, for aviation, and for some sort of "flying lab." Her ideas closely matched Elliott's.

Before the evening was over, Dave Ross offered to donate $50,000—not to Earhart but to the Purdue Research Foundation—toward the cost of a modern airplane suitable for a "flying lab."

Further offers of help totaling $30,000 in cash and equipment came from Purdue Trustee J. K. Lilly, from Vincent Bendix, and from the Western Electric, Goodrich, and Goodyear companies. The inventor Bendix (1882-1945) had long contributed to automobile and aviation progress. His Bendix Company of Chicago had produced more than 7,000 cars before 1909.

The surge of ready cash caused PRF to start its "Amelia Earhart Fund for Aeronautical Research." PRF stated the fund's mission, as a depository for money to buy the plane, would be to "develop scientific and engineering data of vital importance to the aviation industry."

Ross and Lilly further influenced the Trustees to grant Earhart use of the Purdue Airport as a base for a flight around the world she had in mind. She planned to publish a book about the flight and about the results of its research. After her return the "flying lab" plane she had flown would become PRF property. PRF would use income from exhibitions of the plane and royalties from Earhart's book for pure and applied research in aeronautics (Freehafer, 59).

From Hazelden during the fall of 1935, George Ade responded to the usual steady stream of letters asking for his advice, his opinions about politics or the Depression, or for his memories of days gone by. In one rare response that he wrote on October 25, he aired certain views about religion:

> I am not affiliated with any church. However, I do think that the church is necessary in modern life because people cannot get the comforts and consolation and the promises for the future which they find in church relationships by scientific research or a study of philosophies. Our churches inspire faith and arouse emotions which are useful to the well being of the world. (Tobin, 187)

An author named Harry Martin invited Ade to contribute to a sports book Martin was assembling to be titled *Fifty Years of American Golf*. In Ade's reply in early November, 1935, he revealed that infirmities were setting in:

> I began to try to play golf in the 1890s...I was crazy about the game for years and it makes me sad to realize that I am no longer permitted to play. (Tobin, 188-189)

Coach Noble Kizer's Purdue football players won four games and lost four in 1935. The team played just twice in Ross-Ade Stadium that season. There were upwards of 7,000 empty seats both times. Purdue lost seven to nothing to Carnegie Tech in front of 15,000 and beat Iowa twelve to six before 16,000. At the end of the season, 25,000 saw the Old Oaken Bucket game in Bloomington. Indiana won seven to nothing.

Weeks before the Bucket game, though, Purdue campus excitement swelled, but not because of football this time. The hoopla had to do with Amelia Earhart's arrival on Wednesday, November 8. The *Journal and Courier* assigned reporter Herb Heimlich:

> Amelia Earhart, often called the "Lindbergh" of women flyers, will have no respite from hard work during the next three weeks which she will spend at Purdue University as teacher, advisor and consultant on "careers for women." She will also consult with the Department of Aeronautics in the School of Engineering and with male students in that field.
>
> The distinguished aviatrix had time before a luncheon engagement to squeeze in a brief interview, a glance at her schedule indicating she will have little opportunity for leisure during her

sojourn on campus. She came to Purdue after a long lecture tour, speaking twenty-nine times last month.

Her new endeavor in the educational field will prevent her from planning any flights, she said, because even a simple flight requires long preparation. Speaking of pioneering, Miss Earhart holds that there is as much opportunity for her in her new work at Purdue as there is in flying uncharted courses.

She glided into campus life with a perfect three-point landing, settling immediately down to work after her arrival late Wednesday night. She was assigned a desk in the office of the Dean of Women, received her schedule Thursday morning and began a busy round of conferences.

Thursday noon she attended a luncheon for heads of the Home Economics Department. Friday noon she was guest of honor of Mortar Board at luncheon, and in the evening was to be a dinner guest at Cary Hall. Saturday noon she will attend an Iron Key luncheon.

One gains the impression that she may listen as much at Purdue as she will speak. Although a seasoned lecturer she apparently is not given to talkativeness. Her economy of words is more than made up for, however, with her ready smile and engaging personality.

Teaching is not new for her. She admitted that from 1926 to 1928 she had been in charge of girls' work at Denison House, Boston, which she explains was largely a teaching position. From 1927 to 1928 she was a teacher in extension work for the Commonwealth of Massachusetts.

She was brought here, for one thing, to consult with co-eds on "careers for young women." She points out that this is a subject which colleges should be teaching. True, courses are offered in the many sciences, arts and languages to fit women for careers, but the subject of careers in a broader sense, has been neglected.

Will teaching be dull for her after many air adventures? She says not. For her, she explained, flying is merely a means of transportation. She did admit, however, that she found adventure in flying. A person is just as likely, she said, to meet adventure and dangers in an automobile as an airplane.

During her three weeks on the campus now she will not hold regular classes, as such. Instead she will work through interviews and conferences with individual girls and groups.

Her work, however, is not to be entirely for girls. As might be expected of one so prominent in aviation, the university will make use of her knowledge in this field by having her speak before aeronautical engineering students on Nov. 14-15.

Her formal introduction to faculty and student body has been set for Monday evening November 11 when she will speak at a special convocation in Memorial Gymnasium. Under her contract with the university, she will return to the campus two or three times later for similar periods, when her work will be continued. (*Journal and Courier*, November 9, 1935)

An Earhart biographer more than half a century later described Purdue as "almost a period of rest." Mary Lovell would write in 1989:

Of the six thousand students on campus almost one thousand were women and female faculty members were as scarce as female students. Her lectures were oversubscribed but it was in off-duty hours that the students felt they got to know her. (Lovell, 222)

The director of the women's residence hall where Earhart stayed was Helen Schleman, later a Purdue dean. Schleman recalled:

> [Residence hall] students vied with each other to sit at Miss Earhart's table in the dining room. Buttermilk became an overnight favorite beverage because it was her choice. These were the days when table manners were considered somewhat important. One thing you were supposed to do was keep your elbows off the table. Amelia's posture at table when she was deep in conversation was apt to be sitting forward on the edge of her chair—both elbows on the table—and chin cupped in hands. Naturally the question was *If Miss Earhart can do it why can't we?* The stock reply was *As soon as you fly the Atlantic, you may.*
>
> After dinner as many students who could would follow Miss Earhart into my room and sit around on the floor and talk and listen. She sat on the floor too—she was adaptable, easy and informal. It was during these times especially that we got go know some of the underlying beliefs and hopes and dreams that motivated our distinguished guest.
>
> The conversations invariably centered around Miss Earhart's belief that women should have and really did have choices about what they could do with their lives. She believed, and said, that of course women should be engineers or scientists, they could be physicians as well as nurses; they could manage businesses as well as be secretaries to managers. She believed in women's intelligence, their ability to learn, and their ability to do whatever they wanted to do. She saw no limitations on the aspirations of women students.

> There was no question that she, through her own achievements and persuasiveness, was an effective catalyst to heretofore unthinkable thoughts for all of us. (Lovell, 222-223)

A few critics, mostly wives of Purdue professors, expressed shock that Earhart would wear slacks around the dormitories or in local stores. Once she even went down to the residence hall dinner wearing slacks, and this was not accepted dress in the conservative Midwest.

Purdue's engineering dean, A. A. Potter, opined that Earhart was not "scholastically qualified" to be a member of the faculty. However, a woman faculty colleague rebutted that Potter was "a scholar who didn't recognize the importance of motivating young people as well as educating them." Earhart calmly mentioned that she had taught Harvard University extension courses as long ago as the mid-1920s and felt qualified (Lovell, 230).

In late November, owing to the efforts of Paul Mantz (1903-1965), a noted air racing and movie stunt pilot, consultant, and friend in California, George Putnam and Amelia Earhart obtained a quote for a Lockheed 10E "Electra" in their price range. George also weighed a bid from Igor Sikorsky for an S-43 flying boat that would cost $110,000 (Lovell, 224). The pontooned S-43, while expensive, did need to be considered for a world-girdling flight over ocean.

By the end of 1935, Dave Ross had obtained patents for a new method of constructing metal buildings, for a way of fastening metal shapes, and for that compact warm air furnace that an installer could carry through a doorway.

A Ross Gear financial statement for 1935 showed improved earnings of more than $245,000—good in a Depression year—and a treasury surplus of nearly $364,000. But serious debate arose over whether Ross Gear ought to start a pension fund for employees. In a tense stockholders' meeting on November 29, Dave Ross offered

5,000 shares of his Ross Gear stock on the condition that 6,100 more shares held in the company treasury be added to the fund. Company counsel Rochester Baird, a Lafayette lawyer holding proxies for more than 33,700 (300 of them his own) voted "nay." Almost 105,000 shares still sided with Ross and favored the plan. But Ross, wishing to head off the damaging effects of dissension, withdrew his offer. At a board meeting four days later, Ross then donated his 5,000 shares to start a fund "for those in the company employ who may not become entitled to the proposed national 'Social Security' legislation." He added the proviso that "should this trust be terminated the unused portion should become the property of the Purdue Research Foundation at Purdue University" (*The Gear*, 13).

Social Security, in fact, was about to take effect. On January 4, 1935, President Roosevelt's message to Congress had called for a law to help the unemployed, the aged, destitute children, and the physically handicapped. The U.S. House introduced the Social Security Bill on April 4. The measure passed it fifteen days later 372 votes in favor to thirty-three against. The U.S. Senate passed the law seventy-seven to six on June 19. Roosevelt signed the act into law on August 14, but appropriations for Social Security remained enmeshed in time-consuming debate at the end of the year.

The "Flying Laboratory"

President Elliott and R. B. Stewart put George Putnam in charge of buying the airplane for the Amelia Earhart/PRF "flying laboratory." In March 1936, Putnam informed Lockheed he was ready to make a first payment on a 10E "Electra" (Lovell, 230). In a biography of Elliott, Frank K. Burrin wrote:

> Although she was never on the campus at any one time for more than a few weeks the days [Earhart] spent at Purdue were busy. Elliott asked her husband what he thought most interested Miss Earhart in the field of research and education beyond academic matters. Putnam said she was hankering for a bigger and better plane to use as a laboratory for research. Earhart discussed this with Elliott, Dave Ross and others, and there was established in April 1936, within PRF, an Amelia Earhart Fund for Aeronautical Research. From this fund was purchased a Lockheed "Electra" [that] became known as the Purdue Flying Laboratory.

Lockheed had introduced a ten-passenger Model 10A "Electra" in early 1934. The 10A was an all-metal, cantilever low-wing monoplane with twin engines, two rudders, and retractable wheels. Lockheed classified the "Electras" as "short-range light transports." Four-hundred-fifty-horsepower Pratt and Whitney engines powered the 10As. Those engines gave the planes a maximum speed, at 5,000 feet, of a bit more than 200 miles per hour. An "Electra's" ceiling limit was 19,400 feet and range 810 miles. The wings spanned fifty-five feet, body thirty-eight feet seven inches, and height ten feet one inch. Lockheed built about 150 "Electras," following the 10As with progressively better 10Bs, 10Cs, 10Ds, and 10Es. By March 1936, 600-horsepower engines were powering the 10Es when Putnam and Earhart were ready to buy.

George Ade's fan mail, whether he was wintering in Florida or summering at Hazelden, still contained pleas for advice from budding writers. One of them, Stuart Gates, received this counsel when Ade wrote to him from Miami Beach on March 18, 1936:

> The way to learn to write is to keep on writing, and when you are reading keep a dictionary at your elbow and check up on the words which are new to you or whose meaning might be in doubt. Build up your vocabulary but do not strive to put into your stock too many long, unusual or freakish words. A simple and direct style is always the best. (Tobin, 191-192)

One federal Depression-era relief program already up and going—the Works Progress Administration (WPA)—announced plans in April 1936 to build a circular concrete swimming pool in Lafayette's Columbian Park. Meanwhile, Purdue, mostly through R. B. Stewart and PRF, was applying for much more WPA help for several ambitious building projects. Grandstand construction at Ross-Ade Stadium in 1936, for example, raised seating capacity from about 23,000 to about 32,000.

On June 17, Eleanor Roosevelt visited Purdue to learn about housing research and to speak about the issue of housing to 6,000 people crammed into the Purdue Armory. The nation's first lady—wife of U.S. President Franklin D. Roosevelt—attended a Science and

Leadership Institute. Many in her audience were Purdue Summer Session students. A good many others were curious onlookers. The Institute drew leaders in science, business, journalism, and religion.

Indiana Governor and Mrs. McNutt, Mrs. Roosevelt, and her secretary arrived in West Lafayette about nine-thirty a.m. The four with Purdue guides inspected several of the experimental homes west of Ross-Ade Stadium and a wheeled mobile home designed by W. B. Stout, of Detroit. The party spent more than an hour in talks with President Elliott and Frank Watson, director of the housing project. "I came to Purdue," Mrs. Roosevelt told the Armory crowd, "to learn as much as possible about your interesting experiments in housing."

> I am no expert in housing, and can only talk of a few of the reasons why it seems all of us should be tremendously interested in the subject.

> I think we can all agree there is nothing more important than the homes of the country. There are many problems before us, but none seems more important to me than the possibility of acquainting our citizens with the realization that many of our people live in homes where they cannot possibly be comfortable and have a reasonably happy home life. If that be true, then we have not achieved the objects for which our forefathers founded the country.

The smiling first lady quickly gained rapport with her audience. She named three housing problems in America: rural slums, city slums, and "the great group which could own their own homes if the price could be brought down to the possibilities of their incomes:"

> Bad housing begins to tell first on the women. They are the first to become old before their time and their thoughts turn first to the effects on the children. Most homes cost too much for peo-

ple with average incomes. The extraordinary thing about such experiments as those at Purdue has been to show industries what [how much] housing costs. But more interesting will be to see what can be done to moderate costs.

Mrs. Roosevelt emphasized the importance of getting the public interested in the problem of housing and insisted this was necessary before progress could be made. She asserted that the basis of any change in many phases of American life had its foundation in better housing. She quoted the Federal Bureau of Investigations Director J. Edgar Hoover as saying that "prisons and asylums are filled with people who come from homes where the environment was bad, where they never had a chance to become anything except a warped human being."

President Elliott said that Mrs. Roosevelt's visit had given a great impetus to the Purdue experiments. He introduced Dave Ross to her as "the father of the housing project." While touring the research houses, Mrs. Roosevelt declared that American industry had been "stupid" about housing. However, she questioned the practical value of pre-fabricated houses unless there were "pre-fabricated families" in which the number of children is regulated. She said too many houses were planned with no thought of where or how furniture would be placed. There should be no wasted space in any home and every spot should have a specific use. She specifically disliked rooms without doors (*Journal and Courier,* June 17, 1936).

After the Armory address Purdue officials drove Mrs. Roosevelt past the Women's Residence Hall, then over to the Elliotts' home in Lafayette for lunch with the McNutts and others. At one-thirty p.m. she was taken by car to Indianapolis in order to board a train for New York City.

For Dave Ross, Eleanor Roosevelt's visit was just another busy day. During 1936, he was getting three more patents for his construction methods. His Rostone investment, economically speaking, was only treading water. Fairfield business was drifting as well in the general Depression malaise. But Ross Gear was a brighter story. Ross Gear was ending its thirtieth year in 1936. That year, in defiance of general conditions, Ross Gear would earn more than $347,000 and show a surplus of nearly $411,000. Sales of "twin cam and lever" steering gears for cars and smaller off-road vehicles were rising so fast that at one point the Directors doubled the quarterly stock dividend to sixty cents a share.

In West Lafayette, some of the vacant land Dave Ross had given to Purdue, or had helped Purdue acquire for future use, still stood south and east of Ross-Ade Stadium. Although it had been reserved for the Purdue Master Plan since the early 1920s, the land remained undeveloped in 1936. Part of it then became the site of choice for an athletic field house. The federal Public Works Administration (PWA) would foot much of the cost as part of its aim of Depression relief.

The hottest weather ever recorded at Purdue struck between July 5 and 27 in 1936. Fifteen times temperature reached 100 degrees or more Fahrenheit. Purdue instruments measured the official numbers. The all-time record high of 111 occurred on July 14. The intense heat damaged certain city streets paved with bituminous or "blacktop" material. The Wabash River between Lafayette and West Lafayette reached its lowest level since measuring began in 1870. Where "flood stage" was calculated to be a mean depth of eleven feet, the river in the heat dried to six inches. Purdue agriculture specialists predicted Indiana's smallest corn crop since 1881.

Among some of his oldest friends and fans, George Ade's absence from the public eye was beginning to be conspicuous. He conceded the point in a letter from Hazelden that he dated August 5, 1936, in reply to a question:

> I am compelled to say that the literary work I am doing at present is not sufficient in bulk or importance to bear any important relation to present trends in the work by American authors. We may discover by looking over recent outputs that there is a tendency among American writers to favor biographies dealing with our more eminent people, novels that try to illuminate some of our more important periods...It seems to me that all the 'trends' are encouraging and educational and will help us to better understand our own country. The fact that many fiction writers favor mystery stories is not to be deplored because most provide good entertainment. (Tobin, 194)

The central plot in a little remembered motion picture—released in 1936 both as *Freshman Love* and *Rhythm on the River*—came from Ade's old stage play *The College Widow*.

Ade wrote and spoke little in public on the subject of religion. Yet he did respond from Hazelden, in the fall of 1936, to inquiries from George Vaughn, a law professor at the University of Arkansas:

> I doubt very much if I am qualified to speak with any authority regarding the need of a "spiritual awakening." I think our greatest national handicap at present is the willingness and the desire of so many people to live at government expense and get money from the government on any sort of pretext. If you would define a spiritual awakening as a renewed enthusiasm for the activities of the orthodox churches, and especially those of Protestant persuasion, I must say frankly that I do not discover any tendencies in that direction. I think we need a revival of the spirit of independence and unselfish patriotism and a return to the old-fashioned virtues of economy and saving. I fear that we are suffering from a lack of moral fibre and have taken the wrong slant on what our government really should undertake to do for us. Frankly I have no recipe for insuring a return to the cardinal virtues. (Tobin, 194-195)

That hideous 1903 train wreck would have seemed tragedy enough. Yet a new, tearful chapter in Purdue football took place on September 12, 1936. The football team was involved in practice and conditioning routines at the Ross Engineering Camp. The first game of the season against Ohio University was scheduled for September 26. An explosion and fire in a dressing room the young men were using killed two players and injured four. Some players had been using gasoline to remove adhesive tape, a precaution against spraining ankles or other joints in practice. After workouts a plugged shower drain accumulated the gasoline rinsed to remove tape from players' skin. A water heater clicked on. A spark from the water heater controls ignited fumes from the pooled gasoline. In the blast Carl Dahlbeck, a football guard, died almost instantly; halfback Tom McGannon died of his burns five days later.

In the midst of the all-campus mourning about the football tragedy—on September 19—Amelia Earhart landed her shining silver "Electra" 10E at Purdue Airport. News reports vaguely mentioned that the plane was to be loaded with "additional laboratory equipment for various flight tests" and let it go at that.

Coach Noble Kizer's stunned players recovered from the training camp deaths enough to drub Ohio forty-seven to nothing in the season opening game in Ross-Ade Stadium. About 17,000 fans watched. This game started the 1936 season that ended with five Purdue wins, one tie, and two defeats. The Old Oaken Bucket game against Indiana before a crowd of about 30,000 in Ross-Ade Stadium ended in a twenty-to-twenty tie on November 21.

During the football season, President Elliott announced that Purdue had received another PWA grant. It would be coupled with donations and proceeds from a bond sale to finance a multi-purpose athletic field house northwest of Stadium and Northwestern avenues. Dave Ross, behind the headlines, gave $100,000 toward the field house, but typically he insisted that his name be kept secret. "Just let it appear that the money came from various alumni," he said, "and then others will take more interest."

∞

The first national referendum on President Roosevelt's drastic New Deal approach to government, with all its Depression-era programs, took place on November 3. In office since early 1933, Roosevelt now ran for a second four-year term and won by more than eleven million votes. The Republican challenger had been Alf Landon, businessman and governor of Kansas. In electoral votes Roosevelt won 523 to eight, but in Tippecanoe County races, a record 26,800 people voted, and Republicans scored wins almost as decisive as before Roosevelt.

∞

There was one more note of sadness about Purdue football. Failing health—kidney trouble—forced Noble Kizer to retire from coaching at the age of forty. Since the 1930 season his strong Boilermaker teams had won forty-two times, lost thirteen, and tied three. Kizer's top assistant coach, Mal Elward, took over. Elward would serve Purdue as interim, and then head coach in football, and as athletic director for one year, until 1941.

∞

Just before Christmas in 1936, a Chicago-area man named George Hiram Brownell published *Revived Remarks on Mark Twain*. The volume, its printing limited to 1,000 copies, commemorated the centenary of Mark Twain's birth. Five hundred copies were numbered, Ade autographed them, and the other 500 went out unsigned. Ade contributed four articles: "Mark Twain: A Quarter Century Later" (dated Hazelden Farm October 21, 1936); "Tribute to Mark Twain" from *North American Review* June 1910; "Mark

Twain and the Old-Time Subscription Book" from *American Review of Reviews* June 1910; and "On the Death of Mark Twain" from the *Chicago Tribune* April 22, 1910.

Pride, sadness, mystery, hope

The year 1937 brought moments of pride, sadness, mystery, and a few glimpses of hope for an end to the Great Depression.

Floods in late January swamped many a southern Indiana and northern Kentucky Ohio River town. During the worst of it "Cap" Aretz took leave from teaching students and managing Purdue Airport to fly emergency food and medicine. Even in the Depression "bad times" when money was short, Lafayette, West Lafayette, and Purdue donors raised $5,000 for flood relief.

At Hazelden, George Ade responded on March 6 to a letter from Miriam Nesbitt. Long ago Nesbitt had played the female lead in Chicago and New York productions of Ade's *The County Chairman*. In his letter Ade, at seventy-one, discussed literature and his own immortality:

> I read *Gone With the Wind* with the greatest interest and think it is a wonderful book to have been turned out by a young woman with so little training in the game of fiction writing. It has drama and sustained interest and good dialogue and distinct characters and everything needed to make it a book of absorbed interest.
>
> You ask if I am writing anything. I regret to say that since my illness I have not had enough ambition to sit up to my desk and

do a blessed lick of work. I live in hope that later on I may have more pep. (Tobin, 195-196)

A few weeks later, Ade replied to Quincy Howe of the Simon and Schuster publishing house in New York. Howe mistakenly had been led to believe that Ade was writing his memoirs. Howe wished to consider such a book for publication. Ade responded:

> I regret to say that my good friend was not very accurate when he said that I was hard at work on my memoirs. I should be but I am not for the simple reason that I am not feeling sufficiently rugged and ambitious to do very much work and I cannot make any definite promises for the future. (Tobin, 196)

When nine-year-old Dickie Freeman met Amelia Earhart on the Purdue campus in March 1937, he was already smitten by the glamour of flying. "When she said something about my having pretty blue eyes," Freeman said, "I said, 'Yes and I'm interested in airplanes,' and she replied 'I encourage you to continue'" (Mayer, 26-27). The boy's dad was Verne Freeman, Purdue agriculture professor and associate dean. Seventy years later, Dick Freeman, at age seventy-nine, from his home in California, reported:

> My wife Jane and I recently donated about seventy-five thousand dollars to Purdue to make possible a display of Amelia that will appear in a cafe to be installed in the new Aero and Engineering Building. This cafe is to be called "Amelia's" in her honor.

And he still remembered:

> I was too young [in 1937] to be more than just a "flying thought" in [Amelia Earhart's] mind. I still have a letter that E. H. Skinner, then Dean of the School of Agriculture, had sent out to his people about her, saying that A. E. has seen more land from the air than any of his professors had ever seen from the ground. My dad worked for Dean Skinner who made sure I met Amelia in the

Purdue Armory just before her last flight. (Dick Freeman to author, June 26, 2007)

After various test runs early in 1937, Earhart flew the "Electra" from Purdue around to selected cities to add equipment for—and to promote—her world flight. After the world flight and all the expected accolades, Earhart already had agreed to lecture at Purdue about "What Next in the Air?"

During this same season, in a short ceremony, Purdue mortared in place a cornerstone at the building site of the multipurpose athletic field house.

Her Purdue obligations behind her for the moment, Earhart and her consultants, advisers, and helpers focused on the first leg of her world flight. It began well. She flew the "Electra" from Los Angeles to Oakland, California. She then set an Oakland to Honolulu, Hawaii, record of eleven hours and forty-seven minutes on March 17. However, when she left Honolulu for her next stop—it would be tiny Howland Island near the equator in the western Pacific—on March 20, Earhart "ground looped." This mistake during takeoff heavily damaged the "Electra." In pilot jargon, a "ground loop" is an uncontrollable turn by a plane—either during takeoff or landing—when it is rolling over the ground at a speed too low for the rudder to be effective. An eyewitness at Honolulu reported:

> As the airplane gathered speed it swung slightly to the right. Miss Earhart corrected this tendency by throttling the left hand motor. The aircraft then began to swing to the left with increasing speed, characteristic of a ground loop. It tilted forward, right wing low and for 50 or 60 yards it was supported by the right wheel only. The right hand landing gear suddenly collapsed under the excessive load, followed by the left. The airplane spun sharply to the left sliding on its belly and amid a shower of sparks came to

rest headed about 200 degrees from its initial course. (Lovell, 250)

Earhart had the presence of mind to cut all switches when she lost control. A fire truck following along the side of the runway reached the "Electra" within seconds. In touch with Putnam in California by telephone from Hawaii, Earhart insisted that she wanted to try a world flight again. In general, the nation's newspapers were kind, but a sour note sounded from Major Al Williams. A respected flier and leader in aircraft development, Williams, author of a 1940 book *Airpower,* wrote a blunt article syndicated for newspapers:

> Like every other human enterprise, aviation suffers from a great number of ingeniously contrived rackets. Daring, courageous individuals with nothing to lose and all to gain have used and are using aviation merely as a means toward quick fortune and fame. The worst racket of all is that of individually sponsored trans-oceanic flying [where] the personal profit angle in dollars and cents and the struggle for personal fame, have been carefully camouflaged and presented under the banner of "scientific progress."

> Amelia Earhart's "flying laboratory" is the latest and most distressing racket that has been given to a trusting and enthusiastic public. There's nothing to that "flying laboratory" beyond duplicates of the controls and apparatus to be found on board every major airline transport. And no one ever sat at the controls of her "flying laboratory" who knew enough about the technical side of aviation to obtain a job on a first-class airline...

> Nothing is said about the thousands of dollars which she and her manager-husband expected to get for thousands of stamp cachets carried in the "flying laboratory." Nothing at all was hinted of the fat lecture contracts, the magazine and book rights for sto-

ries of the flight...No, the whole affair was labeled "purely scientific" for public consumption.

> She lost control of the plane during a takeoff on the concrete runway on a standard Army airdrome and wrecked the "flying laboratory." And there again the public got a garbled story and a cleverly contrived explanation...plus a heroic story about cutting the switches and saving the lives of her crew. That ship got away from her on the takeoff—that's the lowdown.

Williams was voicing what an element in the aviation industry felt about Earhart's constant media exposure. Earhart's only comment: "I'm glad it wasn't a woman who wrote it" (Lovell, 252).

Lafayette's recovery from the long, painful Depression could be said to have begun on April 2, 1937. That day the Aluminum Company of America, or "Alcoa," announced that it had bought ninety acres at the southeast edge of the city. There it would build and open a "metal-working plant." The plant would employ a projected "several hundred" people making aluminum products. Construction would begin in two weeks.

For Earhart there followed a stretch of about nine weeks while the broken-up "Electra" was repaired in Honolulu enough to be shipped by Pacific Ocean freighter in pieces to Burbank, California. There the Lockheed factory people set about to make it fly again. One of the private donors toward these repairs—twenty thousand dollars—was the same Vincent Bendix who, with Dave Ross, had put up the money for Putnam and Earhart to buy the "Electra."

After discussing a second world flight with her flying friends, Earhart decided to reverse her first plan and go *eastward* because of midsummer weather in the Caribbean and Africa. The decision pressured George Putnam to dive into making arrangements for new or extended diplomatic clearances, permissions to fly over alien land, relocations of land-based fuel, oil, and other supplies or spare parts. Putnam worked with U.S. Navy and Coast Guard authorities to line up a string of ships on water and for radio and direction-finding apparatus on land.

One of Earhart's friends, Harry Manning, a Navy captain who had taken a leave-of-absence to ride along to help on her Oakland-Honolulu flight, informed her that he could not be present for the second try. He was to say years later that he made that decision because he had so little faith in Earhart's ability as a pilot:

> Amelia Earhart was something of a prima donna. She gave the impression of being humble and shy, but she really had an ego, and could be as tough as nails when the occasion required it. I got very fed up with her bull-headedness several times. That's why she brought [navigator Fred] Noonan into the picture—in the event that I would give up on the flight. AE herself was not a good navigator, and Noonan was a happy-go-lucky Irishman. He wasn't a "constant" navigator. I always felt that he let things go far too long. (Lovell, 255).

After such distracting debate and time-consuming and expensive repairs, pilot training, and test runs, Earhart and Noonan left on her second try on June 1, 1937. Purdue had been left out this time and somehow had dodged all the occasional bursts of "flying lab" flak. This time the advance work had taken place in Los Angeles, Oakland, and Burbank and then cross-country via Tucson and New Orleans to Miami, Florida.

༺ ༻

President Elliott, Dave Ross, and her other Purdue friends, Americans most anywhere, and the curious around the world all traced Earhart's adventure by commercial radio bulletins and daily newspaper stories. Earhart and Noonan flew from Miami to San Juan, then to Carapito, Paramaribo, Fortaleza, Dakar, Gao, Fort-Lamy, El Fasher, Khartoum, Massawa, Assab, Karachi, Calcutta, Akyab, Rangoon, Bangkok, Singapore, Bandoeng, Soerabaja, Koepang, Port Darwin in Australia, and Lae in Papua New Guinea.

By the time they reached Lae, Earhart and Noonan had flown for four weeks. It was June 29. They had gone 22,000 miles. On July 2, they left Lae aiming once more to reach the small and remote Howland Island for fuel and service to equipment, and then fly to Honolulu, and on to Los Angeles in triumph. That was the plan. However:

> There is no evidence that Amelia had ever taken off with such a heavy fuel load prior to this. For the Oakland-Honolulu flight Electra [had] carried 947 gallons but on that occasion Paul Mantz had been at her side working the throttles and retracting the landing gear.

> The runway at Lae ended abruptly with a twenty-five-foot drop to the waters of the Huon Gulf and witnesses said the takeoff was hair-raising for there was not a breath of wind to help the Electra into the air on that hot, clear morning. Commercial pilot Bert Heath who was flying into Lae…watched the Electra's lumbering takeoff run from high above the field. He recalled that close to the seaward end of the runway a dirt road crossed it. There was a high camber on this road and as the Electra hit the crest it bounced into the air and over the drop-off, flying so low over the sea that the propellers were throwing spray. The dust kicked up by the Electra over the dirt road hung about in the still air for some time and did not disperse. (Lovell, 276-277)

After the takeoff Earhart made several routine radio contacts over the ocean, but neither the "Electra" nor its occupants would be seen again. Earhart's and Noonan's disappearance entered the pages of U.S. and aviation history, of mystery, and of legend. Theories about the event persist to this day.

However, in 1937, concerns about national economic recovery prevailed over any reports of two missing fliers half a world away. In July, the Roosevelt era's new Social Security Administration opened a Lafayette branch. Social Security joined the Post Office as an occupant of the gray stone Federal Building at Fourth and Ferry, and at Purdue the talk of new buildings created more excitement and anticipation. The designer of the campus Master Plan, Walter Scholer, recalled:

> There were six projects built at one time during the Depression years when they had the PWA when the government made grants to the universities, or states, or counties, or what have you. Then they went ahead and let contracts, and there was very little interference from the government. Alison Stuart [the Purdue Trustees' attorney] R. B. Stewart and I went to Chicago and filed these applications with the government office. The general idea was that if you filed six, you might get a third of them or a fourth of them, or one, so we better file plenty; and all of these projects had been discussed and were needed.
>
> President Elliott called me one day and said that he had just got word that all six had been approved...
>
> Let me give credit to R. B. Stewart for pushing that, and Dr. Elliott. As Dr. Elliott referred to it, we "slipped [the applications] in under the door before they opened the offices" and that was almost literally true. And we got them all approved...
>
> That shocked me because all of them had a date on them, and they had to get work under construction.. We started with the field house, then Cary Hall, and we jumped around and got the [west addition to the] Union Building started—and the Chemical

Engineering Building. The Music Hall was the last one. Well, how was a little architect's office in a little town going to get these out? We had also a practice outside of Purdue, I thought at the time, unfortunately.

So I divided our office into two sections, one that did the work outside which stayed at 1114 State Street [in Lafayette] and I opened an office in the Executive Building with Purdue's blessing. That whole top floor was open, nothing but a rough concrete floor with steel rafters showing. So I had an office right over Dr. Elliott's office and we had quick communication.

That was in 1937 and we used the remainder of that year and 1938 and 1939....I ordered about 45 tables and went to Chicago and hired 50 draftsmen. (Scholer, 24-25)

The July 29 edition of the *Journal and Courier* contained an interview with the old Purdue legend Clarence H. "Big Robby" Robertson. At age sixty-six, Robertson was enjoying retirement from his long YMCA career as teacher and Christian evangelist in China and Japan. Since the early 1930s, those nations had waged various levels of war, and now in 1937, Japan was bearing the brunt of world criticism for its notorious "Rape of Nanking."

Journalists interviewed "Big Robbie" about such events, considering him an authority on Far Eastern political relations. In the story, Robertson predicted that eventually, by "assimilation," China would prevail and regain any territory lost in war. "China," he said, "is the anvil which has chipped many a hammer."

Retirement was giving Big Robbie time to concentrate on what he considered his "three hobbies—people, inventions and golf." Friends said he had rigged his personal car with sixty-some gadgets he had made, and he built and used one of the first wheeled caddy carts to make it easier to carry a bag of golf clubs.

Like Dave Ross, Robertson also remained serious and curious about education. He continued to study academic successes and failures and techniques by which one's subconscious mind might be fed instructional materials during sleep. He often told how, in his first three years in China, he despaired of ever learning the language. But then one morning he wakened after having dreamed in Chinese. "After that," he said, "I knew I would learn it." He remained for the rest of his life intrigued by how and why some students learn and how and why others don't. The theory of teaching by "consciously stimulating subconscious processes" fascinated him.

The economic upswing showed again in Ross Gear's 1937 business performance. Profit rose to more than $458,000, but R-H-K Corporation limped along $42,000 in debt with little prospect of recovery. R-H-K didn't have the people capable of completely designing and building houses. Furthermore, the failure of Rostone Circle, a group of houses put up in 1936 just south of Lafayette to stimulate sales, and Ross's insistence on building ten show homes there instead of one, compounded the situation. Ross had insisted that a circle was the way to go. His theory was that the homes all face into the center. "His idea was to build them and sell them," Paul Jones said. "But you don't do that," Jones continued. "You build one and sell it to a *woman* who then tells every other woman about her great house. You let her sell your next houses. Dave wasn't interested in that."

In any event, with profits from Rostone slow and R-H-K losing money, it made sense for the companies to merge. That was no problem; Ross owned 611 shares of R-H-K stock, and Louis Alt, Floyd Wymer, and Vincent Bliss owned five shares each, Richard Harrison one. Ross dictated the merger action carried out on October 12. Ross named the merged business the "Rostone Corporation." He gave it an operating budget of just over $24,000 and took over as Chairman of the Board. Harrison became President and

Treasurer, Jones and Wymer Executive Vice-Presidents, and Maurice Knoy Secretary.

Assistant Coach Allen H. "Mal" Elward, having succeeded the ailing Noble Kizer, led the 1937 Purdue football team to four wins, three losses, and one tie. In Ross-Ade Stadium, the team beat Butler thirty-three to seven, Carnegie Tech seven to nothing, and Iowa thirteen to nothing, all before average home crowds of 20,000 fans.

Former Indiana Governor Harry Leslie, President of Standard Life Insurance Company in Indianapolis, died on December 10, 1937, at the age of fifty-nine, in Florida. The next day, George Ade, wintering nearby, dictated and addressed a "news letter from Miami Beach" to a roster of his favorite friends in the North. In the letter, Ade referred to "our old friend 'Skillet' Leslie."

> I received a phone message from Mrs. Leslie on December 9 saying that he was in the St. Francis Hospital here in Miami Beach. She said he was very tired from the railway ride and weak because of a recent heart attack. When I went into his room at the hospital about 10 o'clock next morning I found him propped up in bed and smoking a cigarette. He greeted me with his usual cheerful grin and reported that he had passed a fairly good night. The ride on the train from Indianapolis had been bumpy and tedious and he sat up most of Thursday night. A recurrent attack of angina pectoris (old fashioned "heart disease") induced Mrs. Leslie to move him to the hospital as soon as they arrived...

> [Now] there has been nothing much for any of us to do except stand aside and experience a lot of real sorrow over the departure of a genial companion, an able executive, a square shooter and a good scout in general. (Tobin, 202-203)

A new season of pride

The federal relief programs—especially the PWA—dominated talk and action at Purdue. On January 15, 1938, the University dedicated its new PWA-built field house with its concrete block walls, iron girder skeleton, and glass brick ends. More than 8,000 fans seated on wooden bleachers, set up on the packed sawdust floor, howled with delight that winter night. On a basketball court knocked together in portable sections before them under powerful lights, the fans saw "Piggy" Lambert's 1937-1938 team nip Indiana thirty-eight to thirty-six. Fred Beretta, Pat Malaska, Johnny Sines, and Jewell Young led the Purdue team that won eighteen of its twenty games that season.

Around town a number of other PWA jobs were occurring. They resulted in a yellow brick West Lafayette High School on the "Burtsfield's Folly" land, and on the Purdue campus the Memorial Union west addition, the Chemical Engineering building, and the grand Hall of Music with its two balconies and upholstered seats for more than 6,000 patrons. It was a new season of pride for Purdue, and Dave Ross was in no way forgotten. Two top Purdue people—Public Relations Director Thomas R. Johnston and President Elliott's Secretary, Helen Hand—were compiling *The Trustees and the Officers of Purdue University 1865-1940*. In its profile of Ross the co-authors wrote:

> Under the guidance of [Ross and President Elliott] the university has forged ahead in enrollment, expansion of physical plant, scholastic standards and public services to the people of Indiana

in a manner unexcelled in the annals of higher education. (Johnston and Hand, 312)

Another chronicler of Purdue history later would write:

> Dave Ross, who had been one himself, was much concerned about the "poor boys" at Purdue who, without adequate funds, could not afford to live in the residence halls. Ross and [R. B.] Stewart agreed that a good solution would be a program for low-cost housing that would "help students help themselves." They started with a gift of money from Ross and funds advanced for the purchase of houses by PRF and the Ross-Ade Foundation. The Purdue Student Housing Corporation was organized in August 1938. (Freehafer, 64)

Highway, street, and open road travel all sped up, too, with the opening on January 22, 1938 of the six-mile stretch known as the "Road 52 Bypass." It circled Purdue and West Lafayette to the north, crossed the Wabash River on a new steel and concrete bridge, and rounded Lafayette to the east on the ever-busier road between Chicago and Indianapolis. Work had been going on since 1932.

In 1937, the merger of Rostone and R-H-K allowed the Rostone Corporation to go on selling building materials, conducting research, and marketing its cold-mold Rosite to meet a growing motor control demand. On February 14, 1938, Rostone contracted to supply internal parts for a new Allen-Bradley overriding electrical relay system. Allen-Bradley wanted it, no matter the cost, so Rostone started to build these products that eventually became the best in the industry. Rostone did, however, lose nearly $37,000 in 1938.

In early March, Dave Ross opted to resign as President of Ross Gear and to revive and assume the duties of the vacant Chairman of the Board position. The Directors elected long-time employee Eugene Gruenwald as company President. As a result, Ross Gear, in 1938, did turn a slim profit of $168,000.

In a Gala Week affair in May, Purdue friends honored Ross with a bound book of testimonial letters from alumni all over the world. At the Purdue Alumni Association's dinner, Ross accepted the book titled *A Purdue Tribute to David Edward Ross*. It was no ordinary book. The esteemed fellow townsman and Purdue alumnus—Bruce Rogers—had designed it. The book contained an original cartoon by John T. McCutcheon, by now a Pulitzer Prize winner with the Chicago *Tribune*. The remarkable volume, produced in a limited edition of twelve folders, came from Lakeside Press in Chicago, the text set in Rogers' Centaur type:

> To Dave Ross: We, the sons and daughters of Purdue, stand and salute you as our most useful alumnus. No one else wears as many service stripes. No one else has labored so prodigiously in behalf of the school we love and brought about such happy results. Our enthusiasm for you is so real that we shall not hesitate to slop over and use extravagant adjectives. You are entitled to our most superlative praise. We have watched your career with pride and growing wonder. We have rejoiced at your success as a captain of industry and have been compelled to marvel when we saw you bring your well-earned profits and lay them, without one gesture of ostentation, at the feet of the University. Your modest manner cannot hide the fact that you have performed miracles. We glorify you because you have formed a Damon and Pythias comradeship with our esteemed President. Your team-work has been perfect. Together you have worked, like a couple of cipomatic Trojans, to upbuild Purdue's standing as a foremost school of technology, establish friendly relations with important industries, fortify and enrich our research departments, maintain a cheerful morale among faculty members and undergraduates and give proper but not undue encouragement to Purdue's ambition to en-

joy athletic supremacy. In all of your efforts you have been wise, sagacious, tactful and persevering. You have done the right thing at the right time during every forward movement which has brought Purdue to its present eminence and widespread renown. We cannot chronicle all of your good deeds because they have been too numerous and some of them have been artfully concealed. You have avoided self-glorification, but the results of your unselfish labor are so manifest and of such huge proportions that they must not be under-rated. You have been the answer to our prayers and you have made our dreams come true. That is why we insist upon laying a laurel wreath on your unruffled brow, giving three hearty cheers and winding up by adding a fervent "God bless you." - GEO. ADE, '87

One of Ross's wealthy Lafayette friends, Dr. Richard Wetherill, had retired from medical practice to devote time and money to long trips for studies of Africa, game hunting, and archaeology. When Ross would get Wetherill's postcards from far-off places, Ross would shake his head and remark, "It's too bad about Dick Wetherill. Think what he could do with the money he wastes on travel!" (Kelly, *Ross*, 158). However, in due time, Ross did persuade Wetherill to join him in several beneficial acts on behalf of the University, and when the doctor died in 1940, he left his over-five-hundred thousand dollar estate to Purdue.

On May 19, 1938, one of the nation's more notable novelists, Thomas Wolfe, spoke at the annual all-campus literary awards banquet in the Purdue Union where PWA expansion work—a ballroom and other amenities—was still underway. Wolfe had written *Look Homeward, Angel* and *Of Time and the River,* among other works. A native of North Carolina, Wolfe delivered one of the few public lectures in his life. He died of rare brain tuberculosis only months later at age thirty-eight.

Purdue Special Collections preserves a copy of a rather mysterious letter, dated August 18, 1938, and signed by Dave Ross on Ross Gear and Tool Company stationery. Ross sent the message to Claude Swanson, the Roosevelt Administration's U.S. Secretary of the Navy in Washington, D. C.:

> The writer is the inventor of a new scientific fact we believe would be very valuable to the Navy. It is so terribly destructive that I will not apply for patents as I would not want to disclose it. It is probable that President Elliott, Purdue University, will be in Washington next week. Could he see you?
>
> President Elliott, Mr. [Stanley] Meikle, director of Purdue Research Foundation, and a research physicist, Dr. [Raymond B.] Abbett, are the only people that know this secret and can be relied upon not to divulge it.
>
> Will you be in Washington next week and can you see President Elliott? This scientific fact is too terrible in its consequences to be divulged; yet I would like to have my government know it.

Coach "Mal" Elward's 1938 football team won five, lost one, and tied two. Team favorites included Gene Britt, Joe Mihal, Paul Humphrey, and Felix Mackiewicz. In Ross-Ade Stadium, the team beat Detroit nineteen to six before 21,000, edged Wisconsin thirteen to seven again for another 21,000, and topped Indiana thirteen to six for the Old Oaken Bucket on November 19. This game drew a stadium record of 32,000 attendees.

The *Journal and Courier* said late in 1938 that Purdue had been awarded more than half of the federal construction grants made to the thirteen colleges and universities in Indiana. Elliott and Stewart always had a list of needed buildings in readiness for any opportunity. Ross, with his ability to acquire land on the periphery of the campus, had provided many building sites before they were even earmarked (Freehafer, 69).

George Ade, thoroughly retired and battling health nuisances from time to time, produced nothing much new after his tribute to Ross.

Golf courses, parties, and war

Purdue's interest in golf courses, George Ade's love of parties, and all the war threats in far-off Europe ended the 1930s.

In January 1939, Germany's leader Adolf Hitler boasted to the foreign minister of Czechoslovakia that "we are going to destroy the Jews." In March, German troops occupied parts of Bohemia and Moravia. In a few weeks, the soldiers entered Prague and Hitler declared "Czechoslovakia has ceased to exist." On April 3, Hitler sent his military directives to invade Poland by September 1. Italy invaded Albania. Japan promised political, economic, and military aid if Germany or Italy were attacked by a power other than the Soviet Union. Starting lineups for World War II were forming. In the U.S., a Gallup Poll revealed that ninety-nine percent of Depression-weary Americans wanted their nation to stay out of foreign wars.

On January 11, 1939, after ten years the Ross Gear Directors voted to withdraw from the Chicago Stock Exchange owing to inactivity. Ross family members owned seventy-three percent of the common stock; no one was buying or selling. Ross Gear earnings for the year would reach a healthy one dollar and forty cents per share. Fairfield Manufacturing was holding its own, too, but Rostone would lose nearly $14,000.

In Miami Beach, George Ade could still dictate his winter letters with wit and sarcasm. In February, he addressed George Hiram Brownell, a Mark Twain devotee and editor of *The Twainian*. In the letter Ade slammed Roosevelt's federal government relief bureaucracy while kidding his own laziness.

> For a time the docs were stumped but now they know what it is—the deadly WPA-itis. You can see the victims everywhere, poor souls, leaning on golf clubs, against palm trees, lampposts, buildings—even against each other. Some are so weak they can't lean. They lie in beach-chairs or flat on the sand sunning themselves. That's my fix. When I once get into an easy chair with a good book the disease is at its worst. I am unable to rise—until next mealtime. (Tobin, 206-207)

In May 1939, the Mark Twain Society of Chicago published Ade's "One Afternoon With Mark Twain" in a limited edition of 350 numbered copies. Ade composed the piece from the memories of his meeting with Twain in New York City in December 1902. In 1941, the Chicago group expanded to become the Mark Twain Society of America and chose Ade as its first national president.

Back home in Indiana in the spring, and still the popular leader of the Hazelden Country Club, Ade promoted a series of monthly parties honoring "suitable" celebrities. The series began in May with Bob Zuppke. Zuppke (1879-1957) had coached football at the University of Illinois since 1913, winning four national and seven Big Ten titles. On fun nights like the ones at Hazelden, the coach pleased crowds with his "Zuppkeisms":

> Alumni are loyal if a coach wins all his games.

Never let hope elude you; that is life's biggest fumble.

Men do their best if they know they are being observed.

Advice to freshmen: don't drink the liniment.

Ade mailed a written report about the Celebrity Night ideas to club members on June 7:

> Well our first party...was a terrific success. We had an attendance of 100 with plenty of singing and good fellowship and Bob stood the boys on their heads. We want to pull one of these parties each month. The next will have to be on June 14. I have tried to get either [pro golfer] Chick Evans or [football legend] Red Grange for June but without success. We don't want to miss a month and so, rather reluctantly, after talking with several members, I am offering myself as a pinch-hitter. Of course I am not a visiting celebrity, just one of the neighbors and another club member. I wonder [if members] would be interested in a parade of celebrities who have visited Hazelden since 1905? The list is rather amazing. It includes William Howard Taft, Warren G. Harding, Charles Warren Fairbanks, Tom Marshall, Uncle Joe Cannon, Booth Tarkington, Harry Leon Wilson, George Barr McCutcheon, Kin Hubbard, Will Hays, Harry S. New, Albert J. Beveridge, Tom Meighan, Elsie Janis and dozens of others.

> "[On June 14] we will assemble at my home and dinner will be served about 6:30 at the usual price, seventy-five cents. I hope that many of you will show up. I know what they say about a prophet in his own country. I am no spellbinder compared with Zuppke. But I do believe I can tell you some interesting things about the headliners I have entertained.

We have booked John T. McCutcheon and Gen. Charles G. Dawes for July 19; Kenesaw M. Landis for August 16; [athletic director] Nobel Kizer and the entire football coaching staff at Purdue for September 13, and Chick Evans for October 11. (Tobin, 210-211)

⁂

The nearest venue for Purdue, West Lafayette, and Lafayette golfers was Linee Fields, a short eighteen-hole course north of Lindberg Road and west of Northwestern Avenue. However, Charlie Linee had a mortgage on the course and in May, unable to meet payments, went to see Dave Ross. Ross called in R. B. Stewart. They all agreed that the ever-useful Ross-Ade Foundation should buy Linee's course for $20,000, the price of the mortgage. At about the same time, Athletic Director Kizer told Stewart he needed a project to provide summer jobs for some Purdue athletes. Kizer suggested to Ross that Purdue could build a golf course on some of the old Marstellar farmland (Freehafer, 63). Work soon began on what became Purdue's hilly and wooded South Course. Stewart and Ross, even then, could envision how the new course could someday connect to Linee Fields and make Linee's a longer and leveler North Course.

⁂

In August, President Elliott issued a report on all the ways the Roosevelt-era New Deal grants, building projects, and spending had helped Purdue since 1933.

The Public Works Administration—PWA—had by 1939 spent $700,000 on five projects. The five included two units of the women's residence halls, later known as Windsor Hall, the Executive Building, later named Hovde Hall, the field house, later named for "Piggy" Lambert, and the Memorial Union west addition.

- The Works Progress Administration (renamed the Works Projects Administration in 1939)—WPA—had spent more than

$413,000 for a Purdue Airport hangar, an addition to the Physics Building (later Peirce Hall), tennis courts, roads, sewers, fences, and other projects.

- The National Youth Administration—NYA—had spent more than $200,000 at Purdue to pay needy students working at various jobs.

All told, Elliott pointed to the construction of twelve major buildings and a threefold increase in total Purdue assets (Topping, 231).

It was clear that the federal government was supplanting Dave Ross as Purdue's biggest benefactor.

Memories of Amelia Earhart remained fond. George Palmer Putnam saw to that. After she disappeared, he arranged for the publication of her book *Last Flight*. He added to the legend by writing her biography *Soaring Wings* in 1939. He then began work on his autobiography *Wide Margins* that came out in 1942.

In 1939, Putnam gave Purdue a full-length portrait of Earhart. Twenty-five years later it would hang in a women's residence hall that Purdue built and named for her (Topping, 234).

Coach Mal Elward's 1939 Purdue football team won three games, lost three, and tied two. In Ross-Ade Stadium, the Boilermakers beat Michigan State twenty to seven before 21,000 fans and lost to Iowa by the odd score of four to nothing in front of 22,000.

The Hall of Music

By 1940, President Elliott was trial-ballooning a whole new wish list for Purdue that might cost as much as ten million dollars. He wanted to enlarge the power plant, put up and equip more new buildings, and beef up a few others already standing.

Meanwhile, just west of Elliott's Executive Building office workers were finishing the elegant Hall of Music. Elliott had talked—maybe daydreamed—as early as 1934 about an auditorium that would seat 5,000. When the Depression hit and New Deal relief money became available, Elliott, Ross, and Stewart went after it. Elliott learned in 1938 from Governor McNutt that Indiana was getting seventy-five million in PWA dollars. Elliott and Company then pondered how Purdue could get its auditorium. Their plan boiled down to this: the University would ask for a PWA grant and a state appropriation to match what it could raise with a bond issue under the 1927 enabling law. Purdue would make up any leftover needs by raising student fees. Elliott also took Purdue's financing scheme to Indiana University to give IU the chance to do the same thing. Purdue and IU lobbied together at a special Indiana General Assembly session in June 1938. Legislators approved the Purdue and IU requests the same day. Scholer's team of draftsmen at their lighted tables in the bare-bones third floor of Purdue's Executive Building began drawing blueprints. Historian Bob Topping later wrote:

> The [Purdue] auditorium steelwork was a textbook in engineering for the community. Local children would gather at a safe

distance from the site after school just to watch the steelworkers throw and catch hot rivets...

>The actual design included two balconies—cantilevered with no supporting posts. The large balcony beams rested on the rear wall of the auditorium and were hooked to the back wall of the large foyer. At the time the Hall of Music seated 6,146 and was the largest such hall in the U.S. The stage was 100 feet wide. Purdue's consultant on sound was F. R. Watson of the University of Illinois. An acoustical engineer, he had designed the sound system and consulted on acoustics for Radio City Music Hall. (Topping, 232-233)

Purdue dedicated its Hall of Music in early May 1940. Two Metropolitan Opera stars, soprano Helen Jepson and tenor Nino Martini, sang at opening concerts. The Hall of Music cost more than $1.2 million. Purdue paid for the building with the PWA grant of $542,000, a $300,000 state appropriation, a $300,000 revenue bond issue, and nearly $63,000 from gifts and miscellaneous sources. The chief architect Scholer remembered the first dedication concert:

>I was down about the twelfth row and I kept looking back at that balcony because I felt better after it was loaded. It had the 40-foot cantilever and I had said that 'I wish I was seated under it because if it falls I would be under it.' I meant every word of it, too. That was one of the longest cantilevered balconies in the country at that time...Those steel beams project out there 40 feet and there is nothing under them...There is a certain rigidity and a certain flexibility, thank God. If it didn't have flexibility it would break. (Scholer, 25-26)

War fears had been rising in the United States since Germany invaded Poland in 1939. By 1940, England was under air attack and the U.S. began preparing for war. America registered men for future military service and quietly let contracts for military equipment, weapons, munitions, and vehicles. Ross Gear and Tool Company positioned itself to be of help, at times even in secret. During 1940, Ross Gear's assets and liabilities balance soared past $2.2 million, but perhaps in the interest of secrecy and its virtual family ownership, the company made public no profit report for 1940.

Ross and two of his top Rostone men—Knoy and Wymer—received a patent in April for a construction materials machine that could press blocks and tiles. Rostone, during 1940, was in fact edging near a break-even point. The company lost $2,400 that year, but the trend was bright. The losses had diminished from nearly $37,000 in 1938 and $14,000 in 1939.

On the courthouse square in Lafayette callers paraded to the narrow Ross Building to see Dave Ross for advice. After one visit, journalist Ernie Pyle profiled Ross by writing, "He made almost a profession of elevating through the power of his character, his knowledge, his energy and his money" (Kelly, *Ross*, 151).

When a community fund drive fell embarrassingly short, Ross gave it enough to meet its goal. "I don't know where else you can get it," he said, "and it would be a disgrace for the community to fail. I don't want that to happen."

Facing a $20,000 debt on its education building one Lafayette church committee dared to ask a non-member—Dave Ross—for help. "Tell your people that if they'll raise half of what's needed a 'friend' will give the other half," Ross told them. "But don't ever let on who the 'friend' is. They won't be able to resist the bargain of paying off two dollars for each dollar raised" (Kelly, *Ross*, 152).

Ross repeatedly said he would rather give than lend money. Scholer quoted Ross as once having said "the way to make an enemy is to loan him money. When you ask him for it, he's always mad at you" (Scholer, 72). Ross seethed anytime a borrower who could repay a debt didn't or wouldn't. Politicians also sometimes asked Ross to endorse candidates. If Ross heard an appeal that someone "needed the office," he would scowl. "The question is not whether he needs the office, does the office need him?" (Kelly, *Ross*, 156).

All through the Depression—despite the Depression—the Purdue Research Foundation returned dividends almost beyond measure. Private companies gave research fellowships in many fields. PRF income the first ten years through 1940 totaled more than $453,000. One year Purdue awarded eighteen of its twenty-one doctoral degrees in chemistry to students on PRF fellowships. PRF researchers solved problems and made discoveries that led to patents in fields ranging from medicine to paint and insecticides. The U.S. government needed a solution to warplane static. The noise was stopping combat pilots from radioing. Purdue men detected that the camouflage colors painted under the wings contained a chemical that blocked the escape of electrical charges and fixed the problem.

Years passed and successes mounted for PRF. Some people suggested that, to encourage wider use of discoveries, PRF should place its patents in the public domain, but Ross argued against that:

> I can name many inventions that never would have been put to general use without protection by patent. Take for example insulin. Irresponsible makers would have produced disastrous results. The highest integrity had to accompany the manufacture and use of insulin to make it available to the public. The public had to be protected from the unskilled who could easily have ruined the reputation and value of insulin. (Kelly, *Ross*, 117-118)

Purdue did in 1940, however, dump Ross's 1932 Housing Project brainchild, citing "national defense research needs"—a timely way of saying "war fears."

On March 27, the rich doctor whom Ross had chided for wasting money on travel—Richard Wetherill—died at eighty-one. The retired Lafayette surgeon bequeathed $615,000 worth of buildings, art, cash, and other property mostly to Purdue.

Another loss hit Purdue harder. His three-year battle with kidney ailments ended in the death of Athletic Director Noble Kizer on June 13 at age forty. As Purdue's head football coach for seven seasons (1930 through 1936), Kizer's teams had won forty-two games and lost thirteen. That winning percentage became the best at Purdue. Shortly, the Athletic Department began bestowing an annual Noble E. Kizer Award upon each football squad's top-ranked student-athlete. President Elliott assumed the duties of Athletic Director for the time being.

The 1940 U.S. Census results, made public on July 18, counted a Tippecanoe County population of 51,020. Toward that total Lafayette boasted of 28,798 and West Lafayette of 6,270. When the fall semester began, Purdue enrollment reached a record high of 8,300.

The announcement came on July 3 that the WPA had granted Purdue $48,000 for airport work "in the interest of national defense." Stanley Meikle, identified in news releases as an "airport executive and head of research relations with industry," said the money would be used as part of a federal Civil Aeronautics Authority (CAA) program by adding to the east end of an existing hangar. The addition built by WPA labor would contain classrooms for pilot training, a workshop, and research lab.

Late summer brought a new season for Purdue Pride. President Roosevelt nominated and Congress approved Claude Wickard as the U.S. Secretary of Agriculture. The forty-seven-year-old Wickard, a Carroll County beef, corn, and alfalfa farmer from near Camden, Indiana, had earned his Purdue Bachelor of Science degree in agriculture in 1915. Success on the family farm had led Wickard to be named a "Master Farmer of Indiana" by *Prairie Farmer* magazine in 1927. Wickard had won election to the Indiana Senate in the Roosevelt-Democrat landslide of 1932. President Roosevelt tapped Wickard as assistant chief of the corn and hog section in the new Agricultural Adjustment Administration. Wickard remained there until 1936.

The "World's Largest Drum" had remained a rolling, thundering point of pride since 1921, but a problem of cracked and cracking drumheads forced it to the sidelines in 1940. The drum's temporary retirement lasted until 1954.

With the big drum rolled off out of sight, a "Boilermaker Special" made its debut as an official mascot on the first day of classes in September 1940. This and all ensuing "Specials" have been Victorian Era locomotives, complete with big drive wheels, puffs of hissing steam, bells and whistles, mounted over a four-wheeled automobile frame and engine. Alumni, faculty, and students have since then raised funds to replace the Special each time it has worn out. Purdue unveiled the fifth one—"Boilermaker Special V"—in 1993.

Ever the political observer, George Ade wrote a letter to Cyril Clemens from Hazelden on September 11, 1940, two months before the national election. In the balloting President Roosevelt would seek an unprecedented third term against Republican Wendell Willkie from Elwood, Indiana. Willkie, a lawyer, had become an international businessman. In his self-deprecating letter, Ade stated:

> I am strong for Mr. Willkie, but I most certainly am not going to take the stump for him or anyone else. I appeared at [a] convocation in the vast Music Hall at Purdue night before last and am quite sure that my act was a flop. I wouldn't get very far as a

stump speaker. For one thing I am a semi-invalid and must take things easy. (Tobin, 222)

Nationwide registration for a peacetime draft of men for military service began on October 16, 1940. The action affected about 10,000 Tippecanoe County men in the twenty-one to thirty-five age group. The registrants included more than 2,500 young men enrolled at Purdue.

On November 5, President Roosevelt defeated Willkie by nearly five million votes. Tippecanoe County, stubbornly true to form, backed the Indiana-native Willkie by about 4,000. Republicans again swept local contests in a voter turnout of eighty-two percent.

Purdue football fortunes shrank like Willkie's political fate and the hide on the World's Largest Drum. Mal Elward's 1940 team won just two games and lost six. In Ross-Ade Stadium, the team beat Butler twenty-eight to nothing before 17,000 and the happily tooting "Boilermaker Special I." However, the players lost to Wisconsin fourteen to thirteen before 22,000 and lost the Old Oaken Bucket to Indiana three to nothing in front of 30,000.

In November 1940, Purdue issued what it projected to be the "first of a series of publications to be known as the *Archives of Purdue University*. The series was intended to preserve the records of the "significant factors in the development of the institution." Thomas R. "Tommy" Johnston, Director of the University News Bureau, and Helen Hand, President Elliott's Executive Secretary, compiled *Trustees and Officers of Purdue University 1865-1940*. The work contained 428 pages, two of which lionized David Ross:

> It has often been said that Mr. Ross devotes more of his waking moments to the interests of the university than any other man who has served as a Trustee; but whether or not this is true, it is a well known fact that he gives tremendously of his time, thought and resources to aid the university...

> Ross first conceived the idea of a recreational field and stadium, and the Ross-Ade Stadium today stands as one of the many campus monuments to his forethought and generosity. His gifts also include the Purdue Airport, the Housing Research Campus, the Ross Civil Engineering Practice Camp, and many important research projects that have meant much to the growth and progress of Purdue.

> Even more important than his material gifts, however, has been the wise action he has taken or suggested on many matters of university policy and direction. His wisdom and common sense, astute business sagacity, and above all appreciation of the needs of aspiring youth have combined to make his services to the university invaluable. (Johnson and Hand, 311-312)

Getting serious

Britain and France declared war on Germany. Russia invaded Finland. Germany attacked Denmark, Norway, Luxembourg, Belgium, and the Netherlands. Italy declared war on Britain and France. France surrendered to Germany. Italy invaded British Somaliland and Greece. Hungary and Romania joined the German-led "Axis powers." Britain invaded Ethiopia. Bulgaria joined the Axis. Germany invaded Greece and Yugoslavia. Axis forces invaded Russia. Now World War II was getting serious.

Seagoing submarines, vessels the Germans called *unterseeboots* (anglicized as "U-boats") threatened to sink strategic North Atlantic shipping by America's friends in Canada, Britain, and other lands. Torpedoes fired from U-boats destroyed ships in waters from the Atlantic coasts of the United States and Canada to the Gulf of Mexico and from the Arctic to Africa. Because of their limited speed, range, and battery power, U-boats had to surface and run on diesel engines, diving only when attacked. U-boats commonly torpedoed shipping from the ocean surface at night. The torpedoes were straight runners fitted with one of two types of exploder. One type detonated the warhead upon impact with a solid object like the steel hull of a ship. Another went off magnetically upon sensing that it had neared a large metal object.

In this context in early 1941, Dave Ross turned his attention away from Purdue progress and factory management to combat U-boats. He designed what he called a "submarine-catching curtain." His idea was to suspend magnets from buoys. In April 1941, he wrote to a friend at Duncan Electric Company in Lafayette about the scheme. In one message the Duncan Vice President, Stanley Green, replied to Ross:

> The basic idea of [your] curtain was to suspend the parts for it along a line to be established at certain points in the sea. This line could be maintained by a cable held taut by tugs, buoys or other means...

> The lines could be made of some light, strong fiber, either wire or cord being suitable. The end of these lines would be weighted down by permanent magnets. The permanent magnet could be designed to produce any desired amount of pull once they had attached themselves to the steel hull of a submarine. From the length of line pulled out and the angle which the line marked with the vertical it would be possible to chart the exact location of any submarine being snared and to release a depth bomb to within a very close distance of the charted spot...

> An electromagnet would be very difficult, expensive and unreliable to maintain beneath the surface of the sea. There has been developed, however, since 1932 a very inexpensive and strong magnetic alloy commercially called Alnico. This is quite capable of doing the contemplated job. We have tried numbers of these magnets of horseshoe shape weighing only one-quarter of a pound and they are capable of lifting 40 times their own weight...10 pounds. With care in design I feel sure that a magnet could be devised in Alnico having a weight of about one pound that would be capable of exerting a pull of at least 30 pounds on the hull of a submarine. The design of such an Alnico magnet would be quite largely a matter of routine and consequently the details of its design need not be discussed here...

> It would appear that the detecting device mechanism through which the line is pulled so that the position of the submarine can be quickly plotted is a matter that should be taken up through the

Navy Department with one of their suppliers who have been accustomed to furnish them with remote control devices...It is possible that there may be something already in commercial production and available which would be entirely suitable for the problem at hand. (Stanley Green to Ross, April 4, 1941)

On April 14, 1941, Ross wrote to Charles F. Kettering, vice president in charge of research at the General Motors Corporation in Detroit.

Enclosed I am sending you rough sketches of two entirely different devices.

A. To attach permanent magnets to the sides of a submarine. The magnets are attached by light lines running up to a float. This indicates the location of a submarine for the fast destroyer boats to drop a bomb at the exact location.

B. A bomb laying on the floor of the ocean, with highly compressed gas in the top of the cylinder—or a chemical reaction like a fire extinguisher. Immediately, when the gas is released it displaces the water in the hollow shell and the out-rushing water acts as a propeller to propel the bomb to the surface. This can be accomplished in two ways, by a small tank of highly compressed gas in the top end of the bomb, or by freeing acid as in a fire extinguisher. Immediately the top of the bomb, being filled with gas, starts to rise to the surface being accelerated by the expulsion of the water from the shell of the bomb. This may be the answer to the so-called German magnetic bomb.

I am handing over all this description to Dean A. A. Potter to give to one of the admirals but want you to know what I'm thinking.

On the same day, Potter, Director of Purdue's Engineering Experiment Station as well as Dean, was writing to Admiral H. G. Bowen, Director of the Naval Research Laboratory in Washington, D. C.:

> Re: Submarine Locator
>
> On April 3, 1941, I wrote to you about an invention by the President of the Board of Trustees of Purdue University, Mr. David E. Ross. Originally Mr. Ross had expected to turn over the details to you through Mr. Kettering. He has come to the conclusion, however, that time may be saved if I sent the enclosed material directly to you. Accordingly Mr. Ross wrote to Mr. Kettering this morning advising him that he is turning over to you through me certain disclosures regarding a submarine locator.
>
> With this communication I am sending a blueprint of the locator, a statement by Mr. David E. Ross of the objectives and the workings of the locator, and copy of a letter by Mr. Stanley Green, Vice President and Chief Engineer of the Duncan Electric Manufacturing Co...
>
> Mr. Ross has absolutely no personal interest in this matter, does not expect to receive any compensation, and the enclosed material will be turned over by him to the government for such use as the government may wish to make of it in connection with national defense.

The Navy never used Ross's plan. It took awhile, but other approaches—advances in convoying, high frequency direction finding, radar, sonar, and depth charges—defeated the U-boats. In the end, Germany lost more than 740 U-boats—three-fourths of its fleet—and 28,000 men.

Through 1941, the U.S. made war preparations, among them a draft of registered men for future military service and the letting of "national defense" contracts for military equipment, weapons, ammunition, and vehicles. A report to Ross Gear stockholders on March 3, 1941 confirmed that the company already had begun "defense work."

From a hillside view above West Stadium Avenue in West Lafayette, Dave Ross, at age seventy, confided to a lawyer friend one day that they were pausing in one of his favorite places. Ross wished out loud to be buried someday somewhere on the campus. "I don't mean the original campus," he said. "That honor belongs to John Purdue. But perhaps an appropriate place might be found." The two sat silently for a moment before Ross continued, "Of course it would never do to have my grave on the grounds of Ross-Ade Stadium. If a Purdue player dropped a punt at a critical moment and the team lost people would say it was because the man had seen the ghost of Dave Ross. It would be said jokingly, sure, but I would hate to think I'd ever be called a jinx. The same [would be true] at the airport. If I were buried there and a pilot crashed it would be said that Dave Ross was 'ha'nting' the field" (Kelly, *Ross*, 175).

Late in 1941, President Elliott reported on even more government contracts for Purdue campus construction. The jobs involved building the final phase of the Electrical Engineering Building, the Duncan High Tension Laboratory, a new Physics Building, and a transmitter for Radio Station WBAA. On September 27, the Federal Communications Commission awarded a license for WBAA to broadcast for unlimited hours at 5,000 watts of power.

Sponsors within the Caxton Club at Knox College in Galesburg, Illinois, issued a collection of Ade's old work under the oft-used title *Stories of the Streets and of the Town*. Named after the first English printer, William Caxton, the Club pursued literary questions and preservation projects. The book appeared in a limited edition of 500 copies dating to November 1941. The contents had, for the most part, been stories collected in the eight series published in 1894-1900 and in Ade's early books. Two pieces from the Chicago *Record* in 1893 and 1896 made first book appearances.

Mal Elward's 1941 football team stumbled again. The team won two games, lost five, and tied once. In Ross Ade Stadium, a team from Vanderbilt defeated the Boilermakers three to nothing before 17,000 subdued fans. Purdue beat Iowa seven to six before 22,000 and tied Michigan State nothing to nothing before 17,000.

At the end of 1941, Rostone showed its first profit, a modest $6,600. The top people explained this newfound success in several ways. First was the method of sales. In the building business, a salesman sells a home, but in the motor control business, the customers came to Rostone. Knoy and Wymer would get a customer's designs and modify them so they could be molded. They convinced customers of Rostone's engineering skill, then designed a tool that the die shop could build. Second was Dave Ross's conviction that Rostone would succeed. Ross kept feeding the money to keep Rostone in the black. Ross attended his last Rostone meeting on February 12, 1940 but maintained close interest.

Meanwhile, in late 1941, production at Ross Gear became more fully focused upon "war work." All three of the nation's steering gear companies were turning out components and parts for war combat. Ross Gear plant workers made millions of track pins for tanks and armored vehicles. In Michigan, the Gemmer plant produced forty-millimeter armor-piercing shells, sixty-millimeter smoke mortar shells, and aileron control units for B24 heavy bombers. The Saginaw Company assembled machine guns beside its gear production lines. By the end of 1941, Ross Gear assets and liabilities balanced at an all time high of $2.6 million.

Then, Pearl Harbor.

Wartime!

Reeling from Japan's attack in Hawaii, Americans every day had to read grim headlines and learn odd new geography every hour by radio. In those far-away Philippine Islands that inspired George Ade's merry musical *Sultan of Sulu* so long ago, the capital city Manila fell to invading Japanese. There were horrible atrocity stories. "Jap" troops landed in the Netherlands East Indies. Singapore surrendered to Japan. Bataan surrendered. Japan occupied Corregidor.

Within weeks after Pearl Harbor, Purdue cut back operations to three sixteen-week semesters, no vacations, and no final exams. President Elliott took up talks in Washington, D. C., with a subcommittee of the National Resources Planning Board. Elliott told students in a Hall of Music address that they were in a Purdue Training Center: where they should prepare for "some meaningful job of war" (Topping, 238).

In June the Purdue Trustees granted Elliott leave of absence. He left for Washington to lead a division of the War Manpower Commission. His task was to coordinate civilian training in all U.S. colleges. In Elliott's absence the Purdue Trustees turned leadership over to a committee of four:

- Vice President and Executive Dean Frank Hockema.

- Vice President and Treasurer R. B. Stewart.

- Engineering Dean A. A. Potter.

- Agriculture Dean Harry Reed.

Purdue enrollment bounced around in wartime. In 1939-1940, 8,373 had attended. The number dropped by more than 200 for 1940-1941, because the military draft had begun taking men. In 1942, enrollment rose again.

Stewart had been helping draw up a national contract for teaching and housing men in what the Navy called its "V12" program. Promising future commanders were being selected for V12 pre-commissioning training and technical education. Purdue also began teaching Navy electricians' mates.

Purdue's Athletic Director and Football Coach Mal Elward resigned on February 19, 1942 to join the Navy. A week later Purdue named Guy "Red" Mackey Athletic Director, and promoted Assistant Coach Elmer Burnham to Head Football Coach.

Mackey had played end on Jimmy Phelan's powerful teams and had won honorable mention All-American honors in 1929. Mackey stabilized the job of athletic director. The ill-fated Noble Kizer, interrupted and aggravated by illness, had directed Purdue sports from 1931 to 1936 and again in 1938-1939. Sports publicist Robert E. "Bob" Woodworth had worked the job on an "acting" basis in 1937. President Elliott also did so during 1940 after Kizer's death. Then Elward took the job. Now Mackey would be Purdue's "AD" for nearly thirty years.

A new Purdue Aeronautics Corporation (PAC), allied with and modeled after the Ross-Ade and the Purdue Research foundations, began operating in 1942. PAC's mission was to develop aeronautical engineering and make better use of the Purdue Airport. The airport runway now stretched across even more of the acres Ross had given in 1931. Purdue began talking to the Navy and Marines about training aircraft pilots.

When Ross Gear stockholders met in March 1942, they received a good report about all the pre-war "defense" business done in 1941. Prospects now were rising for more. Because of the good field record of ruggedness and performance of the Ross company's steering gears, the U.S. government, by 1942, was specifying them in orders ranging from the little general-purpose car designated GP and nicknamed "Jeep," to huge machines that retrieved damaged tanks in battle zones, and for sixty-eight vehicle models in between.

Another piece of good news for Dave Ross was that Rostone was heading for an $18,000 profit for 1942, but Ross never would know that. In July 1942, in his seventy-first year, Ross seemed unusually fretful one day. He was planning to host a meeting of the Board of Governors of the National Farm Chemurgic Council. He had persuaded the Governors to meet at Purdue. He would welcome them at dinner on July 16. At the end of a day, he turned all the plans over to his secretary and drove out to The Hills. A few hours later, a stroke dropped him. The stroke resulted in hemiplegia, from which he never recovered (Kelly, *Ross*, 175-176). Hemiplegia brings severe paralysis to a vertical half of one's body. This attack rendered Ross bedridden without the power of speech or use of one arm or leg. Offers of help came from far and wide but to no real effect.

When Whit Burnett published *This Is My Best* with Dial Press, New York City, in 1942, George Ade selected for his choice "The Joy of Single Blessedness" together with an explanation of why he chose the piece.

On September 24, the motion picture star Dorothy Lamour performed in Ross-Ade Stadium. Lamour stood in as the headliner for glamorous dancer-actress Rita Hayworth who was ill. The occasion was an outdoor rally to sell U.S. War Bonds. Such star-filled entertainment, by this time, was becoming common in America. About 20,000 patriotic people braved the chilly night air to find stadium seats for the variety show. Before the night had ended, they had purchased or pledged to buy more than half a million dollars' worth of bonds.

In October, the West Lafayette public school system, already using the new West Lafayette High School, changed the name of Meridian Field, its Meridian Avenue venue for football games and track meets, to "Leslie Field." The change honored the late Harry Leslie. Leslie had finished classes in what had passed for a "high school" in the 1890s. An accredited West Lafayette High School had opened in the 1899-1900 academic year.

At a meeting on November 2, while their co-founder and leader dreamed away in silent, paralyzed misery, the Ross Gear Directors again weighed the pros and cons of a pension plan. The U.S. Internal Revenue Service had ruled that employees having more than five years' service needed to be included in a company plan. In a letter to stockholders the Ross Gear Directors explained the situation. In response the holders of nearly two-thirds of the company's 144,000 shares of stock supported the pension plan. The majority authorized the company to contract with Aetna Life Insurance Company to set up and run the plan.

In December, a new national war-bond sale campaign, promoted as the First War Loan, commenced. There were a few rays of hope for America now in the war news and more reasons to invest in bonds. Months ago carrier-based aircraft in a daring attack had bombed Tokyo, the capital of Japan, and the geography lessons continued. The Allies won the Battle of Coral Sea. Japan captured Corregidor. The Battle of Midway ended Japan's expansion eastward. Invading U.S. Marines were fighting on Guadalcanal. Allied forces landed in North Africa.

"A multiplier of the power of men"

"Old Mister Ade"—kidding himself about being "rickety in the hind legs"—still escaped the Indiana winters by basking in Miami Beach, but even Old Mister Ade sensed that his days were numbered. Back home at Hazelden his daily affairs remained in the trusted hands of James D. "Jim" Rathbun. Rathbun had married Ade's niece, Nellie, and for years had managed Ade's farms and personal business. Ade wrote candidly in a letter he dictated from Florida to Rathbun on January 10, 1943:

> Dr. Shaw has prescribed for me some kind of sleeping tablets to reduce blood pressure and improve my general condition. He warned me that they might upset me and make me feel miserable and dopy and he was right. I am taking three a day as ordered but feel about three jumps ahead of an epileptic convulsion.
>
> I went to the Kiwanis Club luncheon on Thursday and am booked for the Exchange Club in Miami on Tuesday...But I will spend most of my time at home from now on. I wish I had the ambition and the physical energy to take long walks. Walking would help to kill time and get me to nearby places of interest, but I am so rickety in the hind legs that a trip to the corner and back is about the limit of my venturing forth and such a brief outing does not provide any excitement or change of scenery. (Tobin, 233-234)

On January 29, there went out from Miami Beach to his assorted friends in the North another "News Letter From George Ade":

> This has been a week of stepping out. On Wednesday evening I put on my dinner coat and attended a dinner of the Book-Fellows at the Urmey Hotel in Miami. A majority of the 150 "fellows" were gals. The dinner had a special interest for me because I met for the first time Edison Marshall, author of many novels, who was born in Rensselaer, Indiana, only 12 miles from Hazelden...
>
> Yesterday I attended the weekly luncheon of the Kiwanis, having been advertised as one of the attractions, so I recited "The Microbe's Serenade."
>
> My entire offering was recorded by a sound machine, and the record will be run off at the next meeting. Last evening I was a guest at the dinner opening a drive for the Community War Chest. No less than 500 people were seated at the tables in the very large and palatial clubhouse of the Women's Club in Miami. I was one of several speakers...
>
> My birthday comes on February 9th. I have written some observations regarding my 77th anniversary and they will be released by the North America Newspaper Alliance on Sunday, February 7. (Tobin, 235-236)

Ade stayed in touch with Rathbun again on February 5:

> This is my day for dictating but in as much as I had a rather sleepless night and am feeling below par today I have asked Mrs. Boswell to postpone her visit until tomorrow. She lives out near Coral Gables and is employed each day at the Bath Club so she has to do a lot of miscellaneous bus riding in order to keep her appointments with me. I think you met her down here and will

remember she is a very attractive gal. Also she is a rapid shorthander and a good typist. (Tobin, 236-237)

During four days, in early March 1943, American warships defeated a Japanese supply convoy in the Bismarck Sea. Those waters stretched for hundreds of miles from New Guinea, the same vast expanse of equatorial blue flown by the tragic figures of Amelia Earhart and Fred Noonan in 1937.

At home the war had changed and kept changing many things. The Purdue Field House, for example, sheltered an unlikely visitor. The professional Cleveland Indians major league baseball team, because of wartime travel rules, conducted "spring training" at Purdue. League rules mandated training in the North instead of Florida, Arizona, or California. This limited travel to training sites east of the Mississippi River and north of the Ohio River.

So the Cleveland team came to Purdue. The Pittsburgh Pirates chose the Ball State College campus in Muncie, Indiana. The Cincinnati Reds went to Indiana University in Bloomington. The Chicago White Sox and Cubs visited the adjoining resort towns of French Lick and West Baden, Indiana. The Detroit Tigers picked Evansville, Indiana, and so forth.

On April 18, Purdue graduated 398 seniors in a streamlined commencement more than a month earlier than usual because of war priorities. A thousand male students already had left Purdue to wear military uniforms since the fall of 1942.

The wartime geography lessons instructed many a jittery American that there was a vast northwest territory called Alaska, and further taught that, flung far out into the cold north Pacific, there were Alaska's Aleutian Islands, of which two tiny ones—Kiska and Attu—the Japanese had occupied. On May 30, 1943 there arrived the assuring news that American forces at least had ended Japanese resistance on Attu, but there was far more to be done in the war.

⁂

George Ade made it back home to Hazelden by passenger train in the spring of 1943, but in a few weeks he took ill at a dinner in the Hazelden Country Club. He had to be helped to his chauffeured car. A stroke weakened his left side but did not impair his speech. Jim Rathbun put in a telephone call to President Elliott's office at Purdue to report the distressing news. Elliott's phone was busy because Elliott, back from Washington, was calling Hazelden to inform Ade that Dave Ross had died. Ross had survived for eleven months in his own pitiful state. His death on June 18 came in a singularly mournful week at Purdue. Just two days earlier, death had taken Dean Emeritus Stanley Coulter at age ninety. The next day, Gilbert A. Young, retired head of Mechanical Engineering and a faculty member for forty-two years, died at seventy-one.

Even after his stroke in 1942, Ross had stayed on the Board of Trustees *in absentia*, but his Board Presidency had devolved to James E. Noel, Class of 1892, of Indianapolis. The *Journal and Courier* printed a long account of Ross's life. On the newspaper's front page there appeared a tribute to Ross composed by Henry Marshall titled "A Hoosier Genius." Among the key points:

> This genius in the several fields of activity in which he won renown rightfully belongs in the Indiana Academy of Immortals...

> Much of Purdue's progressive development is the creation of his active intellect, his faith in the institution and his enthusiastic championship of everything worthwhile in modern trends of education. As president of its board of trustee's he furnished stimulating guidance in shaping policies and expanding its fields of service.

Its highly acclaimed research laboratories, its stadium, airport, engineering camp and numerous other improvements may be traced directly to his vision, his interest and his generous bequests.

Many men after achieving success in their chosen field are content to retire to a life of ease and comfort once they have amassed a fortune. To him money was but a means to an end, a medium to be employed in making dreams come true, not for one family or one set of friends, but for the whole of humanity. (*Journal and Courier,* June 29, 1943)

Although he had achieved so much, Ross had earned no acclaim or reputation as a churchgoer. So, when circumstances called for a funeral, the choice was downtown Lafayette's old stone Central Presbyterian Church where the Reverend William R. Graham conducted matters. Ross's sealed casket then was moved to the "Purdue Research Foundation Campus" on West Stadium Avenue in West Lafayette. Except for its important Navy training classes, Purdue ceased operations between two and four p.m. so that faculty and students might attend the memorial program for Ross. There was a long roster of "honorary pallbearers," among them Indiana Governor Henry F. Schricker, President Elliott, top Purdue and PRF figures, and state legislators, but Purdue chose active pallbearers from the student body because of Ross's all-out interest in students.

In legal documents revealed on July 3, Ross left most of his estate, estimated at a value of more than two million dollars, to Purdue, Home Hospital, and to several of his relatives. Ross bequeathed the City of West Lafayette twelve level acres along the Wabash River between State and Brown streets. Ross had pictured that land for a civic center and public park and even had ordered plans to be drawn, but those ideas died with him. Part of the land became a City dump. Ross stipulated that if the City ever sold the land, the proceeds should go to PRF. The West Lafayette schools did once use the land for baseball, but the City did nothing about a park. Eventually, the City sold part of the land to Sears, Roebuck and Company for a department store. PRF used the proceeds from that sale to buy Happy Hollow property, to which PRF added seventeen acres for more than forty home sites (Freehafer, 139).

As Ross wished, Purdue saw to it that he was buried on a knoll toward the southern end of the old Marstellar farm north of Stadium Avenue. Ross had given that land to PRF. PRF now dedicated eleven acres of it around the grave for a David Ross Memorial.

There had been whispers during the last year of Ross's life that President Elliott's relationship with Ross and the other Trustees had privately cooled. Shortly before he died, Ross let his attorney, Alison Stuart, know about the "talk," and that he was thinking about changing the will he had made in favor of Purdue. Stuart conferred with R. B. Stewart about the "talk" and the two visited Ross in his hospital room. Stewart convinced Ross that Purdue would endure long after President Elliott or any individual. So Ross let his will stand. Stuart and Elliott became its executors. PRF remained the main beneficiary.

In the will, Ross gave "The Hills" with his summer home and 197 acres bordering on the Wabash River to PRF. Other property given to PRF was to be added to the well-disguised "XR Fund." Ross also willed to PRF his stock in Ross Gear, Fairfield, and Rostone. The eventual book value of property Ross left to PRF totaled more than $2.5 million. One historian added, "no one can place a dollar value on his interest and encouragement, years of devoted time, and planning for Purdue's future" (Freehafer, 95-97). And Elliott intimated no rancor between them when he eulogized Ross:

This modest man of might for more than fifty years always was ready to act either as a servant or leader of men of good will. He created his own distinguished and useful career and created the careers of a host of others. He was a multiplier of the power of men. Many knew him only as the inventor and maker of steering devices for motor vehicles. Many more knew him as the inspirer of men for the right steering of their own lives.

Ross's burial place came to be enlarged and landscaped as a memorial with a granite slab covering the grave. Carved in the granite:

David E. Ross, 1871-1943

Dreamer, Builder, Faithful Trustee

Creator of Opportunity For Youth

Life went on. After all, there was a war going on. Don Fernando's Orchestra played a stage show in the Hall of Music. Admission was forty-four cents. They put the Hall of Music to use again in September. A variety show in connection with the nation's Third War Loan campaign featured radio singer Rudy Vallee leading his U.S. Coast Guard band. In two shows, 8,500 people bought more than two million dollars' worth of war bonds. For every seventy-five dollars they invested in war bonds, the buyers could get back one hundred dollars after ten years.

For various reasons, for the first time in twenty-five years, George Ade spent the winter of 1943-1944 in Indiana. As the October frost set in, friends moved "Old Mister Ade" from Hazelden to the Harry Hershman home, three miles from Brook. The move took place because Hazelden, with its 1905 oil-burning furnace and limited (because of a wartime shortage) oil supply, was going to be too hard to heat. Ade's old neighbor Hershman was away in California with his own family.

On the night of October 5, Lafayette and West Lafayette neighborhoods went through a practice "blackout" in case of air raid between 8:30 and 9:30 p.m. There was rising fear that Germany or Japan might bomb America. Neighborhood blocks were divided into territories supervised by air raid wardens. Such precautions took place all over the country.

On the night of October 23, young Albert P. "Al" Stewart, energetic Director of Purdue Musical Organizations, emceed the first in a "Victory Varieties" series of wartime entertainments. Two thousand people attended in the Hall of Music. The stars of the show were slapstick bandleader Milt Britton and popular singer "Wee Bonnie" Baker. A month later the singing Vagabonds quartet headlined the second in the Victory Varieties series. Bandleaders Les Brown, Art Kassel, and Tiny Hill kept the series going. Subsequent shows starred a long list of bands and stage show greats until 1968.

World War II treated Purdue kindly at football time in 1943. The war brought Alex Agase to West Lafayette after he had played an all-American season at the University of Illinois in 1942. The Marine Corps assigned Agase to Purdue for officer candidate school along with more than thirty other Navy and Marine Corps athletes. With that much talent, Purdue won all nine of its games, outscored opponents 214 to fifty five, shared with Michigan the Big Ten Conference title, and ranked fifth in the national Associated Press poll.

Head Coach Elmer Burnham molded twenty-six Marines, nine civilians, and seven Navy men into that undefeated squad. "Football is teamwork and we jelled pretty quick," Agase said. "The coaches—Burnham and assistants Joe Dienhart, Sam Voinoff and Cecil Isbell—did an excellent job of putting that team together. That's not easy to do to take people who don't know each other, from various universities, and get them to jell. But it was a talented team and that is the bottom line."

Local fans quickly came to cheer and adore newcomers like quarterback Sammy Vacanti, halfbacks Chalmers "Bump" Elliott and Stan Dubicki, fullback Tony Butkovich, and rugged linemen like Agase and Dick Barwegen. Purdue trampled military teams from the Great Lakes (Illinois) Naval Training Station (the 1942 national champ) and Camp Grant (south of Rockford, Illinois) and romped past collegiate foes as well. In three games in Ross-Ade Stadium, the wartime Boilermakers drubbed Illinois forty to twenty-one, Camp Grant nineteen to nothing, and Iowa twenty-eight to seven. The crowds never exceeded 15,000, however. Butkovich set a Big Ten scoring record for one season by tallying seventy-eight points, but with one game left to play the Navy abruptly transferred Butkovich and eleven other Boilermakers to military assignments elsewhere. Without them, Purdue barely beat Indiana seven to nothing in Bloomington to claim the Old Oaken Bucket.

Even the war news brightened. American troops in the Pacific landed on Bougainville Island and soon the Marines invaded Tarawa. These were the newest lessons in wartime geography.

"Home is the Hoosier"

At Hazelden, in April 1944, an old acquaintance and writer from Cleveland, Ohio, Fred Kelly, visited the enfeebled George Ade. Kelly was writing a biography of David Ross.

Years before, a New York editor had asked Kelly to write a Sunday newspaper feature about Ade at Hazelden. Kelly and Ade had met in Chicago that time and had reached Hazelden by train. "On the way," Kelly said, "Ade apologized for the slow train. 'The stations are exactly eighty feet apart,' he said, 'and it stops at them all.'"

Kelly said he was glad when his son wished to attend Purdue because it would be easy to visit Ade as well. "In the spring of 1944," Kelly said, "I was writing the biography of David Ross. No one knew certain facts about Ross except George Ade and he was too ill to receive callers. But he sent word that I should come to see him. His smile had its old-time warmth when he said: 'I'm not very ambidextrous or acrobatic but the old bean is still functioning and I think I can tell you some things you'll want to know.' A month later he died" (Kelly, *Ade,* Author's Preface).

To interviewers, Kelly said, Ade sometimes turned facetious when he said, "At a time when I might have contemplated marriage, a license cost two dollars and I never had the money...I suppose I lived in a hall bedroom too long and became thoroughly undomesticated. On top of that maybe no woman would have had me."

Kelly said that Ade once wrote that the American bachelor is not a woman hater. "When he comes into the presence of an attractive specimen of the more important sex he is not revolted. He is awe-stricken and rendered numb and dumb...It isn't usually a lack of intense regard and reverence for womanhood that keeps the bachelor single. Often enough it is lack of regard for himself as a fit companion for the goddess up there above him on the pedestal."

Ade would say, "I didn't marry because another man married my girl." Ade's playwright friend Julian Street said if Ade ever *had* married, "his wife would have been the best entertained woman on earth!" (Kelly, *Ade,* 217-218)

⁂

A few weeks after the visit from Kelly, Ade suffered three heart attacks. He died on Tuesday night May 16, 1944. Eulogies in print and on radio bulletins and movie newsreels spread across the nation. As *Time* magazine put it, "Home Is the Hoosier."

Ade had languished in a coma for three days after his third attack. Since that stroke in June 1943, he had been a weak, blanket-wrapped invalid forced to winter in Indiana instead of Miami Beach. "There *is* no climate here [in Indiana]," Ade used to quip, "just an assortment of unexpected weather."

Ade passed away in the Hershman house. With him to the final minute was Jim Rathbun. The Hufty-Crane Funeral Home in Kentland arranged a service at Hazelden for two p.m. on Friday, May 19. In its obituary, the *Journal and Courier* in Lafayette remarked:

> Prolific in everything but gloom, the celebrated wit had played on the world's funny bone for more than three decades in half a dozen venues—newspapers, magazines, books, plays, movies and casual conversation...

Purdue President Edward C. Elliott stated: "The Purdue flag is half-masted—a sign of the loss of this devoted and distinguished alumnus. For more than a generation George Ade represented the clean humor and the healthy laughter that lightened the burdens of life. He was a philosopher skillfully using his slangy satire and his kindly wit to cause men to laugh at themselves, and thereby be protected from hypocrisy and swank.

Today we mourn a friend whose standards of conduct and responsibility and above all his ideals of generous friendship made him a modest master servant of his fellow men. His artistry celebrated the homely virtues. His life is now part of the permanent endowment of his native state.

Hundreds assembled to pay tribute. Those closest to him knew how much Ade had disliked solemnity. Three specially chosen men addressed the standing crowd of neighbors on the front lawn at Hazelden. President Elliott, Kenesaw Mountain Landis, and John T. McCutcheon each said it differently, but said the same thing; they were sorry that George Ade was gone.

The three spoke into the microphone of a public address system set up just inside the house. Ade's remains lay nearby in a flower-banked casket. There were no "funeral orations." Instead, the three speakers spun anecdotes about Ade, many of them funny. The Reverend Voris B. Servies, Pastor of the Methodist church in Kentland, led a short prayer. Mourners carried the casket from the house to a hearse. A motorcade rolled off to Kentland and to the family burial plot. "There was no music to speak of," the *Journal and Courier* noted, "just hundreds of birds singing in the trees around the big English-style house Ade had occupied for 40 years. Ade probably would have said that was music enough."

Six of Ade's relatives—Jim Rathbun among them—carried the casket. The *Journal and Courier* reported:

> Some stores in Kentland and Brook were closed for the funeral and signs hung in the windows: "Gone to the Ade Funeral." Farmers too busy in their fields to attend the service stood at fences when the funeral cortege passed on its way to Kentland, and bared their heads.

Most of the men, women and children making up the 888 population of Brook attended. Friends and relatives came from Kentland, Lafayette, Chicago, Indianapolis and other points.

There were representatives of the Purdue Alumni Association, and Sigma Chi Fraternity. Charles Kiler, of Champaign, Ill., carried out the Sigma Chi graveside ritual in the Ade family lot of Fairlawn Cemetery at Kentland, placing white roses on the casket just before it was lowered into the ground. (*Journal and Courier*, May 20, 1944)

Five days after the funeral, Rathbun and Newton County Assessor Alvia E. Herriman met at a deposit box in the Continental Illinois National Bank and Trust Company in Chicago and opened Ade's will. Rathbun said the box held securities worth more than $100,000 and deeds to six Indiana farms totaling 2,500 acres and valued at more than $300,000. Beneficiaries included a sister, eight nieces and nephews, and other relatives.

Elmer Burnham left Purdue after 1943 to coach football at the University of Rochester in New York. One of Burnham's Purdue assistants, Cecil Isbell, the Boilermaker fullback for the Noble Kizer and Mal Elward teams during 1935-1937, coached Purdue football after Burnham. Isbell's 1944 team won five and lost five while the home crowds remained modest. In Ross-Ade Stadium, the Boilermakers beat Marquette forty to seven, lost to a strong military team known in wartime as Iowa Pre-Flight thirteen to six, and shut out Wisconsin thirty-five to nothing. However, attendance never exceeded 17,000. In the Old Oaken Bucket battle, Purdue lost to Indiana fourteen to six with 27,500 watching.

Hovde for Elliott

On July 1, 1945, Edward C. Elliott retired to the role of "President Emeritus." The Purdue Trustees named Dean Potter Acting President and formed a search committee to choose Elliott's successor. On August 22, the Trustees named thirty-seven-year-old Frederick L. Hovde to succeed Elliott.

Isbell's 1945 Purdue football team won seven games and lost three. In Ross-Ade Stadium, Marquette fell fourteen to thirteen before 11,000 fans. About 20,000 showed up when Purdue beat Iowa forty to nothing. Fifteen thousand came to see a twenty-eight to nothing win over Pittsburgh, and a scant 12,000 saw Purdue beat Miami of Ohio twenty-one to seven.

When he arrived in January 1946, Hovde determined that Purdue University had been "well-managed." The school had benefited from the giving and counsel of Dave Ross; it had pioneered in research through PRF and the Ross-Ade Foundation. R. B. Stewart had learned management from Ross and Elliott, two brilliant, strong-minded men (Topping, 255).

Trustees, having used Ross as their model, helped the Hovde years by staying interested in Purdue's welfare. Several became givers in the spirit of Ross who was "probably the most important one in Purdue history in terms of largess" (Topping, 290).

Before long, Hovde's get-acquainted briefings led to Walter Scholer. The architect told Hovde "you can't do enough to repay Dave Ross for what he did for the university. He was in my opinion the greatest benefactor of Purdue. President Hovde looked at me kind of funny and asked me about this and said, 'Are you sure?' And I said, 'I'll stand on that statement.'"

Scholer explained, "Hovde didn't know what that guy did for the university. It was a recognized fact in his day that Purdue had but one Trustee who was married to the university. This came up [from Trustee Jim Noel] when I designed those steps and all going up to Dave Ross' grave. Dave had left some pretty definite instructions about it. He wanted just a slab on the level of the ground.

"Because this was so important, I wanted the Trustees to look at the design. Jim Noel made the statement: 'It makes no difference what you do, whether you put a nice granite slab. You can put that, or you could build a block thirty feet high and twenty feet square and a lot of decorations and all that. But in twenty-five years you ask the average person around Lafayette who Dave Ross was and he'll say, 'Oh, I don't know, he used to be around here; believe he had something to do with Ross Gear. And they don't even talk about Ross Gear any more'" (Scholer, 59-60).

In twenty-five years, Noel was right. Ross Gear and Tool Company, in 1964, became a division of Thompson-Ramo-Wooldridge (TRW) and eventually "TRW Commercial Steering Systems," without reference to the Ross name.

⁓ ⁓

Purdue campus sightseers can still find Scholer's creative work. The David Ross Memorial and Garden are northwest of Slayter Center, north of Stadium Avenue, south of Tower Acres, and west of Ross-Ade Stadium. David Ross Road climbs to the shady, well-manicured botanical garden on the hill where they interred Ross beneath "just a slab on the level of the ground." The site, made pleasant with manicured grass, walkways, beds planted with spurge, creeping phlox, sedum and tulips among several marble benches, and both young and old shade trees, offers distant views to the east, south, and west.

Isbell coached the 1946 Purdue football team to two wins, six losses, and one tie. In Ross-Ade Stadium, the team beat Miami of Ohio thirteen to seven before 23,000, lost to Wisconsin twenty-four to twenty with 32,000 watching, then lost to Indiana thirty-four to twenty. A new attendance record of 43,000 people witnessed that game.

Fred Kelly, the Ohio author of a popular biography, *The Wright Brothers,* finished his book about Dave Ross. The Alfred A. Knopf Company in New York City published *David Ross: Modern Pioneer* in 1946. The venerable Bruce Rogers designed the book, elegantly printed and bound by Plimpton Press in Norwood, Massachusetts. Kelly dedicated the book "to students with curiosity about the unknown and the initiative to apply new knowledge, the kind that David Ross was always seeking."

Stuart K. "Stu" Holcomb succeeded Isbell as Purdue football coach. Holcomb's first team in 1947 won five games and lost four. In Ross-Ade Stadium, 34,000 saw the Boilermakers upset Ohio State twenty-four to twenty and watched national power Notre Dame beat Purdue twenty-two to seven with 42,000 on hand. Another 42,000 cheered when Purdue beat Illinois fourteen to seven. Purdue topped Iowa twenty-one to nothing before 35,000, then beat Pittsburgh twenty-eight to nothing as 19,000 looked on.

Dorothy Russo's *A Bibliography of George Ade* in 1947 listed about 2,500 entries, virtually all the published results of Ade's prolific pen. At least sixty percent of these listings appear in collections, for Ade "was a superb businessman and as soon as he had enough periodical material to make a book, he got out a pair of covers, stitched the articles between them, and sent them to market" (Coyle, 133). The Ade bibliography contained more than 300 pages. It listed forty-four ephemeral (short-lived, minor) publications between 1901 and 1943, including speeches, remembrances, and even a *Sigma Chi Catechism Number Two*.

The Indianapolis publishing house of Bobbs-Merrill issued Kelly's biography, *George Ade: Warmhearted Satirist*, in 1947. In it Kelly recalled:

> I began to read George Ade in 1893. A youngster in knee pants, I went with my mother to the World's Fair in Chicago...My mother had noticed in a morning paper, the *Record*, a daily department "All Roads Lead to the World's Fair," delightful little stories of happenings at the Fair. She subscribed for that paper and [so that back home in Ohio] we could read about some of the things we missed seeing.
>
> "All Roads Lead to the World's Fair" was succeeded by "Stories of the Streets and of the Town." We continued to take the *Record*...I was entertained by the stories for years before I knew who wrote them. Then when "Fables in Slang" began to appear I was one of the countless number to whom George Ade was a hero.
>
> I first met him in 1896. By that time I was a columnist on a paper in Cleveland. (Kelly, *Ade,* Author's Preface)

Holcomb's 1948 football team won three games and lost six, but attendance boomed. In Ross-Ade Stadium, powerhouse Michigan drubbed the Boilermakers forty to nothing, yet 46,000 fans watched. Thirty-two thousand saw Purdue top Marquette fourteen to nine.

There was a special event in the stadium on Armistice Day (now known as Veterans Day) on Thursday, November 11, 1948. High school football teams from Lafayette Jefferson and West Lafayette—rivals for decades—revived their annual game at Purdue after a long layoff during which they had competed on their high school fields. Years before they had butted heads at Stuart Field. Now in 1948, in Ross-Ade Stadium, an estimated 12,000 spectators—huge by high school standards—saw West Lafayette win thirteen to nothing.

Two days later, 35,000 sat by as Purdue lost to Pittsburgh twenty to thirteen. A new stadium record of 47,000 looked on when, on November 20, Purdue trounced Indiana thirty-nine to nothing.

The 1948 crowds, rising student enrollment, and demand for tickets persuaded Purdue, in 1949, to enlarge Ross-Ade Stadium. The Athletic Department helped pay for the work by selling $300 memberships in the Ross-Ade Foundation in return for lifetime season tickets. On May 12, Athletic Director Mackey announced that 7,000 more seats would raise stadium capacity to 51,295.

On nine summer nights in July 1949, the stadium came into new use as a venue for outdoor drama. *The Pioneer Glory*, a pageant of Indiana history, played evenings on a 100-foot stage. Howard Tooley, from New York City, wrote the pageant and directed a teenage cast of 200 actors, singers, and musicians from Indiana schools.

The cast performed in front of patrons seated in the north horseshoe so as not to interfere with the west grandstand expansion.

Stu Holcomb's 1949 team won four games and lost five. In Ross-Ade Stadium, the team lost to Iowa twenty-one to seven before 32,000. Notre Dame beat Purdue thirty-five to thirteen before a new attendance record of 52,000. Illinois shut out Purdue nineteen to nothing in front of 48,000.

The high school teams repeated their Ross-Ade Stadium "Jeff-West Side" rivalry before several thousand prep fans on Friday, November 11, 1949. "Jeff" won this time, two to nothing on a safety scored after a blocked punt.

The next afternoon, 28,000 watched Purdue beat Marquette forty-one to seven.

Gaining in value

As the years passed, Ross-Ade Stadium became more valuable to Purdue. Periodic upgrades took place. In 1950, Purdue built a larger press box on the west side. Holcomb's 1950 team won two games and lost seven, but one of the wins took place in front of 56,000 shocked Notre Dame fans up in South Bend, Indiana, twenty-eight to fourteen. In the second win Purdue topped Indiana thirteen to six before 45,000 in Ross-Ade.

In 1951, the team won five and lost four. The Boilermakers played games in Ross-Ade Stadium that fall against Texas, Iowa, Wisconsin, Penn State, and Minnesota. Home crowds averaged about 29,000.

The 1952 team won four, lost three, and tied two. Home attendance for games against Iowa, Notre Dame, Michigan State and Indiana jumped to an average of 43,000.

Purdue's 1953 footballers won only twice and lost seven times, but October 24 became another day to remember. Purdue's then-winless team upset nationally top-ranked Michigan State six to nothing. The result stunned college football fans nationwide and ended the visitors' twenty-eight game winning streak. This, coupled with that shocking win at Notre Dame in 1950, gave rise to pundits naming Purdue the "Spoilermakers." Home attendance in 1953 totaled 146,000 for four games, averaging 36,500.

The "Golden Girl" and "Purdue Pete"

In mid-September 1954, Purdue beat Missouri thirty-one to nothing. Only 25,000 attended three Ross-Ade Stadium debuts that afternoon. Two of the new faces were those of the All-American Marching Band's new director, Dr. Al G. Wright, and the band's baton-twirling, crowd-pleasing "Golden Girl." She was a coed named Thelma Carpenter from Lamar, Colorado. In the game, fans cheered Purdue's new sophomore quarterback Len Dawson, later a college all-American and professional star.

The "Golden Girl" was a product of Wright's "show-biz" mind. Paul Spotts Emrick, while still a student, had taken the band baton in 1905. Under his leadership, the musicians claimed to be the first to break military ranks and make a formation while marching on the field. Emrick's block letter "P" became a traditional part of each stadium performance. Emrick, in 1921, had purchased and used that huge base drum. Emrick's bands gained national exposure in motion picture Movietone News shorts during the 1930s. The Band marched at night lit only by lights attached to horns, hats, and uniforms.

The "Golden Girl" was merely the first of Wright's novelties. Others included the "Girl in Black," the "Silver Twins," and the "Golddusters." Under Wright, the band also toured Europe, Japan, South America, Canada, and the Caribbean. Wright decided to name his musicians "the Purdue All-American Marching Band" and to revive the World's Largest Drum that had been stored since

1940. DuPont's invention of Mylar™, as matters turned out, could be used for synthetic drum heads, and soon the monster drum boomed again.

Holcomb's 1954 football team won five games, lost three, and tied one. The biggest home crowd was 55,500 for Notre Dame. For the season, nearly 267,000 fans spun the turnstiles at six home game, an average of 44,500.

In 1955, the Athletic Department contracted to install permanent steel grandstands on the east side. This raised the stadium seating capacity to 55,000. Purdue also upgraded and named the press box in honor of former sports publicist Robert C. "Bob" Woodworth. Holcomb's 1955 football team again won five, lost three, and tied once. Five home games drew more than 218,000 fans— a 42,500 average. All told, Holcomb's teams won thirty-five games, lost forty-two, and tied four.

In 1956, assistant coach Jack Mollenkopf succeeded Holcomb as coach. Injuries limited Mollenkopf's first team to three wins, four losses, and two ties. It would be the only losing season in Mollenkopf's fourteen years as coach. The 1956 season did result in a satisfying thirty-nine to twenty victory over Indiana in the Old Oaken Bucket battle. Attendance at four home games averaged more than 43,000.

Back in 1940, the men who owned the University Bookstore in the West Lafayette "village," Robert W. "Doc" Epple and Murray C. "Red" Sammons, hired local artist Art Evans to draw a "Boilermaker" to use as an advertising icon for the store. When asked for a name for the burly, hammer-wielding figure in Evans's drawing,

Epple coined the name "Pete." In 1944, the editors of Purdue's *Debris* yearbook obtained permission from Epple to use "Purdue Pete" on the *Debris* cover. In 1956, Purdue Pete debuted at Ross-Ade Stadium games as a painted papier-mâché head costume worn by one of the cheerleaders. Later, Purdue used fiberglass to allow the head to stand up to rain.

In 1957, the University removed the cinder track that had circled the playing field since 1924 and installed a chain-link fence between the field and seats. Mollenkopf's second team won five games and lost four. Home games each drew more than 40,000 ticket holders.

In 1958, the Big Ten ruled that member schools could raise money for athletic grants-in-aid. At Purdue, "Red" Mackey, Alumni Association Executive Director Joe Rudolph, and Alumni Scholarship Foundation Director C. H. "Cordy" Hall established a John Purdue Club to generate scholarship money.

The football team improved in 1958 to six wins, one loss, and two ties. Home attendance that year averaged more than 43,000 for games against Nebraska, Michigan State, Illinois, and Indiana, the latter a fifteen-to-fifteen tie. Mollenkopf's next team, in 1959, won five, lost two, and tied two. Home attendance on four dates averaged 43,400 and peaked that year at more than 53,000 for Notre Dame.

"I am an American"

One of Dave Ross's enduring gifts to Purdue University, the Ross Engineering Camp, operated every summer from 1926 until 1960. When the civil engineering curriculum no longer required fieldwork out at the Camp, Purdue made the grounds and buildings available for the Indiana 4-H Leadership Center.

Coach Mollenkopf's next ten teams won sixty-five games and the prestigious Rose Bowl in Pasadena, California, in January 1967. National rankings began to be commonplace. So did wins over Indiana—eight out of ten years. Attendance at Ross-Ade Stadium rarely fell below 40,000 per game.

The 1960 team won four, lost four, and tied once. Attendance at five home games averaged 45,500. In 1961, the team won six and lost three. In four home games, nearly 189,000 fans showed up—more than 47,200 per game.

There had been a long standing rivalry with the University of Texas over which school's band really had the "world's largest drum." In 1961, there was an attempt to stand the drums side by side to determine which was bigger. It was to take place at the national convention of Kappa Kappa Psi band fraternity in Wichita, Kansas. Purdue bandsmen challenged their Texas counterparts to push their respective drums through every large city on the way to the convention. Purdue people pushed their drum through Indianapolis, St. Louis, Kansas City, Topeka—and even Independence, Missouri, where former U.S. President Harry Truman, in retirement, autographed it. However, the Texas students failed to bring their drum. With the default, Purdue continued claiming the "world's largest drum."

The 1962 football Boilermakers won four, lost four, and tied once. Home games drew 186,000 fans—about 46,500 each. The 1963 team won five and lost four, drawing more than 45,900 at Ross-Ade Stadium games.

In 1964, Purdue dug out and lowered the original 1924 playing field by seven feet and added thirteen rows of seats. Contractors poured sloping, semicircular concrete sidewalks to connect the locker rooms to the playing field. Seating capacity now reached 60,000. Purdue also put Fiberglass™ covers on all permanent seats. This gave the stadium an alternating color scheme of gold and black. The word "Purdue" appeared in the school colors on the north end zone seats. In Purdue's tense Old Oaken Bucket win over Indiana on November 21, 1964, the crowd surged to 61,735. This was another stadium record for the game that ended twenty-eight to twenty-two. Season attendance for four home games rose to a record 210,800—more than 52,700 per game.

In a sometimes-critical 1964 book about George Ade, Lee Coyle, of John Carroll University (Ohio), wrote that Ade's body of work was "glutted with ephemeral publications now difficult to find and little worth the trouble. Ade was as generous as he was business-like, enlisting his talent in causes, dissipating his energies on flimsy projects and playing the part of a literary Rotarian."

Coyle continued:

> Ade was unequal to the discipline and intellectual direction needed to make him other than he was. But what he was was quite

enough. He was a skilled journalist, gifted with a talent that he turned to cash...

He was welcome and honored throughout the land until the Depression came, eclipsed laughter and erased the fame of George Ade within his own lifetime.

When he died America was surprised that he had lived so long.

Little of Ade's work has survived. The modern custodians of literary reputation have relegated him to the limbo of vernacular raconteurs who misspelled their way through the second half of the 19th century. That is unfortunate, for much in Ade remains vital and meaningful today. (Coyle, 137-140)

On September 18, 1965, Mollenkopf's tenth Boilermaker team defeated Miami of Ohio before a crowd of 44,800. The football victory marked Purdue's 100th in Ross-Ade Stadium. That year the team won seven games, lost two, and tied once. There were five home games again that year. The turnouts averaged more than 52,500, and a new record of 62,300 saw Purdue and Michigan State play on October 23.

In the mid-1960s, Purdue English Professor H. B. Knoll revived the memory of Dave Ross. In *The Story of Purdue Engineering*, Knoll described Ross as a "hometown boy who believed in the hometown, which became Lafayette." He continued:

He supported public welfare, knew every worker in his plant and treated all with respect and courtesy. During the Depression he found some sort of work for all his employees...not fulltime, but at least Ross kept them nourished.

He felt that "I live here and I want this community to be a good one...one where people will be energetic and happy."

∽ ∽

In 1966, John A. "Jack" Scott, one of Henry Marshall's successors as publisher of the Lafayette *Journal and Courier*, telephoned the Director of Purdue's All-American Marching Band, Al Wright. There was far-reaching student unrest going on because of U.S. involvement in warfare in Vietnam. "At Purdue it was not too bad," Wright has recalled. "But Scott said 'Al, we've got to get some patriotism into these kids—can you help?'"

A former South Bend mayor and a retired Marine Corps general, Scott was a big fan of band performances infused with patriotism. The idea of a short speech that would be spoken over an arrangement of "America the Beautiful" at Purdue football games in Ross-Ade Stadium occurred to Wright, a native of England. "It's a beautiful tune, a nice quiet thing you can read over," Wright said. Inspired by patriotic verses he read either on a menu or a placemat at a downtown Lafayette restaurant, Wright penned this reading:

I am an American,

That's the way most of us put it, just matter of factly,

They are plain words, those four,

You could write them on your thumbnail

Or you could sweep them clear across this bright [September/October/November] sky.

But remember too that they are more than words,

They are a way of life.

So whenever you speak them, speak them firmly;

Speak them proudly, speak them gratefully.

I AM AN AMERICAN

The first time the band announcer read "I Am An American" at halftime, the football fans in Ross-Ade Stadium stood in surprised and hushed respect. Wright felt "pleasantly surprised" by the positive reaction especially from students. He skipped "I Am An American" at the next home game, whereupon a *Journal and Courier* editorial written by Scott asked what happened to the recitation. Letters to that effect flooded both the Lafayette daily newspaper and the student-run newspaper *The Exponent*. So Wright made the reading part of the pre-game flag ceremony for the last two home games that fall. When Purdue played in the Rose Bowl in Pasadena, California, in January 1967, network television broadcast the band's performance of "I Am An American" all over the U.S.

Purdue had played five home games in Ross-Ade Stadium in 1966. A record 269,800 fans averaged nearly 54,000 at each game.

In 1967, Wright decided again to omit "I Am An American." Again a public outcry forced him to restore and make it tradition. Wright did try one more time to reword the script. "But it was like changing the Bible. You can't do it," Wright said and tried no more.

Mollenkopf's football team in 1967 won eight out of ten games. Again, there were five home games, and for the first time season attendance passed 300,000—more than 60,000 per game.

Another eight-win season followed in 1968. Five home games drew a record 61,000 each. In 1969, the last of Coach Mollenkopf's teams again won eight and lost two. A new record 332,800—an average of more than 66,500 per game—enjoyed the team's Ross-Ade Stadium games.

A hallowed centerpiece

As years pass, Ross-Ade Stadium has continued to remain a hallowed centerpiece around which any and all Purdue Athletic Department progress has evolved. On December 2, 1967 Purdue dedicated a basketball arena that superseded but did not replace the vintage 1938 Field House. The circular brick structure southeast of Ross-Ade Stadium with seating for 14,123 fans cost fifty-six million dollars. In 1972, Purdue named it Mackey Arena to honor the long-time Athletic Director. Purdue gave a name to the thirty-year-old Field House, too, in memory of the late Ward "Piggy" Lambert.

The April 1968 issue of a newsletter called *Campus Copy* contained another paean to Dave Ross, but by that time his name drew blank looks from most Purdue students on campus. The article "David Ross: Trustee with a Vision" described Ross as the "guiding light behind the destinies of Purdue." In the article the venerable Dean Potter called Ross "a veritable Benjamin Franklin, a polygon of talents, and that is something to note. Few people can do even one thing well, but Dave Ross did many things well. He gave a lot of money to the university...over $2 million...but it was not the money, it was what he gave of himself." Ross's life, Potter said, embodied two influences—that of the interested teacher and the inspiring orator who insisted that one must "think big things, and then do them."

Purdue built third and fourth levels above Ross-Ade Stadium's fourteen-year-old Robert C. Woodworth Memorial Press Box in 1969. When finished, Deck One hosted athletic donor-boosters known as the Buchanans. Radio stations filled the booths on the second deck. Print media and statistical crews worked on the third deck, equipped to hold 136 people. On the fourth level, television crews from time to time came to West Lafayette for nationally important games and needed working space.

Purdue next replaced the last temporary bleachers at the top of the original seating area in the north horseshoe with permanent stands. This raised seating capacity to 68,000—more than five times the 1924 original. The University also built a new scoreboard above and outside the south end zone.

Purdue Pride took yet another great leap forward. On July 21, 1969, the United States astronaut Neal A. Armstrong became the first man to set foot on the surface of the moon. A Purdue graduate and member of the All-American Marching Band, Armstrong's became a name for the ages, and his signature joined the list of other names signed on both old and new heads on the World's Largest Drum. Purdue-grad astronaut Virgil "Gus" Grissom was another pounder on that drum, and so were Japan's famed Kodo Drummers and former President Harry Truman.

In 1970, Purdue added 1,200 more seats to Ross-Ade Stadium by putting up a grandstand beyond the south end zone

When Mollenkopf retired after fourteen seasons and eighty-four victories, his quarterback coach, Bob DeMoss, a 1940s Purdue star, took over. DeMoss's first team lost six out of ten, yet the largest crowd in Ross-Ade Stadium history—69,357—viewed the November 21 game against Indiana won by Purdue forty to nothing.

By providing handicapped-accessible seating and other amenities to the stadium, Purdue trimmed the total number of seats to 67,332.

There was a dark side to certain American college traditions, and young society back then chipped away to bring about change. A 1969-1970 sports writer for the student newspaper *The Exponent* was a woman—Stephanie Salter from Terre Haute, Indiana. Her experiences led Salter—a future *San Francisco Chronicle* columnist—to recall and to write:

> When I was an undergrad at Purdue, Frederick L. Hovde was president. A former football All-American and Rhodes Scholar, Hovde began his tenure in one era—post-World War II 1946—and ended it in another—the Vietnam War/Kent State/sexual revolution of 1971. You could count on half of one hand the women in his administrative cabinet. Then, the male-female student ratio was about 4-to-1. First-year females in dormitories had curfews, males didn't. No matter how low the temperature dropped, women students could not walk through the Memorial Union wearing slacks. As a sports writer for the student daily *Exponent*, I was prohibited from sitting in the press box of Ross-Ade Stadium because I was female. As Athletic Director Red Mackey explained, the "language up there can get a little salty for a young lady." Never mind that young ladies already were in the press box during football games—as servants. Women in an Air Force ROTC auxiliary delivered Cokes and hot-dogs to the working gents. During my senior year, I was editor-in-chief of the *Exponent*, the first woman in that capacity, I was told, since the campus man shortage of World War II. When my name came up for induction into the honorary society Iron Key—an automatic for the *Exponent* editor—I was blackballed. A male friend who did make it into the Society recounted the little speech of triumph that a member of the Purdue Board of Trustees delivered to his Iron Key brothers

after the vote. One of the terms the Trustee used to describe me still can't be printed in a family newspaper. (Salter to author, May 2007)

When "Red" Mackey's long reign as Athletic Director ended the men's basketball coach George S. King Jr. held the job from 1971 to 1992. One of King's unforeseen first concerns was the Ross-Ade Stadium playing field.

In the 1960s, certain American venues for baseball and football had begun replacing natural grass fields with carpet-like rolls of artificial grass sold as AstroTurf™ and other brand names. This reduced groundskeeping costs but caused games to be played on harder, more injurious surfaces. Several Big Ten football schools converted to artificial grass fields anyway while Purdue bided its time.

Walter Scholer was eighty years old when he suffered a slight heart attack in 1970. He was in a hospital for about a week. Scholer and a Kiwanis Club friend Roy A. Smith had been bantering for some time about how Scholer ought to tape-record his memories of his work for Purdue University. "The much-enlarged campus of 1970 had dozens of new buildings," Smith said, "the Executive Building, the Hall of Music, Mackey Arena and many classroom buildings and dormitories, all designed and planned by Walter Scholer. Most were constructed of red brick. President Hovde once said, 'Those who do not like red brick buildings must argue with the founders of the university.' Hovde had gained great respect for Purdue's architect and knew that Scholer was one of the nation's best designers of educational construction. Scholer and Purdue made certain that projected building plans contained strict and rigid specifications—details that might make contractors grumble but requirements that would save Purdue much money in repairs and maintenance costs" (Scholer, 5).

Scholer recorded his remembrances on January 14, 1971. Smith was there: "Walter admitted that he was not the best public speaker, and a microphone did not help in his thinking. [So] the mic was covered with a newspaper, and he seemed to be at ease and eager to start talking. The results of this two and one-half hour meeting were transcribed."

The session closed with this dialogue:

> SMITH: I'm very happy with what we got.

> SCHOLER: I didn't quite get the idea when we started here, that that's what we were going to do.

> SMITH: We didn't want you all tied up in knots. When you relax you can do right. If you were all tied up in knots and doing all the talking it wouldn't come out.

> SCHOLER: I'd make it more brief. (laughter)

> SMITH: That's one thing I can say about you—you're just too modest for what you've done. (Scholer, 75)

Scholer died a year later, on January 29, 1972. In 1983, the publications committee of the Tippecanoe County Historical Association at last produced *The Building of a Red Brick Campus: The Growth of Purdue As Recalled by Walter Scholer*. The booklet contained an astonishing summary of Scholer's design work at Purdue. It had resulted in construction of twenty-five classroom and laboratory buildings, six sports facilities, thirty-three administration and service buildings, three student-community buildings (among them the Hall of Music), the Memorial Union, Stewart Center, and fifteen residence halls.

Purdue alumnus Arthur L. Hansen succeeded Hovde in 1971 and held the Presidency for ten years. In football, Coach DeMoss's teams compiled a record of thirteen wins and eighteen losses. Before the 1973 season began, Alex Agase, the star Purdue lineman in undefeated 1943, took over as head coach.

The "PAT" era

In 1973, the honor of reading "I Am An American" went to Roy Johnson, a Purdue alumnus serving as Associate Registrar when he retired after twenty-five years. Purdue football fans soon linked Johnson's distinctive reading with the "America the Beautiful" accompaniment.

In 1975, Purdue agricultural staffers W. H. "Bill" Daniel and Melvin Robey developed a natural-turf playing field to counter Astro-Rurf™. They called it Prescription Athletic Turf (PAT). At a cost of about $125,000, Purdue installed the homegrown PAT in Ross-Ade Stadium that year. PAT featured grass sown above a network of pipes sixteen inches below the surface and covered with a mixture of sand and fill. The pipes connected to pumps capable of draining the field to keep it playable in heavy rain or pumping water back to the grass in dry spells. Considered a perfect compromise between natural grass and artificial turf, a PAT field could be kept playable and virtually divot-proof.

Agase coached four Purdue teams to eighteen wins, twenty-five losses, and one tie. In 1973, his team won five and lost six. Six home games—against Miami of Ohio, Notre Dame, Duke, Northwestern, Michigan State, and Michigan—attracted more than 346,000, nearly 57,700 per game. In 1974, the team won four, lost six, and tied once. Six home games drew 338,800—56,475 per game. Next year, Purdue won four and lost seven. Attendance at six home games averaged 59,428. In 1976, Agase's last Purdue squad won five and lost six. Crowds at the six home games again averaged about 59,000.

Before the 1977 season Purdue hired Ohio native Jim Young from the University of Arizona to succeed Agase. Young coached at Purdue for five seasons. In the process he emphasized forward passing to match the talent of star quarterback Mark Herrmann from Indianapolis.

In 1977, Purdue won five games and lost six. Six home games drew crowds that averaged 57,600. This marked a slippage of about 2,000, but Young's 1978 team won eight games, lost two, tied one, and trounced Georgia Tech forty-one to twenty-one in the post-season Peach Bowl game in Atlanta. Home attendance for six games bounced back to nearly 62,250, a new record.

The 1979 Boilermakers won ten games for the first time in school history and lost two. The team edged Tennessee twenty-seven to twenty-two for the tenth win in the Bluebonnet Bowl in Houston, Texas. This Purdue team played six Ross-Ade Stadium games, each before more than 68,900, still another stadium record.

In 1980, Young's players won eight and lost three, beating Missouri twenty-eight to twenty-five in the Liberty Bowl. Home game crowds in Ross-Ade Stadium peaked that year at nearly 70,000 per game.

After Herrmann's graduation, the 1981 team won just five times and lost six, but six Ross-Ade Stadium crowds still averaged 69,900.

Bill Moffitt succeeded Al Wright as director of the Purdue All-America Marching Band in 1981 and remained through 1988.

In 1982, Young resigned and his Defensive Coordinator Leon Burtnett took over Purdue football. In each of Burtnett's first two seasons, Purdue won just three times and stadium attendance lagged. The per-game averages were 66,800.

In 1982, Purdue built an Intercollegiate Athletic Facility north of Mackey Arena. The "IAF" features included a carpeted football locker room rimmed by weight training and football equipment rooms and a players' lounge. There was an underground connecting tunnel to Mackey Arena. Another tunnel connected Mackey to Lambert Field House where indoor track and varsity swimming events continued.

Burtnett's 1983 team won three, lost seven, and tied once, but Ross-Ade Stadium patronage stayed strong. Attendance at five games averaged 65,350. In 1984, Purdue won seven, lost four, then lost to Virginia twenty-seven to twenty-four in the Peach Bowl.

Purdue added an elevator to the south end of the Ross-Ade Stadium press box that year, and seven home game crowds averaged more than 65,200. In 1985, Purdue renovated the home team locker room beneath the Ross-Ade Stadium east stands and built a better visiting team locker in the southwest corner of the stadium. Home crowds at six games averaged 63,400.

In 1985, Indiana University Press in Bloomington published Purdue English Professor Arnold L. Lazarus's book *The Best of George Ade*. The anthology, with a selection of original drawings by John T. McCutcheon, contained samples of Ade's "Fables in Slang," short stories, plays, essays, poems, songs, and letters. "Today, alas, [Ade] remains all but forgotten," Lazarus lamented in his Preface. "It is hoped that *The Best of George Ade* will afford not only entertainment...but also recognition, at last, for George Ade as a humorist of world class" (Lazarus, ix).

For more than sixty years, Ross-Ade Stadium hosted football games played in daytime, but the reality of television and fees paid to U.S. colleges for television rights dictated change. Night television drew vast viewing audiences and huge fees for the rights. "TV" as it came to be known, called many a shot, and schools like Purdue found it profitable to schedule late-day or even night games to accommodate the popular medium.

The first night game at Ross-Ade Stadium took place on October 18, 1986 against Ohio State. Purdue lost that game thirty-nine to eleven. Portable lighting proved to be the only way to illuminate the playing field because the stadium had no permanent lights or towers for lights.

Portable lighting came into use again for a fifty-one to seventeen victory against Toledo, on September 10, 1994, and on September 21, 1996, against West Virginia (a twenty-to-six loss.) Other late afternoon kickoffs requested by TV started in full daylight but required portable lights to finish. The 1986 Boilermakers struggled through three wins and eight losses. Average home attendance was 63,100.

Burtnett's five teams won twenty-one times, lost thirty-four, and tied one. Beginning in the 1987 season, former Texas head coach Fred Akers took over at Purdue. He fared no better, coaching the team to twelve wins, thirty-one losses, and one tie in four years. Three of the losses came in hard-to-swallow Old Oaken Bucket battles against Indiana. Attendance in Ross-Ade Stadium fell to as little as 34,600 for a game against Minnesota. Akers then gave way to Jim Colletto, hired from the Ohio State coaching staff.

The Purdue All-American Marching Band, by now a long-time favorite of Boilermaker football fans in Ross-Ade Stadium, performed under the baton of David A. Leppla from 1988 until 2006.

Colletto coached Purdue football for six seasons but with scant success. His teams won twenty-one games, lost forty-two, and tied three. Moreover, Ross-Ade Stadium patronage faded steadily. The low point appeared to arrive on November 13, 1993, when less than half the stadium seats were filled—fewer than 31,800—for a twenty-seven to twenty-four loss to Michigan State.

Athletic progress did, however, take place off the gridiron. In February 1990, Purdue dedicated the ten-million-dollar Mollenkopf Athletic Center, north of both Mackey Arena, and the IAF, east of Ross-Ade Stadium. The Center featured an indoor football practice field, weight training room, meeting rooms, and coaches' offices. The structure measured 420 feet long, 220 feet wide, and was eighty-six feet high at its peak. In the south end of Ross-Ade Stadium, Purdue also installed an electronic scoreboard and message center, costing one million dollars, and an auxiliary scoreboard on the curving north end.

About the time of the U.S. involvement in the Gulf War in the early 1990s the standing football crowds started chiming in on the last line—"I am an American"—and that, too, become a tradition.

Athletic Director George King retired in 1992. In 1993, President Steven C. Beering, who had succeeded President Hansen in 1983, hired Purdue graduate and swimming letterman, Morgan J. Burke, to run the Department of Intercollegiate Athletics. This department was growing at a runaway rate. Women's sports—swimming, track, volleyball, basketball, softball, and others—were gaining acceptance nationwide. This meant hiring more staff and building and equipping more sports venues. A 1930-1931 Boilermaker halfback, Howard R. "Monk" Kissell, was among the first to help. He donated nearly one million dollars for third floor and mezzanine expansions, in 1994, in the Mollenkopf Center.

That summer, field-level changes in Ross-Ade Stadium included removal of the chain-link fence around the playing field, removal of the paved walkways around the outer edges of the field, and installation of new sod to replace the walkways.

Purdue started an Intercollegiate Athletics Hall of Fame in 1994. After twelve years, there had been ninety-nine inductees, forty of whom were enshrined because of football as players, coaches, or administrators.

In 1996, Coach Colletto's Purdue team upset Michigan nine to three and won its 200th game in Ross-Ade Stadium, but the team was in the throes of losing eight out of eleven games. Only 39,328—far below stadium capacity—witnessed the landmark.

Not your average Joe

For 1997, Purdue hired Joe Tiller, the head football coach at Wyoming.

Before Tiller coached his first season at Purdue—a good one that produced nine wins, three losses, and an Alamo Bowl victory over Oklahoma State in San Antonio, Texas—Purdue replaced the Ross-Ade Stadium south scoreboard message center. In its place went a three million dollar Sony JumboTron™ retrofitted into the main scoreboard. The Jumbotron™ displayed huge live television images and replays from at least four cameras.

Taking over a program that had produced just one winning football season and no bowl game appearances since 1984, Tiller led Purdue to nine post-season bowl berths in the next ten years—nine of the fourteen bowl games in school history. They were the 1997 Alamo Bowl, 1998 Alamo, 2000 Outback, January 2001 Rose, December 2001 Sun, 2002 Sun, January 2004 Capital One, December 2004 Sun, and 2006 Champs Sports.

In 1998, Tiller's team won eight games, lost four, and beat Kansas State thirty-seven to thirty-four in the Alamo Bowl. In a pregame pep rally in San Antonio, Texas, Tiller proposed that fans begin using a new slogan—"Boiler Up!" The fans did, the team won, and the slogan stuck.

In 1999, the Boilermakers won seven, lost five, and lost to Georgia Tech twenty-eight to twenty-five in the Outback Bowl.

With star quarterback Drew Brees returning for his senior year in 2000, the team captured its eighth Big Ten title, sharing the crown with Michigan and Northwestern. Purdue won nine games, lost two, then lost to Washington thirty-four to twenty-four in the Rose Bowl.

Coach Tiller's first five Boilermaker teams rang up forty-two wins and fourteen losses. The average attendance rebounded from 45,300 in 1996 to more than 65,300 per game.

In 2000, Martin Jischke took over as University President from the retiring Steven C. Beering. In seven years, Jischke spearheaded a spectacular fund-raising effort that put upwards of two billion dollars into the Purdue treasury for research, faculty salaries and hiring, scholarships, and construction. Dave Ross would have exuded pure Purdue Pride at the number of donors and the size of their gifts.

In 2001, work began on a massive renovation of Ross-Ade Stadium. The first phase alone cost seventy million dollars. After that ended, the seating capacity for the 2002 season stood at more than 66,000. The renovation work ended in 2003 with a lower seating limit of 62,500, but with the addition of numerous fan amenities. These included more accessible seats, game-day emergency and first aid stations, telephones, will-call ticket spots, group sales, and better lost-and-found service. A Ross-Ade Stadium Pavilion and optional catering services were made available for private functions and meetings. Purdue souvenirs could be acquired at a Purdue Pride team store in the northeast corner of the stadium or from strategically placed kiosks.

In 2001, Purdue won six, lost five, then lost to Washington State in the Sun Bowl in El Paso, Texas, thirty-three to twenty-seven.

In 2002, Tiller's team won six, lost six, and beat Washington thirty-four to twenty-four in a return to the Sun Bowl. During that season, Tiller became the second-winningest coach in Purdue history. He trailed only Mollenkopf, and also ranked second to Mollenkopf with 124 games coached.

In 2003, Purdue won nine, lost three, and in the Capitol One Bowl lost to Georgia thirty-four to twenty seven in overtime.

The 2004, Boilermakers won seven and lost four, then dropped a twenty-seven to twenty-three game to Arizona State in the Sun Bowl.

In 2005, Tiller's team won five games, lost six, and failed to qualify for a bowl game for the first time. The team returned to the bowl scene in 2006 by winning eight games and losing five, then dropping a twenty-four to seven game to Maryland in the Champs Sports Bowl.

During Tiller's tenure, Purdue established a Hall of Glory exhibit in the Mollenkopf Center. The fact is, the list of distinguished Purdue alumni would fill an entire building rather than just a hall. There have been twenty-two astronauts alone, among them Neil Armstrong and Eugene Cernan, the first and last men to explore the surface of the moon, plus the late Virgil "Gus" Grissom and Roger Chaffee.

Others have been U.S. Senator Birch Bayh, Class President from the College of Agriculture in 1951, Nobel Prize recipients Edward Purcell, Class of 1933, and Ben Roy Mottelson, Class of 1947, both in the field of physics, and Dr. Herbert C. Brown, 1979 Nobel Prize laureate in the field of chemistry.

Purdue long ago was nicknamed the "cradle of quarterbacks" because of outstanding football players at that position. That roster includes Bob DeMoss (1945-1948), Dale Samuels (1950-1952), Len Dawson (1954-1956), Bob Griese (1964-1966), Gary Danielson (1970-1972), Mark Herrmann (1977-1980), Scott Campbell (1980-1983), Jim Everett (1981-1985), and Drew Brees (1997-2000).

Jay Gephart began directing the Purdue All-American Marching Band in 2006. The first drums sported heads made from mammoth steer hides imported from South America. Then Remo

Corporation began producing synthetic drum heads which are changed as needed, even for the World's Largest. That drum continues to be maneuvered by a crew of four silver-helmeted bandsmen, selected for their strength and agility, along with two drum-beaters. The crew rehearses every movement of the "Monster" drum to assure its being in the right place at the right time.

On August 1, 2006, Coach Tiller, working with veteran *Journal and Courier* sportswriter Tom Kubat, put on sale the 236-page biography *Tiller: Not Your Average Joe.*

Bermuda and "The Boilermaker"

An odd combination of weather—blistering heat and aging underground pipes—resulted in the PAT playing surface literally coming up in pieces in the fall of 2005. At the conclusion of that season a committee led by Athletics Director Burke and Coach Tiller set out to find a long-term solution. The solution turned out to be a cold-tolerant strain of Bermuda grass long considered better suited to the South. The Purdue men scouted sites in Maryland and Virginia and came away convinced Bermuda was the best fix. Work crews laid Bermuda sod on the Ross-Ade Stadium playing field in June 2006. Purdue's became the first Big Ten stadium to use the material. That fall, an article in the *Purdue Agriculture Connections* newspaper contained a status report:

> After four football games the new grass surface looks even better than it did the day it was transplanted this spring. In May [2006] the Kentucky bluegrass was scraped off and replaced with a new variety of Bermuda that can survive the cold winters in northern states. The new grass is the fulfillment of a goal first espoused by W. H. "Bill" Daniel, a Purdue agronomy faculty member, for whom Purdue's turf grass research and diagnostic center is named.
>
> "Bill said in his turf grass book that the best grass for a traffic area like a football field is Bermuda, if you can grow it," said Pro-

fessor Zac Reicher, Purdue agronomist and turf grass specialist. "But until five or seven years ago we couldn't grow it in Indiana."

Now thanks to years of genetic research that led to the evolution of new grass varieties, the Boilermakers are playing on a new, hardy, durable cultivar of Bermuda called "Patriot."

"Bermuda is the pickup truck of the grass species," says Cale Bigelow, a Purdue agronomist. "If you buy a pickup truck it wants to be driven and it wants to be used. Bermuda is the same way. It wants to be beat up, wants to take the load. It's not the prettiest grass in the world but it's extremely durable when it's actively growing.

"The grass on the field can be kept shorter than in the past," Bigelow says. "Bermuda most likely will be maintained at about three-quarters of an inch, which helps a football team composed of fast runners."

One drawback is that Bermuda does not stay green late in the football season in central Indiana's climate. However, seeding with perennial ryegrass when Bermuda begins its winter dormancy can help keep the fields green and protect the turf from late-season football action.

Bermuda was not the only novelty. Purdue, on November 4, 2005, dedicated "The Boilermaker," an eighteen-foot, 5,400-pound bronze statue of a muscular, helmeted worker swinging a hammer.

The dedication took place at the statue on North University Drive between the IAF and the Mollenkopf Athletic Center. As part of the dedication Purdue honored Eugene R. Grotnes and his family for their ties to Purdue.

"The Grotnes family represents the same roll-up-your-sleeves and get-the-job-done attitude that 'The Boilermaker' depicts," said Purdue President Jischke. "It is this tireless work ethic and intergenerational Purdue pride that we celebrate."

Eugene Grotnes of Atlanta, Georgia, had graduated from Purdue with a mechanical engineering degree in 1951. Since then, three generations of the family brought their work ethic to Purdue.

An anonymous donor commissioned "The Boilermaker," the term linked to Purdue football since 1891, but the statue also aimed to interpret modern boilermakers and skilled tradesmen. Sculptor Jon Hair of Cornelius, North Carolina, began work on the half-million-dollar statue in 2003.

An economic plus

For the steadily growing Lafayette-West Lafayette community—declared a Metropolitan Urban Area after the 1990 federal census—the 1924 gift of Ross-Ade Stadium remains a conspicuous yet easily overlooked economic asset.

The Convention and Visitors Bureau (CVB) commissioned an economic impact study in 2005. The study assumed 55,000 out-of-town visitors nowadays at each Ross-Ade Stadium game. The two cities' 2,300 hotel rooms now host an estimated 4,600 people on each game date. Another 3,000 people stay a second night. These guests spend about $125 apiece on lodging, meals, a total that reaches $950,000.

About 40,000 people—campers, tailgaters—drive in only for game day. However, on fuel and shopping they spend about thirty-seven dollars each, a figure that totals $1.5 million. And so the CVB did and still does estimate that visitors spend nearly $2.5 million in the community each game weekend, an amount that does not include the cost of game tickets.

The Stadium proper is used only half a dozen or so times a year for games and practices, but suites within the stadium installed in recent years are used for a variety of smaller conference and community events.

Purdue's athletic empire in this day and age includes even more:

- The Birck Boilermaker Golf Complex for men's and women's golf houses two eighteen-hole courses, Ackerman Hills and

Kampen. It is the old Marstellar Farm in twenty-first-century clothing. The golf complex also includes the Pete Dye Clubhouse, Tom Spurgeon Golf Training Center, short game areas, and a driving range. Ackerman Hills is the vintage 1930s "south course," and Kampen is the rebuilt Linee Fields of long ago.

- The Boilermaker Aquatic Center for men's and women's diving and swimming was an addition to the Purdue Recreational Services Center in 2001. The Center includes an Olympic sized pool, diving well, dressing facilities, hot tub, and spectator areas.

- The Dennis J. and Mary Lou Schwartz Tennis Center for men's and women's tennis is home to six outdoor and three indoor tennis courts.

- The Intercollegiate Athletics Facility remains the place for volleyball and wrestling competition. In addition to Belin Court, a dedicated surface for volleyball, the IAF houses the Athletic Ticket Office, the Jane P. Beering Academic Learning Center, a weight room, and the football locker rooms.

- Lambert Field is home for the Purdue baseball team, the name again honoring "Piggy" Lambert's baseball coaching years.

- Lambert Field House now is home for indoor track events. Originally home to the 1938 Boilermaker basketball team and the Purdue swimming team, the Field House now is used solely by men's and women's track teams for indoor competition. The original pool has been filled in to make way for a training center for the Purdue wrestling team.

- The vintage 1969 Mackey Arena has been designated for multi-million-dollar enlargement and upgrades in coming years. In March 2006, Purdue Trustees authorized a Kansas City firm to design a much larger Mackey Arena Complex estimated to cost eighty million dollars or more.

- Purdue's long-range athletics facilities plan calls for adding about 8,000 seats and suites in a deck above the east stands of Ross-Ade stadium.

- The Rankin Track & Field Complex provides for men's and women's outdoor competition.

- Purdue also operates a Varsity Cross Country Course for men's and women's meets, a Varsity Soccer Complex for women's soccer, and a Varsity Softball Complex.

Now nearing its fiftieth year, the John Purdue Club became a model that dozens of schools have emulated for sports fund-raising. More than 9,000 John Purdue Club members now raise nearly six million dollars per year to support 500 student-athletes in eighteen varsity sports.

And then some

The inaugural year of Purdue's new theaters—2006—also coincided with the 100-year anniversary of the Theatre Department. Purdue Theatre began in 1906 with the Harlequin Club and, over the next 100 years, transformed itself into the Theatre Department known today.

The Sigma Chi house at 202 Littleton was enlarged and remodeled during 2006 and 2007 at a cost of about seven million dollars. Much of the gift money came from a 1979 Purdue graduate, Keith Krach. A boulder at the House entrance newly identifies the structure as the "George Ade and Keith Krach Chapter House."

Much of the George Ade influence remains, however. Along with original McCutcheon drawings of Ade, a number of Ade's books are found in the Library along with china Ade collected from around the world. There are a couple of oil paintings of Ade in the Library and Presentation room and his Significant Sig plaque in the Library. Ross-Ade Stadium also displays an original portrait of Ade on loan from Sigma Chi. A typewriter at the Sigma Chi house, thought by some to have been Ade's, actually belonged to Booth Tarkington. The Chapter House President in the fall of 2007, Chris Horney, commented, "George Ade definitely is a common topic brought up around the House during pledgeship and with the brothers because of his significance in the chapter, the fraternity, and the university" (Horney to author, September 27, 2007).

Even the memory of Amelia Earhart remained a topic for a Purdue publication in the summer of 2007. *Purdue Engineering Impact*, a magazine published twice a year by the Purdue College of Engineering, contained the following:

> Freeman believes Earhart survived a crash on a different island and was imprisoned for several years in the Shangtung Province of China. When the prison was evacuated in 1945 those released sent 10-word telegrams to family members. One addressed to G. P. Putnam read
>
> CAMP LIBERATED, ALL WELL. VOLUMES TO TELL. LOVE TO MOTHER.
>
> Freeman came to believe that Earhart returned to the U.S., but not to Putnam who had remarried. She lived near her sister in Roslyn, Virginia, using a different name and living to be 104. "I think the American public is perfectly happy believing she went down in the ocean," he says. "We want to believe she was a heroine who plunged into the ocean." (Mayer, 27)

"Freeman" in this report is Richard "Dick" Freeman. According to Freeman, the oft-repeated speculation that Earhart crashed into the Pacific Ocean and died in its depths is not what happened. Freeman believes Earhart landed on a different island than intended and lived until April 2002. Freeman's career began at Purdue as an undergraduate in air transportation, which included learning to fly. He also earned a degree in naval science and tactics and a master's in industrial management. He has twice been honored by Purdue for career achievements. He founded his own consulting company, International Pacific, and lives in Corona del Mar, California.

Name sound familiar? He was "Dickie" Freeman, the lad with the blue eyes who caught Earhart's attention at Purdue in 1937.

In the summer of 2007, Purdue hired France Córdova to succeed President Jischke. In mid-April 2009, Purdue remembered Amelia Earhart, gone but not forgotten since the summer of 1937. Purdue alumna and Purdue Trustee Susan Bulkeley Butler funded a bronze recasting of the forty-year-old sculpture created by California artist Ernest Shelton. The statue shows Earhart standing with one hand holding an aircraft propeller.

"What a beautiful day to bring Amelia Earhart back to Purdue," President Córdova said in an unveiling ceremony in front of Earhart Hall.

Among the spectators was ninety-one-year-old Wilma Kay, a freshman who lived in the Women's Residence Hall (now Duhme Hall) where Earhart stayed in the 1930s. Kay remembered Earhart as having "striking features...tall and with a boyish frame...she wore pants then, and had short hair. She emphasized the opportunities for women and talked about careers in flight, not just being a hairdresser or going into secretary services" (Lafayette *Journal and Courier*, April 17, 2009).

Meanwhile, Ross-Ade Stadium stands as the largest, loudest, most prominent, and modern reminder of the lives of Dave Ross and George Ade.

Ross and Ade, the people so long forgotten by twentieth-century Purdue types, still symbolize the best in the vast Old Gold and Black family. They were among the first great givers and first great generators of Purdue Pride.

To be sure, modern times have produced more givers of more dollars. Purdue has given the world scientists, astronauts, athletes, and engineers who attained greater fame and "household word" stature. However, Ross and Ade set the tone, set the pace, charted the way, and led the parade when Purdue was but "a few lonesome brick buildings out in a field."

Ross-Ade, the eighty-five-year-old name for the stadium, endures, meaning far more than a cool refreshing drink. Ade sometimes joked that naming the place Ade-Ross would have been a mistake "because Ross really doesn't need any aid."

Dave Ross is the Purdue man who bade all people to keep in mind: "There's hardly a thing we do that we can't do better."

While George Ade's "The Yankee's Prayer" left the lines so well worth remembering: "Compel me to see that our organization is a huge experiment in cooperation, and not a scramble for prizes."

References

Babcock, Robert Weston, ed. *Purdue University: Addresses and Records.* Indianapolis: William B. Burford Printing Co., 1928.

Burrin, Frank K. *Edward Charles Elliott, Educator.* Lafayette, Ind.: Purdue University Studies, 1970.

Coyle, Lee. *George Ade.* New York: Twayne Publishers, Inc., 1964.

Eden, Paul, and Soph Moeng, general eds. *The Complete Encyclopedia of World Aircraft.* New York: Barnes & Noble Books, 2002.

Freehafer, Ruth W., *R. B. Stewart and Purdue University.* West Lafayette, Ind.: Purdue University, 1983.

Hepburn, William Murray, and Louis Martin Sears. *Purdue University: Fifty Years of Progress.* Indianapolis: Hollenbeck Press, 1925.

Johnston, Thomas R., and Helen Hand. *Trustees and Officers of Purdue University 1865-1940.* Lafayette, Ind.: Purdue University, 1940.

Kelly, Fred C. *David Ross—Modern Pioneer.* New York: Alfred A. Knopf, 1946.

———. *George Ade—Warmhearted Satirist.* Indianapolis: Bobbs-Merrill Co., 1947.

Knoll, H. B. *The Story of Purdue Engineering.* West Lafayette, Ind.: Purdue University Studies, 1963.

Kriebel, Robert C. *The Gear.* Lafayette, Ind.: TRW Commercial Steering Systems, 2006.

Lazarus, Arnold, and Victor H. Jones. *Beyond Graustark*. Fort Washington, N.Y.: Kennikat Press, 1981.

———, ed. The *Best of George Ade*. Bloomington: Indiana University Press, 1985.

Lovell, Mary S. *The Sound of Wings*. New York: St. Martin's Press, 1989.

Mayer, Kathy. "Volumes to Tell." *Purdue Engineering Impact* (Summer 2007).

McCutcheon, John T., *Drawn from Memory*. Indianapolis: Bobbs-Merrill Co., 1950.

McCutcheon, John T., Jr. *John T. McCutcheon: Tippecanoe County Cartoonist*. Lafayette, Ind.: Tippecanoe County Historical Association, 1974.

Meikle, G. S. "The Ross Marker." *Purdue Engineer* 28, no. 6 (March 1933).

Millender, Dharathula H. "David Ross—Trustee with a Vision." *Campus Copy* (April 1968): 6-8

Russo, Dorothy Ritter. *A Bibliography of George Ade*. Indianapolis: Indiana Historical Society, 1947.

Scholer, Walter. "The Building Of a Red Brick Campus: The Growth of Purdue As Recalled by Walter Scholer." Lafayette, Ind.: Tippecanoe County Historical Association, 1983.

Tobin, Terence, ed. *Letters of George Ade*. West Lafayette, Ind.: Purdue University Studies, 1973.

Topping, Robert W. *A Century and Beyond*. West Lafayette, Ind.: Purdue University Press, 1988.

Index

Abbott, Don, 217-18

Ade, Adaline Bush, 3, 6, 12

Ade, George, "When I was a Small Boy," 4; "A Mother's Intuition," 5; "A Basket of Potatoes," 9-12, 19, 22-24; "The Day I Arrived," 19; "Habit and Character," 25; "Local News," 25; "The Future of Letters in the West," 32; "Only Forty Years Ago This Summer," 27, 146, 158-59; "The Annuals," 39; "The La Gripp," 39; "Some Easy Lessons," 39; "The College Widow," 39-42; "The Dorms," 39; "Ode to John Purdue," 38-39; "The Glorious Touchdown," 39; "Education by Contact," 25-26, 44; "Picnics," 39; "All Roads Lead to the World's Fair," 53; *Tioga* ship disaster, 52; "Stories of the Streets and of the Town," 54-56, 58, 63; "Circus Day," 56; "What a Man Sees Who Goes Away from Home," 55-56; *Circus Day*, 57; travels in Europe, 55-56, 61, "Stories from History," 57; "Fables in Slang," 59-61, 63; "Stories of Benevolent Assimilation," 64; first stage play, 73; meets Mark Twain, 74-75; *Bang! Bang!*, 76, 210; *Clarence Allen, the Hypnotic Boy Journalist*, 76; "Getting Sister Laura Married Off," 77; "Light Opera Yesterday and Today," 77; "The Microbe Serenade," 77-80; *Breaking Into Society*, 77, 91; *The College Widow*, (play) 91-92, 96; *The Bad Samaritan*, 92; "Mr. Peasley of Iowa," 93; "The First Night," 94; *Artie*, 94; "College Days," 95; "The Fountain of Youth," 95, 99; "How I Came to Butt Into the Drama," 92; "The Hoosier Set," 99; "The Night Given Over to Revelry," 101-3; "A Picture Book for Purdue Sigs," 104; *Ade's Fables*, 104-5; silent movies, 111; renominated for Purdue Trustee, 112; "Around the Campus," 112; resigns as Purdue Trustee, 112, 114; *Betty's Dream Hero*, 112; *The College Widow*, 112, 203; *Artie, the Millionaire Kid*, 113; criticizes President Stone, 114-15, helps

Ade, George *(continued)*
   State in World War I, 116; edits *Purdue Alumnus*, 114; menu for summer picnics, 119; "bolster the weak places" editorial, 120; Purdue-Indiana football rivalry, 121; "Chapter Houses," 121; battles President Stone, 107-8,133; writes Governor Ralston, 133; "The Flag, the Salty Seas, the Yankee Sailor," 135; "A Timely Message," 135; "Observations at Random," 135; "dancing shoes" editorial, 136-37; reacts to President Stone's death, 138-39; "Babies," 145; "College Students," 145; "James Whitcomb Riley as I Knew Him," 145; *Back Home and Broke*, 145; "Christmas in London," 146; "Vacations," 146; "Oratory," 146; "Golf," 146; "Looking Back from Fifty," 145-46; *All Must Marry*, 146; "Musical Comedy," 146; Executive Director of Purdue Alumni Association, 151; editor of *Purdue Alumnus*, 151; heads 1922 Purdue Gala Week Committee, 151; make Commencements "a time of diversion and good cheer," 151; Ross-Ade Stadium statement, 152; "To Get Along, Keep On Being a Country Boy," 188; honorary doctor of humane letters, 193; life story installments for *Hearst's*, 194; writes in *Cosmopolitan*, 194; writes in *Atlantic Monthly*, 194-95; honorary doctor of Laws, 203; introduces Elmer Davis, 218-19; speaks at 1934 Purdue Founders Day, 259; views about religion, 269, 282; "Trying to Get Along Without Juice," 230; *Not Wet–Not Dry– Just History*, 238; caricatured by McCutcheon, 267, 281; contributes to *Revised Remarks on Mark Twain*, 284-85; views on religion, 282; movies *Freshman Lover* and *Rhythm On the River*, 282; "The Fountain of Youth," 235; *Maybe It's Love* and *Eleven Men and a Girl*, 228; gifts to Purdue, 229-30; view about Prohibition, 238-39, 304; "Autobiography of George Ade," 251-52; *Thirty Fables in Slang*, 252, 305-6; accumulated wealth, 238; Roosevelt relief programs, 306; Mark Twain Society of America, 306; *This Is My Best*, 329; marriage and Indiana weather, 343-44; ways to learn to write, 278; Harry Leslie's death, 297; 1940 politics, 316-17; retirement life, 333-36, 340; death in 1944, 344; funeral, 345; extent of estate, 346, 389, 391-392

Ade, George, films: *The County Chairman*, 111; *The Fable of the Brash Drummer and the Nectarine*, 111; *Two Dinky Little Dramas of a Non-Serious Kind*, 111; *Two Pop-Up Fables*, 111; *The Fable of the City Grafter and the Unprotected Rube,* 112; *The Fable of the Kid Who Shifted His Ideals to Golf,* 113; *The Fable of the Throbbing Genius of a Tank Town,* 113; *The Fable of the Two Philanthropic Sons,* 113; *The Fair Co-Ed,* 203; *The Hero of Eagle Creek,* (filmscript) 260; *Just Out of College,* 112, 121; *Making the Grade,* 217; *Marse Covington,* 112; *Our Leading Citizen,* 145; *The Slim Princess,* 112, 121; *Woman Proof,* 146; *Young As You Feel,* 239;

Ade, George, plays: *The Sultan of Sulu,* 73, 75-76; *Peggy from Paris,* 76-77; *The County Chairman,* 77, 91; *Just Out of College,* 92; *The Fair Co-Ed,* 96; *Father and the Boys,* 95; *Marse Covington,* 94, 117; *U.S. Minister Bedloe,* 96-97

Ade, George, stories and story collections: *Stories from History,* 57; *"Doc" Horne,* 58; *Fables in Slang,* 61-63; *True Bills,* 91; for *Adventure Magazine,* 218; for *American Magazine,* 145; for *Century Magazine,* 145; for *Collier's,* 94; for *Collier's Weekly,* 91; for *Cosmopolitan,* 121, 145, 211; for *Dramatic Mirror,* 64; for *Hearst's International Magazine,* 188, 203, 211; for *Humor Magazine,* 230; for *Life Magazine,* 145; *Single Blessedness and Other Observations,* 145; for *Pearson's Magazine,* 92; for *Saturday Evening Post,* 67, 94, 145; *The Slim Princess,* 94; for *The Scrivener,* 209-10; for *Sigma Chi Quarterly,* 121; *Forty Modern Fables,* 73; *More Fables,* 73; *The Girl Proposition,* 73; *Handsome Cyril, or, the Messenger Boy with the Warm Feet,* 75; *People You Know,* 75, 77; Strenuous Lad's Library Series, 75; *Rollo Johnson, the Boy Inventor, or The Demon Bicycle and Its Daring Rider,* 76; *Hoosier Hand Book,* 99; *I Knew Him When,* 98; *In Pastures New,* 93; *The Old Town,* 97; *Verses and Jingles,* 99; *Invitation to You and Your Folks,* 113; *The Mayor and the Manicure,* 117, 147; "Broadway," 145; "Old Stories Revised," 91; *Knocking the Neighbors,* 104; *Speaking of Father,* 117, 147; *Nettie,* 117, 147; *Hand-made Fables,* 121, 135; *Old Home Week,* 188; "George Ade Remembers the Good Old Days When One Might Have a Big Night for 45 Cents," 188; *Giant Killer,* 218; *The Old-Time Saloon,* 238; *Fifty Years of American Golf,* 270; *Stories of the Streets and of the Town* (1941 collection), 324

Agase, Alex, 340-41, 370-72

Aitkenhead, Purdue Professor William, 223

Akers, Purdue football coach Fred, 374

Alamo Bowl, 377

Albion College, 101

Ade, John, 3-4, 6, 10-13, 104
Allen-Bradley Company, 266, 300
American Chemical Society, 250-51
Ames, Purdue football coach Knowlton "Snake," 46, 49
Archives of Purdue University, 317
Aretz, Lawrence L. "Cap," 197, 212, 214, 219-20, 222, 228, 257, 261-62, 287
Armstrong, Neal A., 366
Arnett, Dr. A. C., 197, 212, 214
Authors Today and Yesterday, 251

Bayh, U.S. Sen. Birch, 379
Baylor University, 230
Beering, Purdue President Dr. Steven C., 375, 378
Bendix, Vincent, 269, 291
Berg, Purdue football coach Albert, 33-35
Berlovitz, Julius, 199-201
Best of George Ade, The, 373
Better Homes in America, 245, 267-68
Bibliography of George Ade, A, 350
Big Four Railroad, 19, 35, 81, 88-89
Bluebonnet Bowl, 372
Bobbs-Merrill Company, 94, 99, 350
Boilermaker icon, 356-57
Brees, Purdue football star Drew, 377, 379
Broadway, 92, 96
Bronze statue "The Boilermaker," 382-83

Brook, Ind., 76, 97-98, 141, 147, 345-46
Brookston, Ind., 8, 15, 43, 66, 147
Brown, Purdue Chemistry Professor Herbert C., 379
Building of a Red Brick Campus, The, 369-70
Burke, Purdue Athletic Director Morgan J., 375, 381
Burnham, Purdue football coach Elmer, 328, 341, 346
Burtnett, Purdue football coach Leon, 373
Burtsfield, Frank, 144; "Burtsfield's Folly," 145, 299
Butler University, 33, 35, 45, 47- 49, 230, 297, 317

Campbell, Purdue football star Scott, 379
Capital One Bowl, 377, 379
Carnegie Tech, 254, 270, 297
Cary, Frank, 202-203
Centenary College, 239
Chaffee, U.S. Astronaut Roger, 379
Champs Sports Bowl, 377
Chauncey [West Lafayette], Ind., 22, 43
Cheaper By the Dozen, 262
Chicago Record, 51, 54-55, 58, 60-63, 76-77, 93, 99, 211
Chicago, Ill., 17, 38, 42, 51, 53, 70, 73, 76-77, 96, 99, 104, 111
Cleveland, Ohio, 68, 161
Clinton County, Ind., 49, 228
Coe College, 239

Colletto, Purdue football coach Jim, 374-76
Columbian Exposition (Chicago World's Fair), 53-54
Córdova, Purdue University President France, 391
Cosmopolitan, 238-39
Coyle, Lee, 360-61
Crawfordsville, Ind., 32, 36, 45
Curtis, Purdue basketball coach Homer, 191
Curtiss "Jenny," 199-200, 262
Curtiss "Robin," 220
Curtner, Purdue Professor David, 124
Cutts, Purdue athletic administrator Oliver F., 84, 86, 105-7, 147

Daniel, Purdue Professor W. H. "Bill," 371, 381-82
Danielson, Purdue football star Gary, 379
David Ross, Modern Pioneer, 349
Dawson, Purdue football star Len, 379
Delphi, Ind., 36, 99
DeMoss, Purdue football player, coach Bob, 366, 370, 379
DePauw University, 45-47, 49, 165, 167, 188, 207, 210, 215, 224
Dienhart, Purdue football assistant coach Joe, 341
Dietz, Purdue football coach William Lone Star, 148
Doubleday, Page and Company, 104, 121, 135, 145

Durgan, Lafayette Mayor George R., 71, 127

Earhart, Amelia, 197, 213-14, 217, 222, 228, 236-37, 242, 245-46, 262, 265-66, 268-74, 277, 283, 288-91, 293, 309, 390-91
Elliott, Purdue President Edward Charles, 140-41, 151, 154, 157, 160, 192-93, 202, 206, 230-31, 235, 245, 247, 262, 265, 268, 277, 279, 280, 283, 292-93, 299, 304, 308-9, 311, 315, 318, 323, 327-28, 336, 338-39, 344-45, 347
Elward, Purdue football coach A. K. "Mal," 224, 284, 297, 303, 309, 324, 328, 346
Emrick, Purdue Band Director Paul Spotts, 107, 139, 355
Essanay Film Company, 111-13, 121
Everett, Purdue football star Jim, 379
Exponent, The, 107, 363, 367

Fairfield Manufacturing Company, 129-30, 141, 235, 258, 281
Famous Players-Lasky Corporation, 111-12, 146
Fessenden, Purdue Professor Reginald, 49, 123-24,
Ford, Henry, 67, 220-21, 231
Franklin College, 195, 208, 218
Freeman, Purdue Professor Verne, 288
Freeman, Richard "Dickie," 288, 390

Gates Flying Circus, 199, 201
Gemmer Manufacturing Company, 69-70, 191-92, 325
George Ade: Warmhearted Satirist, 350
George, Purdue researcher Roscoe, 249-50
Georgia Tech, 372
Gephart, Purdue Band Director Jay, 379
Gilbreth, Purdue visiting lecturer Dr. Lillian M., 262-63
Great Lakes Naval Training Station, 341
Greater Lafayette Convention and Visitors Bureau, 385
Griese, Purdue football star Bob, 379
Griggsby-Grunow Company, 249-50
Grissom, U.S. Astronaut Virgil "Gus," 366, 379

Hand, Helen, 138, 299, 318
Hanover College, 34
Hansen, Purdue President Arthur L., 370, 375
Harding, Purdue Professor Francis, 124, 249
Hare, Clint, 35, 46,
Harper and Brothers, 77, 91
Harrison, Purdue Trustee and former U.S. President Benjamin, 10
Harrison, Richard, 204, 244, 296
Hazelden Country Club, 97; Celebrity Nights, 306-8, 336

Hazelden Farm, 76, 92, 95, 98, 104, 112-13, 117-18, 145, 267, 269, 282, 287, 336, 340
Heavilon, Amos, 49, 228
Heim, Purdue researcher Howard, 249-50
Heimlich, Herb, 200, 270
Hernstein, Purdue football coach A. E., 105-6
Herrmann, Purdue football star Mark, 372, 379
Hershman, Harry, 340
Hockema, Purdue Executive Dean Frank, 327
Holcomb, Purdue football coach Stuart K. "Stu," 349, 351-53, 356
Horr, Purdue football coach M. H., 106
Hovde, Purdue President Frederick L, 347-48, 367-70

Indiana General Assembly, 131, 311
Indiana Society of Chicago, 95, 98-99
Indiana State Highway Commission, 234, 253
Indiana State University, 195
Indiana University Press, 373
Indiana University, 12, 49, 215, 224, 230, 263, 270, 283, 299, 303, 311, 341, 346, 349, 351, 353, 357, 367, 374
Indianapolis Dramatic Club, 94, 147
Indianapolis, Ind., 45, 48, 70, 88, 94, 99, 116, 126, 144, 151

Innocents Abroad, 93
Iowa Pre-Flight, 346
Isbell, Purdue football coach Cecil, 341, 346, 349

Jackson, Church, Wilcox Company, 69-70
Jamison, Purdue football coach and professor Alpha P., 106-7
Jischke, Purdue President Martin, 383, 391
John Purdue Club, 357, 387
Johnston, Thomas R. "Tommy," 299, 317
Jones, Paul, 205, 250-51, 265-66, 297

Kansas State University, 222, 224, 246, 377
Kellogg, Purdue athletic administrator Nelson, 147-48, 155-56, 224
Kelly, author Fred, 239, 343-44, 349-50
Kemmer, contractor A. E. "Cap," 127, 161
Kent State University, 367
Kentland *Gazette,* 10-11
Kentland, Ind., 3-6, 9-10, 12, 17, 32, 63, 73, 76, 97, 133, 147, 345-46
Kettelhut, Karl, 258, 265
King, Purdue Athletic Director George S., 368
Kissell, Purdue football star Harry "Monk," 224, 375
Kizer, Purdue football coach, athletic director Noble E., 224, 230, 239, 246, 254, 263, 270, 283-84, 297, 308, 315, 328, 346
Kneale, Jack, 44, 66, 68
Knoll, Purdue English Professor H. B., 361-62
Knoy, Maurice, 297, 313
Kokomo, Ind., 67, 70, 197, 212
Kramer, Harry, 37, 42, 51

Lafayette American Legion Post 11, 200, 227
Lafayette *Call,* 36, 87
Lafayette Citizens (Progressive) Party, 71-72, 127
Lafayette *Evening Courier,* 36, 82-83, 85, 87-88, 127
Lafayette Grand Opera House, 23, 28, 31, 37, 64, 73
Lafayette Highland Park Land Company, 46, 48-50,
Lafayette *Journal and Courier,* 145, 199-200, 210, 212-14, 219-21, 225, 242, 249-50, 261, 270, 295, 304, 337, 344, 346, 362-63, 380
Lafayette Main Street Bridge, 22, 30, 157
Lafayette *Morning Journal,* 87-88, 126
Lafayette *Morning News,* 32, 36
Lafayette, Ind., 16, 19, 20, 23, 46, 48, 71, 73, 99, 100, 125, 128, 130, 185
Lafayette-West Lafayette merger talk, 124
Lambert, Purdue basketball coach Ward L. "Piggy," 191, 299, 365
Last Flight, 309

Leppla, Purdue Band Director David A., 374
Leslie, Purdue football star Harry G. "Skillet," 81, 84, 88, 105, 131,
Leslie, Purdue football star Harry G. "Skillet"
185-86; Indiana House Speaker, 195; General Secretary of Purdue Alumni Association, 195; West Lafayette clerk-treasurer, 195, 210; elected Governor of Indiana, 215; starts Standard Life Insurance Company, 249; death in Florida, 297, 330
Liberty Bowl, 372
Lilly, Purdue Trustee Josiah K. "J. K.," 192, 233, 269
Lockheed "Electra," 274, 277-78, 283, 289, 290-91, 293
Lockheed "Vega," 222, 265
Lovell, author Mary, 272

Mackey, Purdue Athletic Director Guy "Red," 351, 357, 367-68
Mahin, Purdue Professor Edward, 185-86,
Marquette University, 346, 351-52
Marsh, "Pink," 56
Marshall, Purdue Trustee Henry, 138-39, 150, 156, 160, 198, 202, 220; "A Hoosier Genius," 336-37
Martin, Charlie, 20-22
McAllister, A. J., 235, 244
McCray, Warren, 133-35, 210
McCutcheon, George Barr, 36, 94

McCutcheon, John Tinney, 16, 29-30, 36, 38, 42, 51, 73, 76, 99, 105, 121, 193, 210, 259, 267, 301, 345
McNutt, Indiana Governor Paul V., 249, 259, 260, 279, 280
Meikle, Purdue staff member G. Stanley, 220, 234, 253, 315
Miami University of Ohio, 349, 361, 371
Michigan State University, 309, 324, 353, 357, 361, 371, 375
Moffitt, Purdue Band Director William "Bill," 372
Mollenkopf, Purdue football coach Jack, 356, 359, 361, 366, 379
Montana State University, 207
Mount Eon, Canada, 132, 137

Neville, Maurice, 236, 256
New York, N. Y., 74, 77, 92-95, 104, 123, 147
Newton County, Ind., 3, 10, 12-13
Nicol, Hugh, 106, 147
Nicol, Scholer and Hoffman, 149
Noble Kizer Award, 315
Noel, Purdue Trustee James, 138, 160, 336
Noonan, Fred, 292-93
Northwestern University, 86-87, 188, 208, 371, 377
Notre Dame University, 86, 106, 148, 224, 349, 352-53, 356, 371

O'Donnell, Purdue football coach Cleo, 105, 129, 148
O'Ferrall, Dr. Robert, 15, 50

Ohio State University, 191, 349, 374
Ohio University, 254, 283
Old Oaken Bucket, 188, 195, 224, 230, 239, 263, 270, 283, 303, 317, 341, 346, 356, 360, 374
Oliver, Purdue Trustee Joseph Day, 138, 222
Outback Bowl, 377

Peach Bowl, 372, 373
Phelan, Purdue football coach James M. "Jimmy," 148, 188, 195, 207, 220, 224, 227, 328
Potter, Purdue Dean Andrey A., 140, 160, 204, 220-21, 231, 274, 328, 347
Prescription Athletic Turf (PAT), 371, 381
PRF Earhart Fund for Aeronautical Research, 277
PRF membership categories, 247
Princeton University, 34
Prisoner of Zenda, The, 94
Purcell, Edward, 379
Purdue Aeronautics Department, 266, 270
Purdue All-American Marching Band, 355, 366, 372, 374, 379
Purdue Alumni Association, 95-96, 99-100, 105, 112, 118, 128, 130-31, 143, 211, 301, 346, 357
Purdue Alumnus, The, 107, 114, 117, 119, 135-36, 143, 155, 211, 224, 230
Purdue Armory, 116, 128, 199, 209, 278, 289

Purdue Athletic Association, 48, 86-87, 105, 154,
Purdue athletic nickname "Boilermakers," 46, 49
Purdue Bands' "I Am an American," 362-63, 371, 375
Purdue Bands' "World's Largest Drum," 139-40, 316-317, 355, 359-60, 366, 379-80
Purdue Board of Trustees, 96, 112, 114, 131, 138, 140, 150, 156, 159
Purdue Boilermaker Special, 316-17
Purdue Cary Hall (Cary Quadrangle), 160, 203, 293
Purdue Chapel, 23, 30
Purdue David Ross Memorial and Garden, 338-39, 348-49
Purdue Dean Coulter, Stanley, 86, 139, 336
Purdue *Debris,* 50, 101, 136, 146, 158
Purdue Department of Research Relations with Industry, 206, 220, 231
Purdue Earhart Hall, 309
Purdue Engineer, The, 230, 253
Purdue Executive Building (Hovde Hall), 308, 311, 368
Purdue experimental television station W9XG, 250
Purdue Field House (Lambert Field House), 293, 299, 308, 365, 373
Purdue fight song "Hail Purdue," 101

404 Index

Purdue Flying Laboratory, 268, 277, 290
Purdue football Ross Camp tragedy of 1936, 283
Purdue football Train Wreck of 1903, 82-83
Purdue Fowler Hall, 85, 87, 94, 115, 145
Purdue Gala Week, 99, 136, 301
Purdue Hall of Music (Elliott Hall), 295, 299, 311-12, 339, 368
Purdue Harlequin Club, 94, 96-97, 112, 114, 389
Purdue Housing Project, 245, 254, 267, 314
Purdue in World War I, 126, 128-29
Purdue Ladies' Hall, 22-23, 27
Purdue Literary Banquet, 218, 302
Purdue Mackey Arena, 365, 368, 373
Purdue Master Plan, 141, 148-49, 157, 158
Purdue Memorial Gymnasium, 87, 93, 116, 188, 191, 211
Purdue Physics Building (Peirce Hall), 309, 323
Purdue radio station WBAA, 124, 191, 323
Purdue Research Foundation (PRF), 232-33, 249, 253-54, 261, 267-69, 275, 277-78, 314, 328 337, 347
Purdue School of Agriculture, 116, 128, 223
Purdue Smith Hall, 71, 115

Purdue Stuart Field, 47, 49, 80, 100, 105, 107, 116, 148
Purdue Student Army Training Corps, 116, 128
Purdue Student/Memorial Union, 107, 116, 130-31, 136, 141, 150, 202, 294, 299, 302, 308
Purdue University Airport, 261, 283, 287, 308
Purdue University, 12-13, 16-17, 19, 21-24, 43-44
Purdue, The, 25, 35
Purvis, Duane, 224
Putnam, George Palmer, 213-14, 268, 274, 277-78, 291-92, 309

Ralston, Samuel M., 114, 133
Rathbun, James D. "Jim," 333-34, 344, 456
Reisner, Purdue football coach G. A., 45
R-H-K Corporation, 258, 265, 296, 300
Rice Institute, 263
Riley, James Whitcomb, 94-95, 145
Robertson, Clarence Hovey "Big Robbie," 193, 195, 221, 295-96
Rogers, Bruce, 242, 301, 349
Rogers, Will, 198-99, 211-12, 260
Roosevelt, Eleanor, 278-80
Roosevelt, U.S. President Franklin D., 249, 278, 293, 325, 316-17
Rose Bowl, 363, 378
Rose Polytechnic Institute, 188
Rosite, 266, 300
Ross Building, 127, 157
Ross Engineering Camp, 192, 359

Ross Gear and Tool Company, 68-71, 123-24, 126; in World War I, 127-30, 141, 192; diversifies product line, 223; profits during U.S. Depression, 223, 230, 235, 237-38, 243, 250, 253, 258, 274-75, 281, 296, 300-01, 303, 305, 313, 323-25, 329-30; acquired by TRW, 348

Ross, David (grandfather of David Edward Ross), 7

Ross, David Edward, 6-8, 15-17, 44; farm manager, 65; Brookston town board, 66; portable boat, 66; telephone company, 67; first patents, 67-68; first car, 70; Lafayette City Council, 71, 118, 123, 138, 140; Purdue Board of Trustees, 130; urges long-range thinking at Purdue, 131; buys "The Hills," 125-26, 133; pushes Purdue research, 132, 141; meets George Ade, 142-43, 149, 187, 191, 193; president of Purdue Trustees, 197; management changes at Ross Gear, 198; reflecting highway signs, 207; parabolic concrete tunnels, 208; need for Purdue Airport, 214; escorts Henry Ford, 220; patent for plow 223, 230; startup gifts to Purdue Research Foundation, 233; gives for "flying lab," 268; gives Purdue land for Airport, 236, 253, 277; patents window sash, weather stripping, and highway marker, 263, patents cornstalk and clod cutter attachment for tractors, 237-38; patents construction methods, 280-81; gives $100,000 toward field house construction, 283-84; patents for constructing metal buildings, fastening metal shapes, and a furnace, 274; gives Purdue $7,500 for student medical emergencies, 234; tells how to pick right men for research, 234; gives PRF Ross Gear stock for Purdue faculty retirements, 236; invents railroad freight car brakes, new type of streetcar, baseboard for homes, mosquito trap, ventilating system for schools, diesel engine, dairy barn design, milk can cooled with dry ice, 255; Indiana Commission on Government Economy, 267; intercampus cooperation, 246, 292, 299-300; "terribly destructive" weapon, 303-4, 308, 311, 313; honored at Purdue Alumni dinner, 301-2; examples of community giving, 313-14, 318, 323; idea for "submarine catching curtain," 319-22; stricken with hemiplegia, 329; funeral, 337; bequests, 337-38; burial; 338, 343, 347-48, 378, 391-92

Ross, David Linn "Uncle Linn," 8, 15, 46, 68-69, 71, 127, 129, 198, 242

Ross, Eleanor, 15, 44

Ross, George Henderson, 7-8, 15, 17, 43, 45, 65
Ross, William Edward "Uncle Will," 8, 15, 17, 43, 46, 68, 127
Ross-Ade Foundation, 159-61, 192, 328, 351
Ross-Ade Stadium 215, 227, 230-31; "double-header," 239, 243, 246-47, 254, 263, 270, 278-79, 281, 283, 297, 309, 313, 317, 323, 330, 341, 346, 349, 351-53, 355, 357, 360, 363-68, 371-78; pavilion, 378; Purdue Pride store, 378, 381-82, 385, 387, 391-92
Rostone Corporation, 204; at Chicago World's Fair, 243-44, 250, 253, 257-58, 265-66, 296, 300, 305, 313, 324, 329
Russell, Dick, 158, 222, 256
Russell, F. H. Company, 63, 73, 75, 77
Russo, Dorothy Ritter, 51, 147, 350

Salter, Stephanie, 367-68
Samuels, Purdue football star Dale, 379
Scanlon, Purdue football coach Arthur "Butch," 129, 148
Scholer, Walter, 149, 156-57, 161, 203, 293-95, 312-13, 348, 368-69
Scott, John A. "Jack," 362-63
Shambaugh Field, 212-14, 217, 219, 220, 222, 228, 257, 261
Shambaugh, Charles, 212, 214-15
Shook, Charles W., 144
Shook, Robert Harding "R. H.," 144

Sigma Chi, 29-31, 38, 44, 77, 95, 98, 101, 104, 121, 346, 389
Smart, Purdue President James A., 21, 35
Smith, Purdue football coach "Andy," 105-6, 129
Soaring Wings, 309
Speik, Purdue football coach F., 106
Stein, Evaleen, 94-95
Stewart, Purdue choral music director Albert P. "Al," 340
Stewart, Purdue Vice President and Treasurer Robert Bruce "R. B.," 140, 154, 159, 202, 230-31, 233, 235, 244-45, 247, 256, 277, 293, 304, 308, 311, 327-28, 347
Stone, Herbert S. and Company, 57, 61-62, 73
Stone, Margaret, 132, 137-38
Stone, Purdue President Winthrop E., 71, 80-81, 85-88, 94, 96, 103, 105-8, 112, 114-15, 132-36; death on Mount Eon, 137, 148
Story of Purdue Engineering, The, 361-62
Stuart, Alison, 231, 338
Sulu Archipelago, 64
Sun Bowl, 377-78

Taft, William Howard, 95
Tarkington, Booth, 259
television, 228, 249-50
Tiller, Purdue football coach Joe, 377-81
Tippecanoe County, Ind., 32, 46, 48, 100, 262

Tippecanoe River, 16, 66
Topping, Robert W. "Bob", 114, 137, 139-40, 157, 202, 311
Truman, former U.S. President Harry, 360, 366
Trustees and Officers of Purdue University 1865-1940, 299, 318
Twain, Mark, 57-58, 74-75, 93
Twentieth Century Authors, 251

U.S. Census for 1930, 228; for 1940, 315
U.S. Civil Works Administration (CWA), 25
U.S. Federal Radio Commission, 228
U.S. National Recovery Act (NRA), 254
U.S. National Youth Administration, 309
U.S. Patent Office, 68, 191
U.S. Public Works Administration (PWA), 281, 283, 293, 299, 302, 308, 311, 328
U.S. Social Security Administration, 275, 293
U.S. Works Progress Administation (WPA), 278, 315
University of Arizona, 372
University of Chicago, 46, 49, 53, 106, 194
University of Detroit, 303
University of Georgia, 377, 379
University of Illinois, 46, 106, 147, 312, 340, 349, 352, 357
University of Iowa, 147, 254, 270, 297, 309, 324, 353
University of Maryland, 379
University of Michigan, 46, 49, 147, 224, 341, 351, 371, 376-77
University of Minnesota, 147
University of Mississippi, 224
University of Missouri, 355, 372
University of Nebraska, 357
University of Pittsburgh, 349, 351
University of Rochester, 346
University of Tennessee, 372
University of Texas, 353, 359
University of Toledo, 374
University of Virginia, 373
University of Washington, 378, 379
University of West Virginia, 374
University of Wisconsin, 49, 106, 147, 195, 215, 230, 239, 246, 303, 317, 346, 349, 353

Vanderbilt University, 324
Vinton, Judge Henry H., 118, 141-42, 152
Voinoff, Purdue assistant football coach Sam, 341

Wabash College, 27, 34, 45, 47, 49, 106, 188, 195
Wabash River, 8, 20, 30, 34, 43
Waldo, Purdue Professor Clarence A., 85, 87
Washington State University, 378
Welch, Purdue football star Ralph "Pest," 224
Welles, Orson, 98
Wells, Orson "Ort," 98

West Lafayette, Ind., 46-47, 81, 100, 104, 130, 144, 148, 157, 158; Happy Hollow, 34; High School,
West Lafayette, Ind.
  299, 330, Hills and Dales, 144-45, 244; Linee Fields, 30
Western Indiana Gravel Company, 236
Western Reserve, 239
Wetherill, Dr. Richard B., 157, 302, 315
White County, Ind., 7, 16, 46
White, Purdue President Emerson E., 29
Wickard, Claude, 315-16
Williams, Indiana Governor James D. "Blue Jeans," 10, 43
World War I, 116, 126; Armistice, 129, 148
World War II, 305, 312-13, 319, 327, 331, 335-36, 340, 367
Wright Brothers, The, 349
Wright, Purdue Band Director Dr. Al G., 355, 362-64, 372
Wymer, Floyd, 205, 250-51, 296-97, 313

Young, Purdue football coach Jim, 372-73

Zuppke, Illinois football coach Bob, 306

www.ingramcontent.com/pod-product-compliance
Lightning Source LLC
Chambersburg PA
CBHW062007180426
43199CB00033B/1140